Introduction

Plans for *Light From the Hearth* began when Marilyn Brinkman enrolled in my heritage preservation course in American Studies at St. Cloud State University during the fall of 1979. As a native resident of Stearns County, where she and her family farm, Marilyn's firsthand knowledge of the region dovetailed with my interest in vernacular architecture as it had developed from my experience as an historian with the Historic American Buildings Survey, Perry, Missouri, summer 1978.

Since the spring of 1980, Marilyn and I have been photographing rural buildings, talking to descendants of pioneers, recording lives of those few who still live in pioneer-like conditions, and researching background material for this book. Our field work has encompassed a seven-county area comprising the region of central Minnesota. We began with the object of finding buildings that represent Nineteenth Century pioneer life in the region (log houses, barns, out-buildings, frame houses, schools, and churches) and followed up by recording from written records and oral interviews the lives of those who used or use those buildings. Some abandoned sites where crumbling log buildings can still be found required library searches to find original occupants; others are active farms whose owners' ancestors homesteaded the land originally. In a few cases modern pioneers, like John and Anna Petrich, are the last living link with the frontier past.

Light From the Hearth is not a comprehensive history of central Minnesota pioneer settlers and buildings. We have selectively chosen a number of buildings and families that we feel represent the wide ethnic background of the region and the range of building types. Until recently, folk and vernacular buildings have been ignored by historians in favor of buildings from traditional, classical sources. This bias toward the elite has resulted in studies that concentrate upon the lives and homes of the well-to-do. Through the influence of scholars like Henry Glassie (*Pattern in the Material Folk Culture of the Eastern United States* and *Folk Housing in Middle Virginia*); Montell and Morse, *Kentucky Folk Architecture;* and Howard Wight Marshall's recent *Folk Architecture in Little Dixie*, a respect for "common" people and their buildings has taken place. We hope that *Light From the Hearth* will augment scholarly studies of folk and vernacular architecture and help others to appreciate those people who built and lived in those buildings.

We have found that the rural landscape is changing at an almost daily pace. Many of the buildings documented here have vanished or fallen into ruin since the day we first saw them. Therefore, an outgrowth of our research has been to interest people in preservation of both their familial heritage and the built environment. Our work has stimulated some owners to hold onto their older buildings or to find adaptive use. "Progress" is the enemy of the architectural and social historian; witness the vast number of contemporary metal farm buildings. As the supply of natural materials diminishes, craftsmanship and uniqueness of form suffer as well. We agree with the poet and preservationist, Wendell Berry, that people suffer, too, perhaps unconsciously, when a landmark—a hill, wooden silo, crumbling barn—disappears. We believe people need visual identification with their own past.

Marilyn and I have used some of this material for slide and lecture presentations at St. Cloud State University, Elderhostel, and at local historical societies. Students and citizens have responded favorably to our work as they recognize their own roots and our shared heritage. We feel that we have expanded our knowledge, not only through field work, but through contact with these audiences.

We hope that *Light From the Hearth* will interest students, architectural and social historians, and the public. We feel that we have documented an important chapter from the pioneer era (1850-1910) in Minnesota. We have recorded 14 family histories, representing descendants of people from Slovenian, German, Czech, Swedish, and English backgrounds, and traced the history of folk and vernacular buildings in relation to lives of the people in the region.

Many people have been most gracious and helpful to our research. We offer a general acknowledgment, first, to all of the citizens of central Minnesota who have welcomed us into their farmyards and homes—many during repeated visits—to photograph and interview. In particular, we would like to thank Anna Petrich, Clara Symanietz, Joe Gasperlin, Math Grausam, Blaise Legatt, and Andrew, Joe, and Tony Gogala, our earliest and most tireless contacts—people whom we now call friends. County historical society staff members have been indispensable: John Decker and Dave Ebnet (Stearns), Gregg Guzy (Sherburne),), Caroline Westrum (Benton), Jan Warner (Morrison), and Marion K. Jameson (Wright). Many scholars, administrators, and personal friends have made our work easier, John Rylander, Eleanor E. Simpson, Dale Olmstead, Wanda Erickson, Nancy Franzen, Lois Thielen, Eileen Garding, Tom Harvey, and Ruth Kneval.

The Instructional Media Staff at SCSU Learning Resource Center has processed our film; special thanks are due to Mike Nelson, Dan Marek, Paul Walsh, and Jeff Harrington. The pictorial work would not have been possible without the cooperation of Nelson's staff and St. Cloud State University. A faculty-development grant and a Hill Foundation Grant made field work and manuscript completion possible.

We hope that *Light From the Hearth* is a contribution to social and architectural history. Central Minnesota has not been documented as thoroughly as have other Minnesota regions. Much more work lies ahead in ethnic, architectural, rural, and oral history. The role of the woman in any given American time period is still a new, though growing, territory for scholars. We also hope that our work will stimulate interest in the elderly. Many of our contacts are older Americans whose stories remain untold. Visiting with these people has been a source of growth for both Marilyn and myself.

William T. Morgan
American Studies Program
St. Cloud State University
January 1983

Methods of lighting cabins and houses varied throughout the villages and rural districts. The flickering light from the hearth was the only illumination provided in the cabin of Edward Drew in the first year that he lived in Minnesota Territory.

Evadine A. Burris Swanson

Light

From the

Hearth

Central Minnesota
Pioneers & Early Architecture

Marilyn Salzl Brinkman

William Towner Morgan

NORTH STAR PRESS   **SAINT CLOUD, MINNESOTA**

Dedicated to

Nancy, Brian, & Karen Brinkman

Bill and Sarah Morgan

For the moment, saying this much will do: we must save the spirit of the land and the people, for the future and for ourselves. Our challenge is, as Henry Glassie has often asserted, to 'rescue from anonymity' the people and their cultural landscapes in order to achieve a more authentic American history.

Howard Wight Marshall

Marilyn Salzl Brinkman is an American Studies and creative writing major at St. Cloud State University. She is co-author of *Centennial, St. Catherine's Parish, Farming, Minnesota, 1879-1979*. Marilyn is a native of Stearns County where she and her husband own and operate their family farm.

William Towner Morgan is an Associate Professor of American Studies at St. Cloud State. Morgan has published newspaper articles on architecture and was Senior Historian for the Historic American Buildings Survey, Perry, Missouri, Summer 1978. He is a native of Pipestone, Minnesota.

International Standard Book Number: 0-87839-038-3

Preface

Thomas Jefferson believed that in order for America to endure, the land had to be plowed and populated. The pioneers and yeoman farmers became the inheritors of this dream. As the pioneers moved west they broke the age-old sod and transformed the continent into farms. Beginning in 1850, 26 years before America's Centennial, settlement began in central Minnesota. Documented accounts of the lives of settlers during the pioneer era are scarce. Much of that history lies long buried in the minds and hearts of those people who chose not to express themselves in diaries, novels, poetry, or song. In the words of Thoreau:

> (The farmers) never took to the way of writing. Look at their fields, and imagine what they might write, if ever they should put pen to paper. Or what have they not written on the face of the earth already, clearing and burning, and scratching, and harrowing, and plowing, and subsoiling, in and in, and out and out, and over and over, again and again and again, erasing what they had already written for want of parchment.*

Light From the Hearth is an attempt to supply the parchment to record the lives of past and living pioneers from their written and oral statements. The photographs focus upon the buildings constructed by and lived in by these people. While many of these structures—now in a state of ruin or partial decay—are relics of a vanished past, some are still used today. From crude pole shelters, log houses and barns, to magnificent churches, these buildings bear testimony to the lives of their occupants.

*Henry David Thoreau, *Thoreau, Walden and Other Writings*, ed. Joseph Wood Krutch (New York: Bantam Books, 1962), p. 29.

Contents

I.
A Brief History
of Central Minnesota

Early History

"For what is the present after all
but a growth out of the past.
Walt Whitman
Passage to India

Central Minnesota lies near the geographical center of North America. The area was part of what the pioneers referred to as the Big Woods of Minnesota: A land covered with hardwood forests and numerous lakes, streams, and rivers; a terrain of hills, rolling land, and prairie, basically rich agricultural land. A varied continental climate of four distinct seasons, cold in winter and hot in summer gave variety to life in central Minnesota.

Dakota and Ojibway Indians occupied the area before the coming of the white man. These Indians lived in harmony with nature in a simple, primitive manner, allowing the land to lie in its natural, virginal state. With the coming of the white man and "civilization," the Indians were displaced onto reservations and the face of the land was altered with the use of the gun, the axe, and the plow.

The first white Europeans to traverse central Minnesota were the explorers, trappers, traders, and missionaries, of the 17th century. The abundance of fur-bearing animals in this area made it a part of the first major industry of the Minnesota region—the fur trade. A number of trading posts were established along the Mississippi River to serve the white and red fur trappers.

As the rest of the nation grew, so did the need for lumber and building products. Central Minnesota's abundance of these products made it an important part of the second major industry of the region—the lumber and logging industry. Numerous sawmills and lumber-related business opportunities soon sprang up in the area.

In time, both the fur-trade and lumber industries declined due to the depletion of the supply of these natural products. The ending of the exploitation of these natural resources led to the pioneer agricultural settlement of the area. Waterways had been charted, ox-cart trails had been routed through the wilderness, and some of the land had been cleared by the logging industry. The region was lying ready for the coming of the farmer to populate and to plow the land.

Furthermore, the United States as a nation was expanding in population and financial growth. There was pressure to move westward. Minnesota beckoned. Many governmental factors were responsible for the initial influx of settlers into central Minnesota: The creation of Minnesota Territory in 1849 and statehood in 1858; the Indian Treaties of 1850—the Indians of the area were removed to reservations, opening the lands west of the Mississippi for settlement; the Pre-emption Act of 1841 and its extension to unsurveyed land in 1854—settlers could obtain land for $1.25 per acre if they made improvements, erected a dwelling, and lived on the land a certain length of time; the Homestead Act of 1862—160 acres of land were made available to anyone over twenty-one years of age, who was the head of a household, a United States citizen, who lived on the land for five years, and who had obtained a government-issued patent.

The land-grant railroads owned land which could be obtained along the approved rights-of-way—the railroad land was more easily accessible to the market; thus, the value of land and products was enhanced. Additional land was made accessible through military bounty land patents—land was given as a reward for a soldier's or sailor's wartime service. Interest in owning land blossomed like the wild roses that abounded in the area.

There were also many personal, human factors which attracted settlers from various parts of the world to central Minnesota. Some, called "Yankees" by Ben Scherfenberg's Sherburne County grandmother, Kate Snow Cater, came from the eastern United States as early as the 1840s;[1]

soon after the Germans came; then the Norwegians and Swedes by the 1860s. The Slovenians immigrated in the 1870s; and eastern and southern Europeans came after the 1890s.

The Yankee New Englanders came because Minnesota was a free state, and had a booming lumbering industry that attracted them. They had an instinct for speculation and investments in towns and lands, and many had money to invest in new ventures. The first newspaper editor of Minnesota, James Madison Goodhue, proclaimed, "We regard this territory as destined to become the New England of the West."[2]

A seemingly endless stream of German emigrants poured into central Minnesota between 1854-1864 because of the promotional efforts of a sixty-seven year old Slovenian missionary priest, Father Francis Xavier Pierz. Peirz was assigned as a spiritual servant to the thousands of Indians in Minnesota Territory, as well as the incoming white settlers. He spent his energy and time seeking spiritual welfare for his people. Father Pierz has been described as "one of those rare individuals who thrive on hardship that would kill most people."[3] He came to love Minnesota and to regard it as God's own country.

Pierz shrewdly foresaw the day in which the settlers would fully populate the area. It was his desire to attract people of his own nationality and faith. He wrote hundreds of letters to his fellow Slovenians urging emigration to Minnesota. Very few responded to his plea. A small group of about fifty Slovenian pioneers came and founded one small settlement near St. Stephen and another near St. Anthony, both in Stearns County, Minnesota.

Disappointed by this initial failure to secure fellow countrymen, Father Pierz turned his attentions toward attracting German Catholic settlers. He wrote articles and advertisements for leading German language newspapers in this country and Europe. Father Pierz wrote in glowing terms of the richness of the Minnesota prairie land, the wealth to be recovered from the acres upon acres of standing timber, and of the healthful climate enjoyed year round.[4] The Germans responded and became the major immigrant nationality group of central Minnesota.

Moreover, Pierz was directly responsible for the establishment of the monastery of St. John's in Collegeville, Minnesota, and the convent of St. Benedict's at St. Joseph, Minnesota. These two religious establishments served to stabilize the first German Catholics in the area and encouraged others to come as homesteaders.

Another immigrant, Swedish born Hans Mattson, as secretary of the Minnesota Board of Immigration, was fundamental to the migration of Swedes, Norwegians, and Danes into Minnesota. The board distributed advertising pamphlets and sent agents to the eastern states and to the European countries. As immigrant agent for the Northern Pacific Railroad, Mattson personally recruited emigrants in Sweden. "The board cooperated with the railroads in efforts to get cheap fares for immigrants and their families."[5] Between 1868 and 1873 Mattson personally organized three shiploads of immigrants to accompany him back to Minnesota, which he described as a land of milk and honey. Likewise, another Swede, novelist Fredrika Bremer, proclaimed that Minnesota would become a "glorious new Scandinavia."[6]

Indeed, groups of various other European nationals came into central Minnesota, making it a hodgepodge of nationalities. Irish, English, Poles, Czechs, French, and others came. The Americanization of the cultures of western and central Europe began to develop.

1   The Cater family is of French and English descent. They emigrated from North Barrington, New Hampshire to Minnesota in 1856. See Cater family history for more information.
2   Theodore C. Blegen, *The Land Lies Open* (St. Paul: University of Minnesota Press, 1949), p. 140.
3   Rhoda R. Gilman and June Drenning Holmquist, eds., *Selections from "Minnesota History"* (St. Paul: Minnesota Historical Society, 1965), p. 179.
4   William P. Furlan, *In Charity Unfeigned* (Paterson, New Jersey: St. Anthony Guild Press, 1952), p. 195.
5   Theodore C. Blegen, *Minnesota: A History of the State* (St. Paul: University of Minnesota Press, 1975), p. 305.
6   Blegen, *The Land Lies Open*, p. 113.

Emigration

I tell you the past is a bucket
of ashes.

Carl Sandburg
The People, Yes

The pioneers coming from the east and other parts of the United States came for new opportunities; the immigrants came for better opportunities. Many of the emigrants left their homelands because they felt their lives could not be improved upon where they were. In interviews with central Minnesota immigrant descendents, many spoke of the contrast between central Minnesota and their European homelands.

Many had been very poor. Joe Gasperlin of Albany said his mother often told him "Here a lady had more lard on her clothes than she had in a pan over there." Math Grausam, a Bavarian immigrant descendent, said "Here they had meat to eat; over there they had only soup." Some emigrants left to avoid forced marriages or unhappy family situations. In one interview, a woman said her mother had told her that she decided to emigrate after her father re-married and the stepmother started to wear her mother's clothes. Many were tired of the feudal land system in Europe where only the wealthy and the nobility could own land. Herman Kohorst, Richmond, Minnesota, said, "If you were born poor in Germany, you stayed poor all of your life. There was no land or opportunity for the poor."

Slovenian emigrants began arriving in central Minnesota in the 1850s. Anton Gogala, Sr., (right) and his family arrived in Stearns County in 1866. Descendants farm the same land today.

Others left their homeland to avoid military conscription. Vincent Symanietz, St. Stephen, said his father left Poland to avoid military punishment because of a minor offense committed during a drinking spree. The potato famine in Ireland prompted a massive Irish emigration. Many sought religious freedom in America, especially the Scandinavians. About 100,000 children came west between 1854 and 1904 on the various children's "Orphan Trains" from the east. A number of the orphans were given homes in central Minnesota, as was Clara LaDue, in Holdingford, Minnesota, in 1900. In many cases, kin already in America summoned relatives to join them in America. Whatever the motives, emigration meant severing old ties and turning toward a new land of promise, fixing courses on an unknown future in an alien land.

The emigrants traveled by ship to America, an awesome feat in itself, as traveling conditions were poor on the wooden-hulled steam and sailing ships. The journey could take many weeks, and depending on weather, even months.

Many of the newcomers reached port in New York Harbor where the Statue of Liberty welcomed them. Usually they could not speak English and needed the help of interpreters to travel west. From New York they would travel via steamboat, covered wagon, or railroad to Minnesota, another difficult leg on their arduous journey from Europe. If the immigrants reached the Minnesota port of St. Paul during the summer months, they could continue on to central Minnesota by steamboat up the Mississippi River, by stagecoach, wagon, ox-cart, buggy, or on foot. The head of the railroad reached St. Cloud in 1866.

If the settlers reached Minnesota in fall or winter, they had to find employment and shelter in or near St. Paul until the spring thaw let them move onto the land. The Anton Gogala family worked in the sawmills of St. Anthony Falls (Minneapolis) until spring 1865, after a three-month journey from Slovenia to Minnesota. One wonders if the promise of a better life helped soften the hardship and privation endured during their journeys. Undoubtedly, the need for faith, courage, and strength was more demanding than ever, in this alien land of their choice.

The very first settlers to put their plows into the virgin soil settled in the safety zones near the established forts. Then, as security from the fear of Indian raids increased, others settled along the rivers and ox-cart trails because that land was easily accessible and the rivers and trails offered a means of escape from hostile Indians still roaming the area.

The settlement of the prairie land followed. The newcomers believed the prairie lands to be the most conducive to farming, although Henry Salzl, a Stearns County retired farmer, said, "Those people thought they had the best land; but once we had all of our trees cleared, we had the best land. The prairie soil soon wore out!"

As more and more settlers came into central Minnesota, they had to move inland from the main trails to the forested regions recently opened up to agriculture by the lumber and logging industries. The last areas to be settled were those lands that were still tree-covered and wild. These wooded acres were the most difficult to clear and break but were, like Henry Salzl's farm, very rich as farm land. Here the axe and elbow grease were the primary tools. Anna Petrich recalled that her father told her many times, that when the Poglajen family came to the Brockway, Minnesota, area, "All you could see was the sky up between the trees— you had to clear it first." The virgin hardwood timber had to be cleared to make room for homes and farms, and the earth did not yield without the sweat of heavy labor seasoning the soil.

Typical of the thousands who came to America, Anna Mari (Johnson) Ryberg emigrated from Hinneryd, Smalands Stenar, Sweden in 1888 with her husband and three small children, her aged mother, and three of her brother's children. She said, during their difficult journey by sea, "If I ever get on land again, I'll never go out on water."

Generally, the pioneers settled among people of their own nationality. Many came in groups. Near Buckman, Minnesota, four families settled together forming a "block" in which each family built their dwellings at the corner of their property facing each other, with their land extending behind the buildings. In this way, according to Sylvester Mischke, neighbors were very near when help was required or company desired. Sometimes a group of people brought up large tracts of land and sold property only to "people of their own kind."

Other types of social bonds brought people to settle together. In central Minnesota, religion was usually a factor in settlement. In Stearns and Benton counties German Catholics predominated, other ethnic Catholics and Protestant groups were accepted only with an uneasy tolerance. In Holdingford, Minnesota, both German-Catholic and

6

Polish Catholic parishes were established. Of St. Stephen, Minnesota, one woman related, "Slovenians walked this way, Polish that way." The church groups were divided in her neighborhood. On the other hand, as Math Grausam stated, "During threshing time we all worked together." The desire to own land and to be independent generally overcame all other obstacles. Just as the settlers had to come to terms with the land they chose, they had to come to terms with their neighbors. A close cooperative community spirit was necessary for survival.

When the pioneers reached their chosen land, the land that was their dream of a glorious future, they beheld a wilderness of enormous stillness, awesome beauty, and toughness. Necessity and the needs of survival would shape their lives, and in order to survive the pioneers needed to be tougher than life. Farming in central Minnesota became the way of life, a way of feeding the family, and a way of establishing security for the family through ownership of land. In the words of Ralph Waldo Emerson, "A true man belongs to no other time and place but is the center of things."

Peter and Martha (Gibson) MacDougall arrived in Morrison County from Ontario, Canada, in 1873. Descendants say they lived a happy and prosperous life on their central Minnesota homestead, "Riverside."

Daily Living

I claim, and act, and am mingled
in the fate of the world.
Wendell Berry
Farming: A Hand Book

The daily life of the pioneers in central Minnesota was not documented in writing by the people. The farming people did not write things down. They thought, as we do now, that their lives were so commonplace that the details were not worth noting. They were engrossed in more pressing and important matters—their work—which was difficult and time-consuming. Each year they helped start new life in the orderly cycle of the waiting earth. These early Minnesota farmers were in a constant contest with the adversity of the weather, wild animals, insects. The cost of equipment, seeds, and materials sapped their meager resources. Dirt, drudgery, and untimely death were among the elements which made life a fearful adventure. Rest came not when darkness crept in but when the day's work was finished.

Very few people kept diaries. Writing letters and personal record keeping was not part of their lives. By pulling together threads of information from letters, newspapers, and the few diaries from that era, plus the stories and traditions of later pioneers, we are allowed to speculate as to what their lives may have been like. Merrill E. Jarchow, a Minnesota agricultural historian, has described what he felt was the "annual schedule" of an early established farmer:

In January or February, our intelligent farmer took care of his stock; he hauled wood to his woodpile; he split rails; he took good care of his machinery; and he hauled out some manure. In March, he might market grain left on hand; sow some vegetable seeds in a hot-bed; plow; and plant some potatoes, spring wheat, and vegetables. April and May were the months for sowing most of the small grains, potatoes, corn, sorghum, Hungarian grass, and some vegetables. In June some late vegetables might be planted, but the main work for June, as well as for July, was keeping the weeds down. Also in July there was haying to do, and sometimes rye and winter wheat to harvest. During August little was done on the farm except in the harvest field, where cutting and stacking wheat and oats was the order of the day, although some grain might be marketed at that time and tools might be put away. During the first part of September harvesting continued; in addition, potatoes were dug and grain was hauled to the mill. Later in September, plowing for next year's

In 1890 men and women worked side by side at harvest time on the Meyer Farm, St. Joseph. *Photo courtesy Stearns County Historical Society.*

wheat crop, sowing winter wheat, cutting up corn, and attending fairs were the usual procedures. In October more potatoes remained to be dug, and other root crops and garden vegetables waited to be gathered. There was threshing to do, corn to husk, hogs to fatten, and beef to "make." Plowing and preparing for winter often continued into November, but that month and December were usually devoted to chores, husking corn, threshing, and marketing grain and other farm produce. At the end of this round of activities, many farmers no doubt could say with John Cummins: [Farmer] "Another year rolled round, and has not added much pecuniarily to my condition, though probably I have benefited some little by experience."[1]

Although Jarchow accurately documented the daily work of the farmers, he did not record their attitudes and values, the mortar that bound the people to this way of life and made it all worthwhile.

The farming pioneers *chose* their lifestyles. These new Minnesotans left an old, traditional way of life for a new way of life that they believed presented beneficial opportunities and advantages for themselves and their children. They were willing to endure hardship and deprivation to accomplish this end. They knew that their heart, hands, health, and head were their only capital. They worked along without complaint; accepting hard work and long hours as necessary to their way of life. The settlers were busy, the people were respected as individuals, the social atmosphere was friendly and easy going, daily concerns were fundamental, and the people were drawn together in fellowship and mutual need. There was a sense of

the patient, quiet wisdom that comes from the continuity of life on the farm. The seeds that they planted annually grew as did their children, marking the cycle of progress.

The farmer-settlers took pride in their work, felling their own trees, cutting their own logs, and driving every building peg or nail themselves. The dependency on the neighborhood compelled everyone to know his neighbors on a first name basis. John Schmitt, an Albany farmer, recalled in an informal interview, that most areas had carpenters, well-diggers, a blacksmith, a doctor or midwife, and even a coffin-maker—"professionals" who helped out anyone who did not have that particular skill or talent. In some regions there were story-tellers who traveled from house to house providing entertainment in the evenings by telling stories. These were usually local people who enjoyed telling ghost stories, Indian stories, humorous stories, tragic stories, and tall tales. In winter whole families gathered together in front of the wood-burning stove to listen. People shared together in work and play since necessity left little other choice.

Generally, the pioneers accepted all people as essentially good. Their prime social test was evidence of good conduct. Frontier hospitality demanded that no one was ever turned away from a doorstep. Friends, neighbors, and strangers were all treated with respect and a natural easy-going hospitality. For example—Ruben Parson says of central Minnesotans in his book, *Ever the Land,*

It was the custom of the frontier of settlement that the traveler be offered food and shelter wherever night overtook him. Rarely was true hospitality compromised, however simple or crude the accommodations.[2]

Ceil Salzl said in an informal conversation at her St. Martin, Minnesota, home, that one time when she and her family were traveling by horse and wagon to visit distant friends, a sudden and severe rain storm came up. They noticed the lights of a distant farmhouse and headed the wagon toward it. The Salzls were warmly welcomed into the home; and, they were asked to kneel down and pray with the family, then in the middle of their evening family rosary. When the prayers were finished, the two newly-met families visited until the storm passed and the Salzls could continue on their journey.

Whereas the early farm people were practical by need, many were clever and some were ingenious. Bertha Rolfes of Farming, Minnesota, recalled that as a young girl she could tell the time by the sun. She recounted that on sunny days when she was working in the fields, if she faced north and she could step on the head of her shadow, it was noon.

Practicality was evident in the manner in which a family living near the Sauk River cleaned their wool. They washed it with homemade soap, placed it in a basket made of marsh willows, and then set it in the river where flowing water streamed through it, rinsing the soap from the wool. Then they hung the wool in trees to dry. Also, logs were mauled out for hog troughs with a corn cob used as a stopper in the draining hole. Sylvester Mischke, a farmer in Morrison County, Minnesota, still living on his family's homestead, said his ancestors had "staked out their house at noon, with the sun." However, they were also sentimental. Mischke said his ancestors had brought peppermint plants from Germany to their new home in Minnesota when they emigrated, these plantings the family has nurtured and kept growing all these years.

Throughout central Minnesota the pioneers took advantage of the natural bounty of the land. The area was naturally rich with wildlife, animals, fish, and fowl; thus, hunting, fishing, and trapping, usually done by the men and boys of the family, provided much of the food for settler families. When any animal was slaughtered for food, all parts of the animal were used. From the hides came mittens, blankets, or leather for shoes. The animal intestines were used for casings when making sausage from animal scraps. Choice animal pelts were sold for cash or bartered with the storekeepers for necessary goods and supplies. Hildegard Salzl said her father, Anton Moonen, shot enough ducks, pheasants, and prairie chickens on one of his trips to Albany, Minnesota, to pay for his needed supplies.

This double-barreled, muzzle-loaded musket, handcrafted for their grandfather the night before they sailed for America, is a prized possession of the Gogala brothers in St. Anthony. Central Minnesota was well stocked with wildlife and hunting provided much of the food for the table; thus, the gun was part of their way of life in the early days.

A unique natural product was found in the years 1859–1864 in Wright County, Minnesota. Men, women, and children contributed to the family income by digging ginseng roots. A forked root plant believed to have medicinal value, ginseng sold well to Yankee buyers from the east. Many farms in Wright County were bought and paid for in this manner. Similarly, all over central Minnesota, as in many parts of the country, vegetables, berries, and fruits from nature were harvested for home use or bartered for staple food for the larder and table. In one instance blackberries were bartered for logs to build a log house.[3]

Examples of the ingenuity of the early farming pioneers of central Minnesota are endless and can be learned of in stories told by living pioneers and their families; from their family histories, or in general conversation with elderly people in the area. They declare that the early settlers lived on the land and with the land they loved. They believed in God, and like Pehr in *Ever the Land*, they "prayed more for worthiness of the gifts than for the gifts themselves."[4]

Math Grausam, a retired farmer from Albany, Minnesota, said his ancestors had left Austria because of semi-starvation, "they had no meat to eat, only soup," when they left their mother country. In their new home in central Minnesota they found an abundance of all that they had ever desired in Austria. Many of the pioneers were God-fearing folks who believed that God made all things

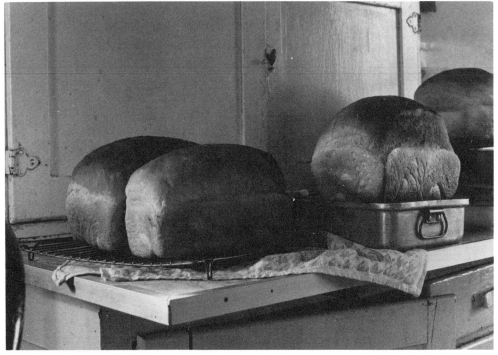

The aroma of freshly baked bread cooling on the kitchen counter permeates the Petrich house on cold winter days, just as it did in the early days of settlement when people prayed more for the worthiness of gifts than for the gifts themselves.

possible; that everything came as a gift from God. Their way of acknowledging their worthiness of these gifts was by silently continuing to work diligently and faithfully on the soil, living a good life and in keeping with their religious beliefs.

Ingenuity and faith were especially necessary for the women in the early days of settlement because they were often left alone on the farmstead while the men and boys were off in the woods or fields working. Throughout central Minnesota the Indians roamed about freely in the early statehood period. Often they appeared unexpectedly at the homes begging for food. One day several Indians visited the Rolfes home. They had a trapdoor in the floor of their house which led to a cellar filled with food that the Indians wanted. Bertha Rolfes said Grandmother Rolfes covered the trapdoor with a rug and "set her rocking chair on it and knitted away" until the Indians left. Irene Voronyak related that her mother was often frightened by Indians but "acted like they were good friends." One time they came to her house in search of freshly baked cottage cheese rolls which they could smell from a distance.[5] Although many of the pioneers feared the Indians, none of the people we interviewed reported any instances of actual bodily harm to their relatives. The settlers treated the Indians with respect and they were repaid in kind.

An impressive number of family histories have been recorded by local historical societies in central Minnesota and are available to the general public to peruse. Likewise, area schools, churches, and families are themselves now attempting to document the lives and events of the early pioneers of central Minnesota. Ben Omann, a prominent St. Stephen, Minnesota, resident, wrote the following account of a fellow parishioner, John Schumer. It aptly describes the attitudes and values of many area early farmers.

But his [Schumer's] goal was not material wealth. He never was the least bit envious of anyone else's good fortune or in the least way belittled his own lifelong work. He was completely happy and satisfied farming up on the hill where his father before him had brought up his family, and I feel sure [he, Schumer] always thanked the Lord for what he had—a living and good family life.[6]

However, although a decent living and good family life were the simple goals of many early central Minnesota farmers, they also changed with the times. In time they ceased to be self-sufficient small farmers. The farms expanded as the people acquired the machines, technical skills, and scientific agricultural knowledge required to meet the increased demand for their products. In the 1978 agricultural census for Stearns County, Minnesota, the average farm totaled 208 acres and

Anna Petrich in her log house kitchen. Like the early pioneers of central Minnesota, Anna chooses this lifestyle where the air is clean, the people are individuals, and concerns are fundamental. *Photos by Mike Nelson.*

was worth well over $150,000.[7] Surely, the pioneers' fulfillment of the dream for better opportunities and advantages for themselves and their children is evident today as one drives through the countryside of central Minnesota. While a few of the original log and stone structures still remain, they are dwarfed by massive barns and out-buildings and modern farmhouses. Streamlined agricultural equipment, machinery, and specialized crops help to feed the people of the world while assuring the pioneer's descendants the good life.

When the early settlers first set their axe to the trees in the wilderness of central Minnesota, the sounds of felling trees and hewing logs began the work that shaped the landscape of the area and established a lifestyle for the generations of people far into the future.

1 Merrill E. Jarchow, *The Earth Brought Forth* (St. Paul: Minnesota Historical Society, 1949), p. 26.
2 Ruben L. Parson, *Ever the Land* (Staples, Minnesota: Adventure Publishing Co., 1978), p. 66.
3 Actually the blackberries were not meant as payment for the logs but "just to be good," as Frances Supan related in a personal interview. See Steve and Frances Supan family history for more details.
4 Parson, *Ever the Land*, p. 243.
5 See Voronyak-Habas family history for details. Bertha Rolfes' stories were obtained during personal conversations with her over a period of years.
6 *"The Church Steeple,"* (St. Stephen Parish and Community Newspaper), 28 January 1979.
7 Orville L. Wilhite, *1978 Census of Agriculture, Stearns County, Minnesota*, U.S. Department of Commerce Bureau of the Census, 78-A71.

11

Women

Better born than married, misled,
in the heavy summers of the river bottom
and the long winters cut off by snow
she would crave gentle dainty things,
"a pretty little cookie or a cup of tea,"
but spent her days over a wood stove
cooking cornbread, kettles of jowl and beans
for the heavy, hungry, hard-handed
men she had married and mothered, bent
past unbending by her days of labor
that love had led her to. They had to break
her before she would lie down in her coffin.
                                        Wendell Berry
                                Farming, A Hand Book

For early pioneer women toughness was essential and pleasures had to be simple. Anna Petrich in her log home in St. Stephen. *Photo courtesy Nancy Brinkman.*

Throughout recorded history women have been largely ignored, especially the rural farm women. These women have not been recognized as an entity; but nevertheless, they were a vital, fundamental part of the history of settlement of the American frontier. They made log houses into homes and they helped turn the woods and stumpland into farms. Without the partnership of women, men would not have permanently conquered the wilderness. Barbara Ann Soloth vividly points this out:

> The scarcity of widows and single girls on the frontier is testimony that men found women to be a valuable asset. It is frequently told that a man would bury his wife at the corner of the fence and immediately begin the search for a new one.[1]

Although central Minnesota, with its terrifying, virginal beauty must have been frightening to the early pioneer women, they wanted to share in the experience of settlement with their men. They emigrated because they felt duty-bound to follow the men of the family, but also because they too wanted free land, new opportunities, and independence. George Kulzer, a Stearns County pioneer, wrote in his personal diary that his wife, Gretl, abandoned a substantial inheritance of land and property in Germany to emigrate to America. She had bound herself to a wealthy childless family for two years to work as a maid and cook in their bakeshop. When her indenture time was over, they told her that if she would stay with them they would will all of their property to her. Gretl refused their kind offer, having decided to emigrate to America instead. George Kulzer wrote that the dream of independence and freedom in America was a

"burning flame" for both of them. Gretl came to America first and he followed.[2] Immigrant women like Gretl Kulzer broke old home ties and traveled many miserable miles by sea and land sometimes in dread and fear of how their journey would end. They endured hardship and deprivation; seasickness and poor food was their lot on shipboard. Exhaustion and fear were their constant companions on the long journey by land to central Minnesota. Feminine frailty had to be abandoned in order to survive.

Only upon arriving after their arduous journey, did women come in contact with the physically demanding, masculine environment of the raw frontier of central Minnesota. Suddenly the reality of the harsh life in this alien land became apparent. Women had to be strong physically and emotionally because "in this new land, everything was different from [their former] home, they were forced to act in new and unaccustomed ways."[3] A woman had only herself and her family to depend on. Home activity and distance made close friendships and socialization with neighborhood women almost non-existent. It is certainly true that:

> The hardships endured by women in isolated areas were sufficient to make homemaking as heroic a task as that performed by her male counterparts.[4]

As with the men, the woman could not accommodate the wilderness to her needs and desires. She had to accommodate herself to the hard realities of living within the limits of a small farm clearing in the woods. The food was plain but wholesome and nearly all of it was raised on the farm. Wild game, and natural plants obtained by digging and hunting in the woods, and fishing the streams enhanced the routine diets. Ceil Salzl, a Stearns County woman, remembers picking and eating wild onions. Others remember picking cranberries, wild strawberries, gooseberries, hazelnuts, or whatever was available. Without refrigeration, meat was kept from spoiling by drying, salting, or smoking. Eventually, "the ability of the homemaker to make the most of the environment often determined the subsistence level of the family."[5] Women were the nurturers and the center of all life around the early farms.

However, the frontier demanded many changes in the role of women. The role of the homemaker expanded to include much of the work generally thought of as, "man's work." Many women, like Gretl Kulzer, helped the men grub stumps, break sod, and construct buildings. In one account of the building of a log cabin, "the cabin was erected by six women and four men . . ."[6] Fortunately, while their own log house was being built families often lived with friends or neighbors. There a woman could learn from another woman, already experienced, of the ways of log house living: Making do with heavy, crude furniture, few utensils and supplies, little space, and cooking an entirely new menu, before she actually moved into her own log cabin. Surely, these new experiences "were unknown, even unimagined, outside Biblical accounts of suffering, by the women pioneers."[7] Ida Ryberg told the story of their quickly constructed log cabin. She said, "The hurriedly cut logs were so fresh that in the warmth of the cabin they began to sprout leaves." She said their eighty-eight acre farm in rural Upsala, Minnesota, was wild, swampy, and tree-covered but it was all they could afford.

The log cabin was usually a basically constructed, monetarily inexpensive dwelling—one room covered with a leaky roof, few windows for light, poor ventilation, cursed by insects, mud or dust, and smoke. All living activity was centered there. Sleeping, eating, working, visiting, laughing and crying, all took place in this one room home. A flickering light from a glowing hearth fire was sometimes the only illumination relieving the stark darkness of the night.

In summer, heat and insects were unbearable; in winter, one woman said she "found ice in a tub at the door over two inches thick,"[8] on a cold winter morning. Cold crept into bed with the sleepers while animals howled outside. Their beginnings were pitifully crude. The cabin was cramped with all their worldly possessions. The furniture was practical and sturdy: Tables, benches, and stools were made of split logs pegged to stout wooden legs. Trundle beds and cradles were slid under larger beds during the daytime to conserve space. Clothes were hung on pegs in the walls. Dale Olmstead writes:

> Paraphernalia of even the simplest living hung from the beams, dripped from the walls, and kept the place forever glutted. Women worked doggedly to keep things orderly. By spring, cabin fever often set in: The monotony of daily living in too close quarters with too much work put men on edge; and women cried.[9]

To offset the drab monotony of cabin life, many women tried to beautify the interior of the cabins by making gayly colored curtains, crocheted floor rugs or bed covers from fabric dyed with berries and roots. Beautifully patterned fabrics, when obtainable in local towns, gave color to rooms and allowed women a chance to express their creative talents. Sometimes cozy furs or warm buffalo or horse hides were put on the floors to help stay the cold.

The women, however, could do little to change the form or appearance of the exterior of the cabins. Therefore, they turned some of their creative and imaginative skills to the grounds surrounding the cabins. They planted vegetable gardens, fruit trees, shrubs, and whatever useful plants they could acquire from friends and neighbors or gather from the wilds. The remains of these early plantings can be seen in many surviving pioneer farmsites in central Minnesota, for example, the Lind farm in Sherburne County. Although only remnants of the Lind farm buildings remain there is a definite line of rhubarb plants, lilac bushes, irises, raspberry plants, chokecherry trees, and Canada plum trees, bordered by stately bur oak trees set in a definite pattern around the buildings. It gives one the feeling of a distinctive air of pioneer prosperity. There was both great satisfaction and perplexity in seeing what growth one could accomplish. Certainly, "on a farm you have a chance to develop your management skills and build your muscles too."[10]

Women met the challenge of building a new life on the frontier because they believed that someday their lives and their families' lives would be richly rewarded, and the sacrifice would be well worth the effort. Almost everything was bearable because it represented the beginnings of a new and better life. The future held bountiful promise. Most things were considered as only temporary. And usually the family was better off within a few years than they could ever have been in their old homeland.

Temperament also played a large part in how these women succeeded. Many living pioneers still believe that toughness was essential and pleasures had to be simple. Anna Petrich, St. Stephen, said, "You have to respect each other and work together." Joy was found in small things like a child's first step, a healthy family, watching children slide down a haystack or playing games. Good crops, or a root cellar filled with canned goods and produce for the coming winter months gave great satisfaction.

A root cellar filled with canned goods and produce for the coming winter was a joy for the early pioneer women.

Patience, courage, and a fierce determination helped women to triumph over the hardships of early pioneer life. They did not complain and soon found that strength and knowledge came from the doing.

Furthermore, they did not rebel because they liked the idea of the family working together; they took pride in being a real helpmate to their husbands. Clara Symanietz, a living pioneer, said proudly, "I don't think he [her husband] could have drove a post in the ground without me. There was no other way. You had to do it." Farming was a family affair, with the women and children doing most of the routine work.

Unlike the pioneer women of the Great Plains of America who suffered from severe isolation and loneliness because they were so remote from friends and neighbors and other living creatures, in central Minnesota, nature was a woman's ally. The Big Woods provided a never-ending supply of work activity and simple entertainment, food stuff and supplies. Animals sometimes became pets. The Gogala brothers said their family had a deer so tame that it came up to them and ate out of their hands, at St. Anthony, Minnesota. Wood for the cookstove and heating was close at hand, often split by the women themselves. And an abundance of fish, fowl, and wild animals was not too far outside the door. Fruits berries, and nuts in season were there waiting to be picked. Syrup and sugar could be obtained from maple trees. Bees supplied honey. Birds could always be heard singing the choruses of the season. Their own vegetable gardens afforded variety; new flavors in vegetables and fruits. Some mistakes were made—"Harriet Pease, during her first winter in Minnesota, asked for dandelion seeds to plant in her garden for early winter growing"—when she wrote to friends back east![11] Few items had to be purchased. With ingenuity and hard work a family could be well fed. These frontier women took great pleasure in turning work into successful productivity.

A safe and adequate water supply was always a problem. Obtaining water was hard, heavy, constant work. In summer it was dipped from springs and streams. After wells were dug, the water had to be raised up in buckets and hauled into the house; and the well was a dangerous hole that worried many a mother, fearing her child would accidentally topple in. During the winter,

The well was a dangerous hole that worried many a mother, fearing a child would accidentally topple in.

snow was carried into the house; and melted on the back of the kitchen stove. Agnes Gertken, from Avon, Minnesota, recalls that every Sunday in winter was the day the girls of the family had to bring in snow to melt for washing clothes on Monday. A large wash boiler was filled with snow and set over direct heat on the back of the stove. Then the melted snow was strained through a cloth and put in tubs to await Monday's washing. Furthermore, since water was often very hard, hands soon became hard, dry, and rough, especially in combination with harsh homemade lye soap.

In winter, kitchens also became bathrooms. Tubs, filled with water heated on the stove, or dipped from the reservoir of the stove and placed in front of the open oven door provided bathing with few amenities. Then, after the baths, the water had to be dumped outside in the snow, creating clouds of steam that tempered the freshly bathed individual.

The interior of a restored log house at Albany Pioneer Village, Stearns County.

In summer, washtubs were often filled in the morning and allowed to sit in the hot summer sun all day for warm evening baths, usually outside or in the out-buildings.

The drinking water supply was held in metal or wooden pails near the wash basin. Consequently, any water that was used for drinking or cooking needed to be boiled to prevent disease and sickness. Later, cisterns and water barrels were used to collect soft water for laundry, but getting an adequate water supply remained difficult and time-consuming work.

Cooking utensils used in early cabin homes were primitive and few. Usually very few

homemaking things were brought along from the old country. Some items could be purchased in St. Paul or in local stores if there was any money. However, tinned copper kettles, hand carved wooden bowls, churns, and ladles, and iron skillets sufficed for most cooking chores in the early homes. Where to store them, also, was a problem. Often the utensils hung from pegs in the walls and beams.

By the time central Minnesota was settled, toward the end of the real pioneering era of America, the industrial revolution had already made its impact felt. For settlers coming into central Minnesota, cookstoves with tin pipes were available, replacing the dangerous fireplaces found in the earlier pioneer era. These early inefficient

The kitchen in a log house or cabin was the center of activity. Cookstoves replaced fireplaces in central Minnesota.

cookstoves made kitchens very hot and smoky in summer; in winter, maintaining an even heat required a constant vigil at the stove. If the fire went out, it was difficult to rekindle. Blaise Legatt, who was born in a log house in St. Stephen, Minnesota, related that on many extremely cold nights his mother was up all night keeping the fire going and heating blankets and clothing to keep the children warm. The early houses were so poorly insulated that often there was rime frost on the inside walls. In the sleeping loft, the children often woke with snow in the beds with them. Many pioneers enjoy retelling of their own unique experiences with snow in their beds in the early, cold sleeping lofts.

While meals were being cooked or water was being heated on the kitchen stove and wet clothes were hung to dry around it, a woman also needed to make time to care for childen, churn butter, make soap, sew, mend, and patch clothes, preserve garden produce, make tallow candles or clean kerosene lamps. A woman's slavish round of activities was never-ending. It is often said that women learned to do at least three things at once: "Rock the baby in the cradle, churn butter, and hear the younger children recite their catechism."[12]

Similarly, a woman had only to look out of her front door to see work she must do outside the house. Since the men spent most of their working hours in the fields in summer and in the woods in winter in central Minnesota, the women and children had to take care of the livestock and all of the routine work involved around the buildings. Women milked the cows, fed the livestock, and often even manured the barns. It is a small wonder that many women in pioneer novels, such as Beret of *Giants in the Earth*, acquired a special closeness to the cattle—live companions for lonely, busy women. While sitting on a three-legged stool listening to the peaceful twashing sound of milk filling the bucket, a woman could relax and think and dream. It was a quiet time away from the noise and activity that filled most of her day.

Usually, women also raised ducks, geese, turkeys, and chickens. Chickens were always considered "woman's work." They required constant care and attention but the work was not strenuous. Oftentimes the girls in the family took this chore off the mother's shoulders as soon as the girls were old enough. Agnes Rausch, born in Farming Township, said that by the time she was twelve years old she had the responsibility for the care of their chickens. She even kept a wood-burning stove going in the cold stone chicken barn during the winter to keep the chickens laying eggs. She recalls that if the men were in charge of the chickens, the chickens would go into a molt and stop laying eggs!

During the planting and harvesting seasons, when help and tempers were short and tension was high, women and children helped with the field work too. At such a time the indomitable spirit of the pioneer woman became apparent. While her husband was incapacitated, writes Barbara Lawrence of an early pioneer woman:

> The harvesting of all three acres of wheat fell to Rebecca. A scythe would have been too heavy for her to use, so a hand sickle was her only implement. When all the

wheat was cut, she and her nine year old son carried it on a litter-like device made of two slender poles to the cabin.[13]

The following year Rebecca was again forced by circumstances to go into the fields, this time she was six months pregnant with twins. Women helped whenever the men "were in a pinch or something," Fred Swan of Benton County, Minnesota related. Many women could handle oxen and horses as well as the men. Anna Petrich said, "I worked with all the horse-drawn equipment I could. When we sold our horses, I just cried." Selling the horses was harder for her than selling the cows, Anna said on the day she and her husband, John, celebrated their 70th wedding anniversary in St. Stephen, Minnesota. Many central Minnesota women could say along with Willa Cather's Antonia as she tells Jim in *My Antonia*:

> We'd never have got through if I hadn't been so strong. I've always had good health, thank God, and I was able to help him in the fields until right up to the time my babies came.[14]

Truly, pioneer women proved themselves not only capable of coping with the rawness of nature, they also experienced the actual manual labor involved with making a home and a farm in the wilderness.

All of this was not accomplished without some sacrifice of ideals and traditions. Farm women did not have lily-white hands—their hands were sun-burned and calloused and strong. "Proper" etiquette, too, was often abandoned for practicality, although not courtesy. Women often married in haste and quite young, with no time for a honeymoon or even a day off. Many were married in the morning and moved into their new homes by early afternoon. When evening came they were milking the cows. They had little time or space for personal privacy, and very little social life. Even letters were rare because the few post offices in existence were remote and time away from the pressing chores to write letters was scarce. Moreover, as Ruben Parson writes in *Ever the Land*—a novel placed in central Minnesota—"The men were so preoccupied with their own struggle that feminine needs generally escaped their notice." Pehr, after their mother died, unintentionally forgot that his daughters had personal needs. His new wife, in time, realized this and—

> . . . appreciated the girls' need of privacy, attractive clothing, and family respect; and it was she who insisted that their father provide the means.[15]

Women's clothing also reflected their austere lives. Styles were not gay but practical. Black and gray dresses with large white aprons were everyday attire and dress clothes were few and plain, as they were not often needed and the amenities in dress were not of primary importance. Probably the only really fine clothing in a woman's life were her wedding gown, usually hand-made with love and care, and the christening dress for her children, also hand-made out of lace and the finest material they could afford. Rough farm work was hard on clothing; therefore, it needed to be practical, strong, and oft-mended. Girls wore dresses much like their mother's, only a bit more colorful, if possible. Many times cumbersome, long dresses were a nuisance and got in the way during their daily chores. Clara Symanietz, Stearns County, Minnesota, related that her mother-in-law was fatally burned when her skirt caught fire while tending a burning grass fire. Undergarments were plain, white, and homemade. Leather shoes were made at home in simple styles. Usually, in summer woman and children went barefooted around the house and farmyard. Sunbonnets were worn to keep the skin white (an attempt at femininity), but were often abandoned in the discomfort of the fierce summer heat.

Pioneer women shared with their men a great faith in God. They developed a rapport with God and nature. Everything was considered a gift from God, to be treasured. Appeals to God through prayer were considered the best known remedies for everything from cabin fever to broken bones. Anna Petrich, who still lives in a log house, recounted that, "One lady had a sick husband and her biggest worry was—would the priest get there in time?" In the isolation and quiet of the woods, it was easy for the farm woman to pray.

However, unlike their urban and city counterparts, the churches of the farming frontier were not outlets for socialization among women since they were often quite distant. Although women were content and busy most of the time, they sorely missed the companionship of other women. They were lonely. Unfortunately because of

propriety, many restrictions were placed on them.

> The code of living in the Victorian Age made the pioneer woman's situation even more disillusioning. The feelings and consideration for women were secondary to the pleasures and whims of the male as the more important half of society.[16]

Thus, the birth of a baby, weddings, and funerals in the neighborhood offered limited sources of socializing for farm women. On the other hand, many women in central Minnesota used their practical ingenuity and combined sociability with work via husking bees, quilting bees, and other work-related group activities in which neighbors helped each other out. They generously visited each other and offered their help to anyone in need. In *Unto A Good Land* Kristina is visited by a woman she has met only once before, "and yet she felt she had known her for years; someone had come to whom she could talk."[17]

These reserved women, however, did not ordinarily discuss personal, intimate problems or concerns. Traditional feminine virtues of purity, charity, and harmony were respected and religiously adhered to in practice. In fact, in central Minnesota, the virtues described were much like Cora's in Wright Morris' *Plains Song*:

> Cora is typically modest—has never consciously looked at her own naked body, has never talked about her sexuality, is more than anything selfless. She values useful talks and fills her days with work.[18]

These women believed that their role in expressing sexuality was to satisfy their husband's natural sexual desires and to bear children. They were supportive and nurturing. Women lived in a male-dominated society, supported by structured religious behavioral standards that suggested they love their husbands with a pure and chaste love, silently acknowledging him as their head. This sanctity of marriage was understood and unquestioned.

Women also needed other women who acted as nurse or midwife in times of illness or disability. A family that did not suffer due to sickness or death was rare. Doctors were scarce, ill-trained, and often believed to be quacks. Medicines were primitive, poor in quality, and few. Home remedies were generally turned to in time of need. Medical equipment was almost non-existent unless one traveled to St. Paul. For this reason much of the burden of doctoring and providing medication also fell to the women. Eva K. Anglesburg offered this gruff reality, no doubt a common experience for the pioneer farmer:

> Blood from his hands was streaming; the yellow lamp-
> light shone
> Upon a thumb half severed, A palm slashed to the bone.
> Although his face was ashen, Quite casually he said,
> "Get out your needle, mother, And take your stoutest
> thread;
> For here's a bit of stitching I'd like to have you do.
> No need to call a doctor when I can come to you."[19]

When birth was imminent, a woman baked, washed clothes, and cooked to surplus to hold the family over while she was in confinement. Efforts were made so that a doctor or midwife could be at hand, but often babies came without help from either. If given a choice, many women preferred the help of a midwife—someone who they felt could identify with their situation and be a friend as well. One woman said that she preferred a midwife because midwives were more considerate and they let everything happen *naturally*. In her case, "Lard or butter was used in you so the baby would slide better and the child came lots easier."[20] Neighbor women or young girls often provided help to a woman during her confinement. This is beautifully depicted in *Unto a Good Land*:

> Kristina and Ulrika embraced like two devoted sisters. They were back at humanity's beginning here tonight, at the childbed in the North American forest. They were only two women, one to give life and one to help her; one to suffer and one to comfort; one seeking help in her pain, one in compassion sharing the pain which, ever since the beginning of time, has been woman's fate.[21]

New babies and children were considered a blessing from God and treasured as such. On the farm, children also represented an economic asset. In the eyes of their parents, they provided an ongoing heritage. Girls were welcomed by women as future companions and persons with whom to share work, experiences, and dreams. Mothers and daughters often became good friends, sharing intimate concerns and fears. Irene Voronyak, from Upsala, Minnesota, said her mother taught her many traditional, ethnic customs and crafts that she has practiced over the years.

Many hours spent working together, especially working in the kitchen while preserving food or while washing clothes, side by side, offered ample time to develop friendship and trust that lasted a lifetime. Girls also took over many of the chores and burdens previously performed by the mother, easing her life somewhat. Very young girls worked; they learned to card wool, crochet, and knit socks; they helped cleaning and filling kerosene lamps, emptying chamber pots, carring out dishwater, bringing in water used for cooking, washing, and drinking, bringing in corncobs and wood to fuel the stove, and occasionally flowers to brighten the kitchen table.

Too often there were moments when women needed each other to share grief. A death in the family was one of these times. Unfortunately, death was a common reality among the early pioneers, especially among the very young, as evidenced by the larger number of children's graves relative to adult graves in local cemeteries. The help and support of one's neighbors was comforting when death came to a family. A vacant place at the table was hard to bear. For this reason many farm people still rationalize concerning the reality of death—if death must come, let it come outside the home; among the animals. It was difficult for the bereaved to return to an empty house to face hardships of frontier life without the loved one, often a child, "the light of the home."[22] Women found needed comfort from the presence of other women. In *O! Pioneers*, Willa Cather depicts such psychic support,

> In time of trouble Signa had come back to stay with her mistress, for she was the only one of the maids from whom Alexandra would accept much personal service.[23]

Signa stayed on with Alexandra for three months, until she had time enough to accept her beloved brother's death.

After a difficult period, in houses quiet under drifting snow or softly falling raindrops, life continued. There were also happy times to be treasured and enjoyed amid the hardship and turmoil. Holidays, like Christmas and Easter, came and went and their festivity depended on the ability of the women to brighten the cabins and the spirits of the family. Ethnic traditions were carried on in small details of special foods and hand-made clothing; special gifts were made or gathered by the women and children to add cheer to the holidays. Women made special attempts to retain those aspects of culture and tradition that did not interfere with progress because home industries did not change as quickly or as drastically as did farmwork related industries.

The making of quilts is probably one necessity that evolved into an art form in pioneer America, and has continued on throughout the generations. Women could use their creative abilities and imaginative skills and apply them to quilts both utilitarian and beautiful. Many women responded to quilt-making as being fun! Ceil Salzl said that in summer she often sewed quilts in their barn. She cleaned the barn up a bit and set up her frame there where it was cooler and roomier than in the house.

A woman's tools—scissors, needle and thread, thimble, and quilt cards, used to disentangle fibers prior to spinning or to raise the nap on a fabric.

Today many nursing homes and women's groups in central Minnesota pride themselves on the lovely "patched," stamped, or embroidered quilts and coverlets they stitch together. Patterns are continued and skills learned from their mothers and grandmothers are practiced and still enjoyed by the social groups.

A seldom recognized fact is the monetary contribution pioneer women made to their family's livelihood. Besides doing their routine household and farmyard duties, helping in the fields, and raising the family, women sold the surplus from many products they raised; they sold geese, ducks, turkeys, chickens, eggs, garden produce, berries, fruits, and nuts picked from the wilds; home-made items of fancy work, including quilts, feather pillows, clothing, butter and baked goods. Often this was traded in barter or sold for cash to buy needed

supplies for both the farm and the house.

As time and progress allowed, life became relatively easier for women. Homes were enlarged, became more spacious, and were better equipped with devices which eased the immediate labor demands. However improved farming conditions have become, farming has remained a family oriented economic operation, with women and children still doing many of the routine chores. Fortunately, Hiram M. Drache acknowledges a recognition of the contribution of the services women and children made to farm economics. He wrote:

> By the 1920s it was obvious to the professional economist that the then apparent prosperity in American agriculture had resulted chiefly from two causes—the steady rise in land prices and the "unpaid services of women and children."[24]

Although many aspects of the pioneer farm woman's life were hard, seemingly unbearable at times, those women persevered in their dual role of homemaker and farm helpmate because they, like their men, usually chose this life and they were willing to sacrifice and work hard to make it successful—and enjoyable. They had faith in the future. As a rule, the pioneer women and men were economically and physically better off in two years than they ever would have been had they remained in the old country.

In a 1978 study of rural women in Minnesota, a forty-seven year old woman reflected on her life. She indicated that for her, as for most women all over, family and friends were important; but, she said—

> Family comes first and around that you build everything else. There really is nothing else. Just the normal life with its ups and downs, but there's nothing you can do about that, just make the best. I wouldn't trade with anyone.[25]

This woman was speaking of her life as a farm woman in central Minnesota today. Still today, on the farm, family members depend on one another and share life and work experiences together. "Family comes first" because they all need each other.

Just as living pioneers told us in numerous interviews that their ancestors never spoke of a desire to return to the old country, most farm people today have no desire to change roles and would likely say, with the modern farm woman, "I wouldn't trade with anyone."

Women who grew up on a farm, and also their men, recall childhood days as pleasant memories; they are convinced that their experiences shaped their character and gave them an awareness concerning the world that would not have been quite so sharp had they grown to maturity in another place.

Hopefully, modern historians, as they recognize the impact pioneer and modern farm men have had and will continue to have on American history, farm women will also be recognized for their contributions.

1 Barbara Ann Soloth, "Women on the Farming Frontier of Minnesota, 1849-1890," (Unpublished Master's Thesis, Mankato State College, 1965), p. 35.

2 "George Kulzer, 1831-1912, A Continuing Story of a Stearns County Pioneer," *The Albany Enterprise*, 15 June 1976, p. 1B. (Personal diary of George Kulzer, translated from German to English by daughter-in-law Mary Kulzer in 1935 and continued and completed by grand-daughter Ramona Kulzer in 1970. Serialized in *The Albany Enterprise*, 1976.)

3 Vilhelm Moberg, *Unto a Good Land*, (New York: Popular Library, 1964), p. 91.

4 Soloth, Preface.

5 Soloth, p. 15.

6 Betty I. Madden, *Arts, Crafts, and Architecture in Early Illinois*, (Urbana: University of Illinois Press, 1973), p. 40.

7 Marie Campbell, "Frontier Women: Pioneers or Outcasts?" Paper presented at Popular Culture Association, Eleventh Annual Meeting, Cincinnati, Ohio, 27 March 1981, p. 3.

8 Peg Meier, *Bring Warm Clothes*, (Minneapolis: Minneapolis Star and Tribune Company, 1981), p. 60.

9 Dale Olmstead, "Benton County Log Structures," Unpublished paper for St. Cloud State University American Studies Course, December 1980.

10 Clay Anderson, Ronald M. Fisher, Stratford C. Jones, Bill Peterson, Cynthia Russ Ramsey, *Life in Rural America*, (Washington D.C.: National Geographic Society, 1974), p. 19.

11 Margaret Snyder, *The Chosen Valley*, (New York: W. W. Norton & Company, Inc., 1948), p. 215.

12 Laino Alatalo, "Life in a Log Cabin," *The Gopher Reader: Minnesota Story in Words and Pictures—Selections from the "Gopher Historian,"* (St. Paul: Minnesota Historical Society and Minnesota Statehood Centennial Commission, 1966), p. 92.

13 Barbara Lawrence, "Two Women: Good News and Bad News," Paper presented at Popular Culture Association, Eleventh Annual Meeting, Cincinnati, Ohio, 27 March 1981, p. 4.

14 Willa Cather, *My Antonia*, (Boston: Houghton Mifflin, 1918), p. 342-3.

15 Ruben L. Parson, *Ever the Land*, (Staples, Minnesota: Adventure Publications, 1978), p. 243.

16 Soloth, p. 15.

17 Soloth, p. 260.

18 Campbell, p. 3.

19 Hiram M. Drache, *The Challenge of the Prairie*, (Fargo: North Dakota Institute for Regional Studies, 1970), p. 270.

20 The individual who said this asked not to be identified. Typical of most central Minnesota living pioneers, she was very willing to discuss her life but matters of personal propriety were delicate topics never to be made common knowledge.

21 Moberg, p. 297.

22 Everett Dick, *The Sod-House Frontier 1854-1890*, New York: D. Appleton Century Company, 1972), p. 254.

23 Willa Cather, *O! Pioneers*, (Boston: Houghton Mifflin, 1941), p. 275.

24 Drache, p. 106.

25 "Life Cycle and Personal Goals: Rural Women Talk about the Past, Present, and Future," *Rural Women in Minnesota: A Needs Assessment*, (St. John's University, Collegeville, Minnesota, Center for Human and Community Development, 1978).

The hearth of a home is wherever family life and activity are centered.

Churches

"Christianity is the root of all democracy,
the highest fact in the rights of man."
—Novalis

God was an ever-present source of inspiration for the early pioneers. They truly believed that it was God's will that had brought them safely into the new wilderness. Religion was the sustaining force in their lives. It enabled the settlers to cope with the fundamental processes of their natural world. They believed prosperity was a blessing and they were willing to work for it. They loved their land and had a simple, almost childlike, faith in God, believing that God was at the beginning and at the end in their dealings with nature. Concerning the land, the pioneers might also have said:

> Yes, we love it; we care for it; we own it; But it belongs to the Lord. That's why it smells so good and looks so fine. We come from it, and we go to it. It's the beginning and the end.[1]

The farmer's God was in the soil, in the fields; he found him everywhere. The co-attachment to the land and religion ran deep. However, spiritual leadership and guidance and churches were desired; therefore, established settlers welcomed newcomers into their areas to help ensure the establishment of churches. Churches represented a place where a believing community of faith could gather together to celebrate the Word of God.

In central Minnesota, missionary priests and pastors served the spiritual needs of the early settlers. Services were few and settlers had to travel great distances to attend—women seldom did. Family and housework kept them at home. Anna Petrich, St. Stephen, Minnesota, said: "The ladies, they had to stay home. There was so much work to do."

Log cabins served as the first churches. However, in time, these became too small and inconvenient. Larger churches were needed. In Wright County, John McDonald gave his barn as a place of worship until a church could be erected. In some areas schools functioned as churches.

Built by the people themselves, these first churches were modest log structures about twenty by thirty feet, cold and bare, mortared with

sacrifice and faith. People diligently applied their own time and skills to their church's construction in a spirit of dedication and devotion to their God. They strongly believed that their church deserved a share of their best; they donated land, lumber, altars, windows, statues, bells, and vestments; everything that was needed to provide a dignified and elevating worship celebration. The Gogala family at St. Anthony, Minnesota, donated twenty acres of land for the church in early St. Anthony. This was the practice in many small towns and villages. Land, a most prized possession, was not too much to give for the construction of a church. Anna Petrich, even today, takes personal care of the altar flowers in St. Stephen, raising them in her own garden.

The early churches were mission parishes without resident pastors, but they were the outward signs of the faith of the people who built and attended them. Faith and perseverance were the life-blood of these people. They believed the Lord would work with them to meet their needs.

Very few of these original log churches still exist; however, the parishioners of one such church in Santiago, Sherburne County, Minnesota, had the foresight to preserve their structure. It stands at the rear of a new brick church. The pioneer building is in very good condition, and it is presently used as a Sunday school.

The missionary priest, Father Pierz, resolved the problem of mission parishes among the German Catholics of central Minnesota by requesting his superior, Bishop Cretin, to procure a religious community of priests for the area. Benedictine monks from St. Vincent's Abbey at Latrobe, Pennsylvania, heeded the call and arrived in central Minnesota in 1856. They established themselves permanently at Collegeville, Minnesota, founding St. John's Abbey. This helped to stabalize the German Catholic population in the area.[2]

Reverend Sherman Hall built a Congregational church in Sauk Rapids, Benton County, Minnesota, in 1855. He was spiritual leader and pastor of his church for twenty-six years and became affectionately known to many people in Minnesota as "Father Hall," according to local memories.

Substantial frame churches replaced the early log churches. These frame buildings were generally

painted white and they were graced by a small
steeple over the main entrance. The church with its
spire pointing heavenward, which could be seen for
many miles, was the landmark of a Christian
community. Sylvester Mischke, a Buckman,
Minnesota, farmer said his family built their family
farm home facing the direction of the village
church in the distance. They could hear the noon
Angelus Bells ring each day from the farm house.

The early church services were usually
conducted in the native language of the
predominant ethnic group who attended them.
Native language services lasted well into the
1900s. English began to be used more and more in
the twentieth century. St. John's Lutheran Church
in Livonia, Sherburne County, Minnesota,
celebrated its annual mission festival in 1916 with a
German service in the morning and an English
service in the afternoon, according to records.

As the population and prosperity of the people
grew, so did the size of the churches and their
congregations. Imposing church structures of stone
and brick were constructed. They were:

> Monuments that seemed to dwarf the man who entered
> it. Space, light, and sculptural effects of the masonry
> were so organized as to produce a transcendental and
> awesome character, visionary in scale.[3]

Frank Lloyd Wright said that buildings are
"corporal extensions of personality."[4] If viewed
against the background of the times, the churches
of central Minnesota illustrate the strong,
unbending, Christian faith of its people. Many of
the churches are impressive architectural
achievements, often decorated with definite ethnic
motif. The village church is a symbol of a living
community of faith; the center of social life. The
church bells ring out their place of prominence in
the lives of a trusting, believing people.

The doors of St. Francis Catholic Church, Buffalo, Wright County, Minnesota, reveal the degree to which construction can be an art form. These doors, handcrafted in Mexico, were installed after a fire partially destroyed the 66-year-old edifice.

The white frame churches of the late nineteenth century are rapidly disappearing from the American landscape. If these neat clapboarded churches escape the bulldozer, they often fall prey to unsympathetic remodeling. This Benton County, Minnesota, church has the lancet window element common to Gothic Revival architecture.

The first St. Anthony's Church, St. Anthony, Stearns County, was a 25' × 40' log structure built in 1879 on land donated by Anton Gogala. A frame church was built in 1893, and the present brick structure in 1897-1900. The building is an interpretation of the Gothic Revival built of yellow brick.

1   Maisie and David Conrat, *The American Farm: A Photographic History* (San Francisco: California Historical Society, 1977), p. 168.

2   William P. Furlan, *In Charity Unfeigned* (Paterson, New Jersey: St. Anthony Guild Press, 1952), p. 195.

3   Richard E. Perrin, *The Architecture of Wisconsin* (Madison: Wisconsin State Historical Society, 1967), p. 72.

4   Perrin, p. 138.

Probably the only central Minnesota log church still in use is the 1888 South Santiago Lutheran church, Santiago township, Sherburne County. Used today as a Sunday school, it was the original church for Scandinavians who settled the township in 1882.

St. James' Church, Jacobs' Prairie, Stearns County, represents the pattern of architectural development in central Minnesota. The church makes use of granite slabs set in mortar—an unusual interpretation of ecclesiastical architecture for this region.

One of the most beautiful churches in central Minnesota stands on a wooded knoll near Clearwater Lake, Corinna Township, Wright County. The organization and construction of the church were initiated by Octavius Longworth and Rev. David B. Knickerbacker, members of St. Mark's Church, Brooklyn, New York, before coming to Minnesota. Longworth came to the township in 1859 where he settled in a log house that also served as the first church. The present sanctuary was built in 1871 and consecrated by Bishop Henry B. Whipple the following year.

Constructed of wood frame with board/batten siding painted brown, the church blends in with its natural setting. The church is Gothic Revival and contains elements common to that style: pointed lancet windows, arched entries, and a bell tower with arched openings. The interior has an exposed truss work ceiling, a raised altar, wainscotting, and straight-back, narrow pews. St. Mark's is an architectural gem.

Schools

Our todays and yesterdays
Are the blocks with which we build.
Henry Wadsworth Longfellow
The Builders

Along with churches, schools were an immediate requirement for the early settlers in central Minnesota. Some of the immigrants had a substantial education, some had very little, and most had no formal education at all. Part of their dream for a better life in the new world included an education, if not for themselves, at least for their children. They felt it necessary for the children to know how to read, write, and to "figure." In several of the townships of central Minnesota, a school was built even before a church parish congregation was formally established.

Like other early pioneer buildings, the first schools were poorly ventilated log or stone buildings which were poorly heated and poorly equipped. The schools had rude benches for seats, few books and few teaching and learning materials. They were, however, the forerunners of the more substantial educational system of frame buildings and better equipment which came as conditions improved in the years that followed.

These frame school buildings once dotted the countryside of central Minnesota. They were of a traditional American design not easily mistaken for any other type of building. Early schools were rectangular, one-room structures with small entry halls to hold coats, boots, lunch buckets, and wood for the stove. They were practical structures with windows placed the length of the building high above the eye level of a sitting student for light and ventilation, to provide space for maps and art to be displayed at the pupil's eye level, and to eliminate distraction—the opportunity for a pupil to look out the window and daydream. All eight grades were taught in one room. Often the room was very crowded. Rural families tended to be quite large so whole family groups would be in the same room. There was no age division classification. Students advanced at individual paces. Math Grausam, recalling his rural school days, said the one-room school he attended near Albany, Minnesota, had ninety-two students attending at one time!

The North Prairie school, Morrison County, is unusual because of its style, size, and use of materials. The symmetry and proportions, as well as the hipped roof and double chimneys, denote Georgian Revival, an uncommonly elegant style for a country school. Two-story schools are also rare as is the use of brick. This structure has been converted into a home without too much loss of its original integrity.

Historically, American rural schools are usually depicted as "the little red schoolhouse;" however, white was a more prevalent color in the Minnesota region. The interior dimensions of the room determined by the range of the human voice, usually thirty to forty feet.[1] Often, George Washington's picture graced the front wall near the American flag. Pupils moved to the front of the room for recitations. As a rule, almost everyone who ever attended a rural school remembers it as a pleasant learning experience.

The following is a poem written by Joseph L. Brady of Sherburne County, Minnesota, published in 1923 in his book entitled *Philosophy in Verse*. It provides an insight into the nostalgia generated by the early schoolhouses:

FIRST SCHOOL OF PIONEERS
Near the winding banks of a meadow stream,
    Where murmuring waters gently flow,
On the edge of the frontier's extreme,
    Was the pioneer's school of long ago.
The rude school house was made of logs,

And block and slabs were used for floor;
The roof of shakes held down by clogs,
And woven elm bark made the door.
The seats were planks hewed flat on top,
None had backs, but boards in front,
Fashioned at the woodman's forest shop;
But for a plane he did not hunt.
An old style box stove warmed the room,
When blasts of blizzards frigid grew,
Two small windows lessened the gloom,
And through the roof was a stove pipe flue.
And when spring and summer's sun and rain,
Unfolded cell life from dormant rest,
And heat too great indoors to remain,
There's school under the trees and songster's nest.
There were no charts or maps at all,
And though books were few—yet studied well,
One small blackboard adorned the wall—
There's lump chalk, but no teacher's bell.
A barrel used also for a chair,
The front upper part cut half way down:
The seat was made from skin of a bear,
Trimmed with red oak leaves of richest brown.
There were no slates, but in their place
Birch bark was used for writing tabs;
Homemade ink served for copy trace,
And weasel skins for blotter pads.
And there the master taught his school,
Made cube root blocks and goose quill pens;
Proved the intergral unit rule
And ciphered decimals by tens.
And there essential rudiments were taught
From A B C to the Old Rule of Three;
And there was trained the development of thought
That to future advancement was the key.
It matters not where one first saw the light.
Or first was led in paths of knowledge;
Those who in a log schoool house recite,
May soon be teachers in a college.

The earliest rural schoolhouses were built of logs. Later stone, milled lumber, brick, and sometimes area granite were used as construction materials. In Sherburne County, Minnesota, "during the 1880s a brick school house was built in the Swede Hollow area. The lintels on the school below the windows, were solid granite blocks."[2] In areas where stonemasons were available, stone was the most popular building material for schools—the St. Joseph, Collegeville area of Stearns County, Minnesota, for one. In fact, two walls of a little stone schoolhouse one mile north of St. John's University still stand in a hollow amid trees and thicket. This school was built in 1895 in the wake of a cyclone that destroyed a log school that had been there.[3]

Most country schools followed the style of this rural Albany building which has been moved to Albany Pioneer Village. Windows were placed high for light and ventilation and to prevent distraction.

Children started school at about age six and continued until they were "through their readers." Ida Ryberg, who attended a rural school in the Upsala, Minnesota, countryside, said theirs were McGuffy's Readers; if they were in grade five, it meant they were using the fifth reader. There was no real class structure in the present day sense. When a student graduated, it meant he or she had satisfactorily completed the required number of books to graduate.

Because of farm work, the school year was often shortened to accommodate the farm schedule. Attendance at school was sometimes poor, and children often had to discontinue their education at an early age to help on the farm. Anna Petrich lamented, "You just stayed home, but there were tears," when she had to stay home to help with the farm work.

Children walked to school, carrying their lunch in a bucket or pail. Math Grausam said he carried "dry bread with lard and syrup" in his pail. Often they pulled sleds to school to provide winter fun during recess and after school. They played games requiring little equipment but much imagination. Joseph Gogala recounted his school days and said, "We had to make up our own games." They played Drop the Hankie, Hide and Seek, Hide the Thimble, Ante, Ante Over, Tag. Blaise Legatt, Rice, Minnesota, remembers sledding on a big hill near the schoolhouse.

The teacher was hired by the district school board. The teacher was usually looked up to both by the students and the community as a person of high intelligence and abilities. He taught the basic subjects with an emphasis on conduct and fellowship; and if the teacher was a woman, household crafts were taught to the girls. Simple values and attitudes were carried into the school curricula. Irene Voronyak, a former Stearns County, Minnesota, teacher, said, "kids were more independent in rural schools. They learned to work on their own. . . . There was more family and more people were interested in what their kids were doing." Religion was routinely taught in the public schools by the local ministers or priests.

Moreover, work, play, fresh air, sunshine, home-grown food, and a sense of belonging and sharing in family life all contributed to a healthy farm child, one very capable of learning and grasping new ideas and knowledge in the school atmosphere. Also, because all of the children were in one room, they were exposed to various levels of learning—what was taught to one grade was heard by all in that school. This constant repetition was conducive to retentive learning, recalled Viola Flynn, another Stearns County teacher. School plays, pageants, and religious programs were presented, as cooperative ventures between students and teachers, to the community, thus enriching the community life experience.

In time, expanding educational demands, changing economic and social conditions—better roads, transportation, and a declining rural population—resulted in the consolidation of small rural schools into larger single units. The consequence of this move was the closing of most of the neighborhood school buildings. Many people feel some of our ability to transmit the basic American values was abandoned with those buildings. Irene Voronyak said, "When the rural schools went in about 1967, I just hated to see them go. It seems like part of our lives, our independence, went."

Very few one-room schoolhouses remain standing in central Minnesota. None are operating as schools. Most have completely disappeared from the landscape, although a few have survived because of changed use. They have been converted into homes, animal shelters, or storage sheds.

Some of those still standing are crumbling shells. Their window panes have been knocked out and the frames appear as empty eye sockets. Their walls look like broken down, forgotten old toy buildings, standing amid tall grass and weeds, suffering the ravages of time and neglect. They are silent reminders of a past not so long gone. Only light and darkness come inside now.

Broken windows cast shadows downward, like closed eyes, on:
"Sweet childish days, that were as long
As twenty days are now."
William Wordsworth

Perhaps their nostalgia and importance can be summed up thus:

> Country schoolhouses are icons of such treasured American values as simplicity, equality, and self-reliance. . . . Country schoolhouses are also cherished symbols of a life-style gone from most parts of the United States: Independent, family-centered, agrarian and more consciously tied to the soil and the season than to far-off powers and technologies.[4]

1   Fred E. H. Schroeder, "Educational Legacy: Rural One-Room Schoolhouses," *Historic Preservation*, vol. 29, (July–September, 1977), p. 7.
2   Elaine Anderson, "History of Sherburne County" (Sherburne County Historical Society, n.d.), p. 125.
3   William Bell Mitchell, *The History of Stearns County, Minnesota* (Chicago: Cooper and Company, 1915), vol. 2, p. 1360.
4   Schroeder, p. 5.

Towns

"The history of a nation is only the
history of its villages written large."
Woodrow Wilson, 1900

The pioneers coming into central Minnesota stuck their roots firmly and deeply into the rich soil of the area. The first settlers were self-sufficient farmers who raised their own food and built their own buildings, using the abundant products of nature in the region. Land, labor and livestock were factors which shaped their lifestyle.

Few immigrants, however, brought the necessary implements, tools, and supplies required to practice their trade when they emigrated from Europe or other parts of the United States. Most of them came with only the clothes on their backs. Coming through St. Paul or St. Anthony Falls, they could purchase a few things, such as a plow, an ox, and the food staples needed to begin their new lives in the wilderness of central Minnesota. But, once established on a homestead, St. Paul was over 100 miles distant from many areas of central Minnesota. A trip there by oxen consumed six or more days of precious time. The farmers needed towns or villages within easy traveling distance to supply their basic needs.

A few Minnesota towns such as Clearwater, St. Cloud, Sauk Rapids, Little Falls, and Elk River had been established along early trade routes, ox-cart trails, Mississippi River steamboat routes, and stage coach terminals. Even these towns were inconvenient for the farmers in the early days, however, because roads were almost nonexistent and travel was very difficult, had money and time been available.

The European emigrants had lived under a feudal class system in which the farmers were members of the lowest class, bound to the land and fief-bound to the lord of the manor. Irene Voronyak, an Upsala, Minnesota, immigrant's descendant, said her ancestors worked for landed gentry who controlled most of the land. They left Czechoslovakia for central Minnesota because they wanted to own and control their own land.[1] In early New England, farmers lived in villages and farmed the outlying arable land. For a brief time these lands were held communally. Some vestiges of the medieval land system carried over into the new world, however, in the colonial period in the form of large family estates or royal land grants. The Baltimores in Maryland and the Roosevelts in New Amsterdam are examples. However, Minnesota was populated primarily by poor and middle class people who settled on scattered farmsteads throughout the state, thus impeding the establishment of large family holdings and estates.

By the time Minnesota settlement reached its peak, land-holding was based on more democratic principles. The Pre-emption Act of 1841 and the Homestead Act of 1862 had been enacted, laws that opened up opportunity for settlement with a minimum of capital and few legal requirements. Because of these laws, the population of central Minnesota swelled between the 1850s and the 1880s, increasing both the number of small farms and the need for specialized rural villages and towns. With the obliteration of class lines and with a sense of loyal self-determination in the new world, many small villages and towns began to develop.[2] These early settlements were small, geographically close, and generally tied to the land use patterns of the immediate area. They provided those farm-related services that were essential to the population and encouraged the growth and progress of the towns. Life in these towns was truly related to nature, following a classic, rural lifestyle.[3]

Many central Minnesota towns were formed when clusters of people settled together at a crossroads and an ambitious entrepreneur opened a general store, a blacksmith shop, or a sawmill to serve the needs of his fellow neighbors. Flour and grist mill sites along a river's edge often determined the location of a town. In other cases towns began with the establishment of churches—a staying power resulting from the large number of national religious groups in the region. As roads improved and bridges were built, towns evolved around small hotels or boarding houses along central service roads between major transportation routes, convenient stopping places for weary travelers. Other settlements grew out of town halls where farm or community organizations met to promote the common good, and where the pleasure of one another's company was a binding force. A raw village with dirt paths and a handful of businesses could evolve into a successful town because of the interdependence of rural and urban society. In central Minnesota, as in most sections of the United States, the early towns were a nucleus around which social and economic needs revolved. Consequently, as Minnesota historian, Lowry Nelson, points out: "The completely rural society was short-lived as the urban-industrial world soon appeared and gradually emerged into predominance."[4]

The railroad became the vital link between the settler-farmer and towns and cities. The industrial revolution was well under way by the time Minnesota became populated. In this new country there was a shortage of labor and farmers needed labor-saving devices and machines. Technology and mechanization, even in its early stages, made farmers dependent on towns for steel and chilled-iron plows, grain drills, mechanical harvesters, and other tools and machinery, as well as cookstoves, cast-iron pots and pans, and factory-made furniture and household goods.[5] Railroads made it possible for these items to reach the rural people in central Minnesota. The growth and development of rural America was keyed to the introduction of railroads into the countryside—transportation and communication enabled men to conquer the land spatially and mechanical inventions enabled them to stay on the land permanently.

In Minnesota, the first railroads were chartered as early as 1853 with active building after the early 1860s. Lines reached St. Cloud in

The Paynesville (Stearns County) depot, c. 1887, is typical of small frame depots throughout the middle west. Stripped of all ornamentation, they served the dual purpose of passenger and freight service. This depot has been covered with asbestos siding manufactured to look like brick.

1866 later expanding to the north and west. The names of early railroads are unfamiliar to modern Minnesotans as a score or more of the pioneering railroads were consolidated in the 1880s. The names commonly found on maps are the Minneapolis, St. Paul and Sault St. Marie Railway, or the "Soo" Line, the Great Northern, and the Northern Pacific.[6]

As construction of railroads in central Minnesota proceeded—

> They opened lands, built towns, forwarded trade, and strengthened the economy. Railroads eased the conveyance of immigrants, gave jobs, sold land, conveyed goods to trading centers, carried products to markets, and helped people keep in touch with the world they left behind.[7]

Impromptu towns mushroomed at the end of these lines, often little more than a main street with a depot and a few beer halls. Aggressive railroad promotional campaigns lured people to towns and railways were "eager to sell their town lots and to create a demand for alternate sections which they [railroads] had been granted along the right of way."[8] Sometimes railroad companies donated land for churches, schools, and public buildings. The railroad network expanded with industrialization and the towns which had been peacefully contained for years started to grow and flourish into commercial and manufacturing centers. At times, town lines were defined by a radius from a depot—the distance convenient for farmers to transport their products to the nearest depot.

Towns were laid out on the basis of a surveyor's township, 6 miles square, containing 640 acres, divided into 36 sections. Each section was one mile square. Railroad companies or their subsidiaries laid out many of the towns. In the Midwest, two types of town planning pre-dominated—the linear plan and the grid plan. In the linear plan a town grew along a single major thoroughfare—perhaps a main street that fronted on a railroad track, as in Albany, Minnesota. In the grid plan the application of a rectilinear plan was used, regardless of natural terrain. The grid took the form of rectangular blocks, straight streets, and right-angle intersections.[9] After the late eighteenth century, most American towns and cities followed the grid plan. Railroads preferred the simple, efficient grid plan because:

> Here was a 'labor saving device' without peer: the grid could be planned from a distance, even without exact knowledge of local topography; the grid was easily surveyed and lots conveniently numbered for sale; the grid, rapidly extended in any direction and for any distance, was tailor-made for future growth and exploitation. Not the least of it, the grid plan expressed the order, regularity, balance and predictability most admired by the rationalists of the early nineteenth century.[10]

In burgeoning Minnesota towns, the grid plan was generally simplified and abstracted in response to the demands of expediency because the area was basically agricultural and the useful rather than the beautiful was preferred. While many critics have attacked the grid system for its monotony and its lack of rapport with the natural terrain, one critic, Vincent Scully, defends the grid as a dramatic *contrast* between the natural landscape and orderly settlement by saying:

> . . . the crossing of two streets makes a place in the emptiness . . . false fronts of the wooden buildings masked their gable ends to provide a true street facade, reaching for urban scale, for a shape in the vastness.[11]

Historian John B. Jackson, however, expresses a far more common feeling:

> . . . Dozens of villages sprang up along the railroads— some of them immediately shabby and swarming with flies, others neat and inviting. Widely scattered throughout the landscape—at crossroads, on the banks of streams, at railroad stops—were small churches, small factory houses, a new Grange Hall, a mill, and sometimes a small factory where farm equipment was made. Whether the land was hilly or flat, the same dispersed pattern seemed to repeat itself—friendly, peaceful, vaguely untidy under its opulent trees. It was easy for the outsider to discover monotony in the Midwest and to think of monotony as its significant characteristic.[12]

Once a town was established, it functioned as a marketplace, a meeting place, and a crossroads for commerce and communication. Main street became the focal point for these activities. It was the axis of the town and success was identified with building up the main street. Carol Rifkind writes that, "Main Street was always familiar, always recognizable as the heart and soul of a village, town, or city."[13] Buildings of every size and shape formed the face of main street. Towns changed and

adapted to serve the needs of the commercial middleman as farming became more commercialized. Dealers, suppliers, merchants, itinerant peddlers, mechanics, lawyers, doctors, and teachers teemed into new towns, encouraged by opportunity and new-found freedom.[14]

The general store was the most frequented establishment in early towns. It was the center of the town's business life. Farmers came to sell crops, purchase a keg of nails, tools, farm equipment, tobacco for chewing or smoking, or a glass of beer. For women it meant a change from isolation and daily chores. They could barter or sell eggs, butter, maple syrup, dried fruits, garden produce, and hand-made items. The town became a place to buy clothing, dishes, steel knives and forks, pewter spoons, jars, crocks, pans, brooms, salt, sugar, soda crackers, coffee, tea, spices, rice, or candy for the children. The availability of these staple items as well as items possibly raised or made at home eased the work load of the farming men and women. With the general store's readily available supplies, self-sufficiency became somewhat less necessary.

The general store provided a place to socialize as well as buy, barter, or sell. The north end of the Evens store, Farming, Minnesota, served as a bar. The family lived upstairs.

The false front provided a standard cornice line for any main street. In the T. J. Anderson store, Belgrade, Stearns County, Minnesota, the cornice was embellished with a pediment and brackets. *Photograph courtesy Stearns County Historical Society.*

29

Many living pioneers remember the stories told by their ancestors about the general store. Joe Gasperlin said his family sold strawberry crab apples for $1.00 per bushel. Anna Petrich said her parents traded butter, cordwood, and eggs for garden seeds, axes, grub hoes, shovels, and pitch forks. Irene Voronyak's father cut and sold railroad ties for $3.00 per load to purchase supplies at the general store.[15] The general store was also a place to meet, to gossip, play cards, or exchange stories while warming hands over a wood-burning, pot-bellied stove.

Often the general store building served multi-purposes. Perhaps a makeshift post office was located in one part of the building, before rural delivery mail was introduced into Minnesota in 1896. Post offices, then, as now, keep people in touch with the world by way of letters, bulk mail, and parcel post packages.

Many times the shopkeeper's family lived upstairs over the general store; sometimes a saloon or tavern was located in one end of the building; often specialty shops such as barber shops, beauty shops, shoe shops, or drug stores were located in other parts of the building. In a few instances, newspaper offices began in general stores. The local newspaper was an active voice in the life and politics in the early towns. Weekly tabloids advertised the community, recorded its history, and promoted its interests. The Melrose, Minnesota, *Record*, as one example, printed its first newspaper in June, 1877.[16]

Flour and grist mills, usually located near the railroad depot, often rose above the treetops in early towns throughout central Minnesota. Local mills transformed bushels of grain into flour. From these mills tons of wheat flowed from the heartlands of Minnesota to the mills that lined the Mississippi River during the years when Minneapolis was an international flour milling center.

A most important service was provided by the local blacksmith shop. Farmers depended on the blacksmith for services and repairs on a daily basis, year round:

> [The blacksmith] did plow-lay sharpening in fall, horse shoeing, sled repair, and wagon building in winter, and wheel and drill repair in spring. In summer he was the general handyman to have around for all kinds of daily repairs.[17]

The local blacksmith shop provided services vital to the needs of a growing rural community. The Herman Athmann blacksmith shop, Farming, Stearns County, Minnesota.

The blacksmith also made and sold hardware, tools, farm equipment, and his shop was a place where men would congregate to discuss everything from politics to local gossip. A masculine atmosphere pervaded the shop.

Towns were often built around churches because they offered spiritual strength and consolation for the pioneers. Churches offered a link with the traditions of the past without affecting progress. Religious worship and church-directed activities between residents of a town and the farmers in the immediate area brought about an easy acceptance of the two economic groups for each other and an appreciation for their common bond. The churches were built as monuments that fly up to God, like their prayers. In the grid of a town, churches usually occupied valuable space, often on the main street. Because central Minnesota has a high number of national and religious groups represented in its population, in many towns, more than one church graced its main thoroughfares. In Holdingford, Minnesota, for example, a Polish Catholic church and a German Catholic church can be found, both on main street. In Melrose, Minnesota, an Irish Catholic church and a German Catholic church were soon followed by a German Lutheran church. In the small village of Pearl Lake, Minnesota, the town evolved around the only church.

Schools were also a focus which brought people together. In early towns, the schools were usually located near the churches, but the distance a six-year-old child could reasonably be expected to

30

walk determined where rural schools would be built.

Today, because of school consolidation in Minnesota, most rural schools have closed. Larger schools in towns and cities with facilities to accommodate progress have replaced the rural schools, bringing all the area children into towns and cities. In the towns which have a consolidated school, the school is a strong investment that helps assure that the towns will not fade away. People still want their children educated as near by their home as possible.

Local hotels or boardinghouses were an important asset to any town that hoped to attract new residents or businesses. Though built to accommodate people, they were by no means luxurious, and were often furnished only with necessities: A heavy bedstead with a lumpy mattress and a stiff pillow, a washstand with a washbasin and pitcher, and sometimes an armchair or a small chest of drawers. Usually board was provided with the cost of the room. The guests were served simple, light meals in the downstairs dining room. The hotel was always a popular gathering place for newcomers and townspeople alike. Hotels accommodated settlers finding homes, visitors, working men and women, and traveling salesmen, as well as land merchants and sometimes immigrant women with children in tow, stopping to rest before journeying onward.[18]

Furthermore, as John B. Jackson points out, the local hotel was both a social center for the community and a permanent home for single men, women, and even entire families because of the shortage of homes in post-Civil War America.[19]

Banks also enrich the rural midwestern landscape. In most towns they occupied a coveted corner on main street. Americans have traditionally identified security with structures that are architecturally imposing. The conservative farmers of central Minnesota were no exception. They believed that if banks looked structurally sound on the outside, they were financially sound within. Hence, early banks had thick, solid walls and barred windows. They were often constructed of brick, granite, or marble with impressive columns and pedimented facades in classical temple form.

This bank in Rockville, Stearns County, still serves its original purpose. Classical facades, like this one in local granite, adorned hundreds of small town banks throughout the middle west. Solidity of form symbolized internal solvency.

Today,

> Banks still occupy a prominent corner on Main Street in many small midwestern towns. Even where the banks have moved to new quarters in outlying shopping centers, the original structures remain as symbols of security, strength, and character.[20]

Early towns sprang up because of the presence of lumberyards and sawmills. These businesses while providing a necessary service for the farmers also provided the lumber they used to build the town. Farmers brought logs to the mills to be sawed into lumber for their own use or they sold the logs to the mills for cash with which to buy other farm supplies and equipment. Sawmills and lumberyards, in fact, were major contributors in turning the Big Woods of central Minnesota into the agricultural center it is today.

The Sauk Centre House, 1863, built by Warren Adley, burned in 1900. The extremely wide gable ends, returning eaves, window symmetry, and heavy raking boards are Greek Revival characteristics. The graceful veranda provided a sense of grandeur to the entering traveler. *Photograph courtesy Stearns County Historical Society.*

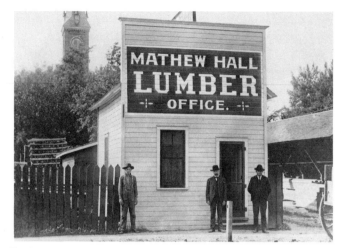

Business office, Mathew Hall Lumber, St. Cloud, *c.* 1900. The wide use of pre-cut and store-bought lumber in place of on-site cutting hastened the development of vernacular architecture. Still extant, this building awaits restoration. *Photo courtesy Mathew Hall Lumber Co.*

As towns prospered, new businesses, stores, and shops were established. Grain elevators, usually of cribbed construction with clapboard or tin covering wood planks, reached into the skyline along railroad tracks. The elevator had storage capacities that enabled millers to buy wheat in large quantities in fall, the time when farmers were most eager to sell, and store it for markets in other parts of the world.

After the 1880s, creameries were common in most central Minnesota towns. As more farmers

turned to dairying, cream separated from milk on the farms was brought to town by wagon and churned into butter at small frame creamery buildings on the outskirts of town. Later, the frame creamery buildings were replaced by larger masonry structures. Although today most creameries in small towns have been vacated and abandoned, many still stand as imposing, solid structures some distance from main street.

Co-op stores, farm implement dealers, hardware stores, livery stables, shoe and harness repair shops, and feed stores also served farmers. Specialty shops such as meat markets and butcher shops, tailor shops, women's dress shops, drugstores, book stores, and even coffin shops were established along newly laid out streets and sidewalks. Post offices, grange halls, fire departments, and town halls served the common good. Taverns, cafes and restaurants, opera houses, and dance halls provided entertainment, food, and drink. Various small factories offered limited employment to people.

Services provided by towns always harmonized with the needs of the people. Interior, Aloys Willenbring shoe and harness repair shop, Farming, Stearns County, Minnesota.

A mainstay of the community was the cooperative creamery. Along with the bank building this was often the most solidly built structure in town. The Farmers' Cooperative Creamery, 1911, Brooten, Stearns County, is Greek Revival in style. *Photograph courtesty Stearns County Historical Society.*

For outdoor entertainment and diversion circuses came; traveling salesmen showed their samples as they passed through. Itinerant peddlers stopped by the farm and village to trade or sell. Traveling sideshows and parades were community entertainment. Stages drawn by beautiful horse teams could be watched coming and going on the dusty main street. Churches held bazaars and festivals in the summer and at fall harvest to earn money and lighten the village life a bit.

Fourth of July parade, Belgrade, 1910. The essentially linear quality of town streets is shown here. *Photograph courtesy Stearns County Historical Society.*

In the early small towns social and business relations were informal and personal. Much business was carried on a credit basis. "Agricultural goods flowed into the cities from the farms for storage or processing, and for ultimate distribution, either locally or in distant places."[21] The small towns in central Minnesota were established to serve the agricultural needs in the area. Rural people feel a sense of loyalty to institutions and enterprises which are geographically close to them, which serve their own needs, and perpetuate their own ethnic, religious, or social patterns.

With the passage of time many towns grew and experienced progressive change. Village street lights were installed to light main street and the lateral side streets. Concrete sidewalks were built to replace wooden ones. Ground was set aside for public parks. Sewer and water lines were put in as public sanitation gained importance. Police and fire protection were inaugurated. Gradually the *cities* of the central plains evolved.

On the other hand, a great number of small towns still exist in central Minnesota as hamlets, villages, or unincorporated towns because they serve only the agricultural needs of the immediate area. They did not expand with industrialization.

These villages began as dirt paths in the wilderness and they still exist as crossroads. There is little more than a main street lined with a few stores or specialty shops, a tavern or saloon, maybe a blacksmith shop or a garage, a church, sometimes a school, and a few residences. Fairhaven, Minnesota, at the edge of Wright County, began as a very prosperous grist-mill town on the north side of the Clearwater River. But, when the "Soo" line railroad built a rail line two miles south of Fairhaven, South Haven, Minnesota, was born; Fairhaven remained static. These small towns, with many unique old structures still remaining, are scattered throughout the central Minnesota countryside. Fairhaven still has its old mill site. The mill building is in the process of being restored, and it has been entered on the National Register of Historic Places.

However, some towns failed completely, either because of poor site location, cutthroat competition, poor business acumen, or because towns spawned by one mode of transportation failed with the development of a new one; for instance, those towns along the Red River ox-cart trail were soon replaced by towns along the railroad lines.

Towns and cities are where people go to work, to shop, to be entertained, to meet friends, or just to pass time. They are " an aggregation or collection of houses for living and buildings for working."[22]

An old blacksmith shop as well as a brick church or a corner bank can reflect the true character of a town. Many unique or individual structures in the old towns should be saved, restored, or reconstructed to original conditions and functions, on original sites, such as the Fairhaven Mill. These buildings are reminders of the rich heritage early small towns have given to central Minnesota. The aging vernacular structures in towns and cities are our link with the past.

1   Personal interview. See Voronyak-Habas family history.

2   Lowry Nelson, *American Farm Life* (Cambridge: Harvard University Press, 1954), p. 6-7.

3   Anthony T. Rozycki, "The Evolution of the Hamlets of Stearns County, Minnesota," (Unpublished Master's Thesis, University of Minnesota, 1977), p. 46. [This thesis was donated to the Stearns County Historical Society and is their property.]

4 Lowry Nelson, *The Minnesota Community: Country and Town in Transition*, (Minneapolis: University of Minnesota Press, 1960), Preface.

5 Vincent A. Yzermans, *The Mel and The Rose*, (Melrose, Minnesota: Melrose Historical Society, 1972). This is a comprehensive history of a small Stearns County town that grew and prospered with the coming of the railroad. It is the centennial history of the town, 1872-1972. Unfortunately copies are difficult to locate.

6 Theodore C. Blegen, *Minnesota: A History of the State*, (St. Paul: University of Minnesota Press, 1975), p. 296.

7 Blegen, p. 304.

8 Carole Rifkind, *Main Street: The Face of Urban America*, (New York: Harper and Row, 1977), p. 58.

9 John B. Jackson, *American Space: The Centennial Years, 1865-1876*. (New York: W. W. Norton, 1972), p. 68.

10 Rifkind, p. 17.

11 Vincent Scully, *American Architecture and Urbanism*. (New York: Praeger Publishers, 1969), p. 76.

12 Jackson, p. 62.

13 Rifkind, Introduction.

14 Rifkind, p. 17.

15 For more personal information on persons and conditions mentioned, see Gasperlin, Petrich, and Voronyak-Habas family histories. Personal interviews.

16 Yzermans, p. 59.

17 Marilyn Brinkman and Marcelline Schleper, *Centennial, St. Catherine's Parish, Farming, Minnesota, 1879-1979*, (Albany, Minnesota: Weber Printing, 1979), p. 87.

18 Joanna L. Stratton, *Pioneer Women: Voices from the Kansas Frontier*, (New York: Simon and Schuster, 1981), p. 192.

19 Jackson, p. 69.

20 William T. Morgan "Strongboxes on Main Street: Prairie-Style Banks, *Landscape*, vol. 24, no. 2, 1980, p.35.

21 *Minnesota Trends: A Report to the People*, (St. Paul: University of Minnesota Social Science Research Center of the Graduate School, 1954), p. 27.

22 Lowry Nelson, Charles E. Ramsey, and Coolie Verner, *Community Structure and Change*, (New York: The MacMillan Company, 1960), p. 9.

23 Warren Upham, *Minnesota Geographic Names: Their Origin and Historical Significance*, (St. Paul: Minnesota Historical Society, 1966), rpt.

II.
An Analysis
of Folk and Vernacular Shelters
in Central Minnesota

Primitive Shelters

An early wooden building usually has more to tell us than the average person sees.

Eric Sloane—*A Reverence For Wood*

The need for shelter was the most immediate task for the settlers arriving on the early American frontier. In some cases the men went ahead to search out claims and construct rude shelters before their families joined them. If there were other settlers or relatives already in the area, new families could move in with them until a shelter of their own was built. Usually, however, entire families stayed together from the outset of their journey to the time when the homestead was settled. In this way the whole family faced both the innocence and the violence of nature on the frontier.[1]

Often the frontier settlers improvised shelters with any materials at hand, including tents, wagon boxes, and the canvas from covered wagons. These temporary shelters were soon replaced by brush and meadow hay structures, caves, dugouts, or sod houses. The use of these primitive shelters built from crude, available materials followed a long tradition in the American frontier movement. Beginning with settlers in the seventeenth century and continuing through the various stages of frontier settlement from east to west, the building pattern was for an improvised shelter to be used for one season or shorter time period, a sod or log house for from three to five years (ten or longer in the case of log), and a stone, frame, or brick shelter after that. The erection of a white, clapboarded farmhouse became the sign of success for the individual settler and marked the end of the frontier movement for society in general.

Because the central Minnesota frontier period (1850-1900) came late in the national movement, settlers had easier access to mid- and late-nineteenth century technology. Progress thus accelerated the time span from improvised shelter to frame house in this region. Because of the abundance of timber wood, however, the log period, especially for use in barns and out-buildings, was long, extending in many cases well into the twentieth century. Because many structures from this time period still stand, central Minnesota is an ideal place to study log architecture.

During the course of the journey to the new home, the prairie schooner, or covered wagon, provided living space for the settlers, who slept either in or under their wagon boxes.[2] Sometimes the box made an immediate shelter at the homesite, as in the case of the Ferdinand Mielke family who dug a hole in the ground in which to live and used their wagon box for a cover when they arrived in Maine Prairie township, Stearns County, in 1869.[3] A four-foot deep hole covered with slough grass, bark, and sod was the first home for the Ole Hedman family in Cottonwood County in 1870.[4] Because central Minnesota was so heavily wooded, the use of dirt structures, either above or below ground, was short-lived and probably limited to treeless areas like western Stearns County. On the prairies of southwestern Minnesota and the plains states, however, more elaborate types of sod structures were utilized.

On flat, treeless land settlers built a "soddy" (sometimes spelled "soddie"), a free-standing structure made from three-foot strips of sod called "Kansas brick" or "Nebraska marble,"[5] which had been cut from the untilled ground and laid in brick-like courses, grass-side down. A common plan called for a building 16 feet deep and 20 feet long constructed from sod strips. A wooden door, window frames, and forked posts were set at each end to support a ridgepole. The pole rafters were covered with separate layers of brush, prairie grass, and sod.[6] According to Merrill E. Jarchow, an authority on soddies, western Minnesota in the 1860s, 70s, and 80s and later was dotted with sod houses of various types and sizes.[7] Although crude in construction and difficult to maintain, these structures were not only inexpensive and fireproof, but also warm in winter and cool in summer.

Another rude shelter type common to the prairie but less common in wooded areas was the board shanty or shack. This type of structure was widely used in the late-nineteenth century, and usually served to house a male settler, or sometimes an entire family, during only the initial homesteading season. Under one of the provisions of the Preemption Act of 1841, a settler was required by law to build a shelter at least 12 feet square with a door

John and Beret Hagebak lived in this sod house near Madison, Mn., in 1872. Beret (below) was born in Selbu, Norway, in 1810 and died in 1903. The photographer was on his way elsewhere to take a family portrait. Stopping at the sod house to rest his horses, he took this classic picture instead. Widely reprinted, it is often used to symbolize the bleakness of prairie life and the special hardship it placed on women. *Information from Kathy Worth, great-granddaughter of Beret Hagebak.*

and a window. Homesteaders often built plank shanties of 12-inch wide pine boards using the overlapping style board/batten construction. These shanties had flat or sloping roofs. Their thin construction made shanties hot in summer and cold in winter.[9] Often, the ceiling of the shanty was so low a person could not stand upright. Their light construction made them easy objects to the thief when left unoccupied, though when permanent

shelter was built they were often used as firewood or animal shelters.[10] In Stearns County, J.E. West and his neighbors spent the winter of 1885 in various shanty shelters of this type. West later wrote that only one inch of lumber protected the settlers from the extreme winter cold.[11]

However adverse the conditions of climate and locale, the early settlers had to accommodate themselves to their situations and surroundings.

The Conly family lived in this sod house, located west of Jasper, Pipestone County, Minnesota, for 13 years. This 1889 picture dramatically depicts the stark prairie landscape. Only the facade of the hut appears to be of sod. The side wall utilizes a wood frame with stone-block infill with earth piled up against both. *Photo courtesy of Pipestone County Historical Society.*

The stories told by the sod-dwellers depict the extremes of pioneer life as it was lived between the dirt walls. Their accounts describe roofs that tended to collapse during heavy rainstorms or snowfalls, the dirt fall from ceilings (a sheet was often strung beneath the rafters to catch debris), and the continuous battle against pests—including prairie dogs and snakes which made their way up through the dirt floor in spring.[12]

Whether soddy or plank shanty, life in these crude shelters was especially hard on the women whose daily routine of household chores and child-care was never-ending. Meals were prepared on makeshift hearths; clothing was laundered in nearby rivers or streams; the children had to be watched constantly to be kept away from open fires or prevented from wandering off into the forests; and if husband or father called for help in the fields or with the animals, that came first, and everything else was dropped. The frontier farmstead was no place for delicate, fragile women. In this ostensibly male environment, a physical constitution beyond that required of most civilized men was called for.

As in ancient times, life centered around the light and warmth of the hearth—tended by the women.

A homestead claim shanty in Pipestone County. Of board/batten construction, the shanty's thin walls and cramped quarters made its use short-lived. Mill-sawn (rather than hand-crafted) lumber, including a paneled door, represent the presence of technological change even in semi-primitive conditions. A canvas lean-to provided cool shelter for food. *Pipestone County Historical Society.*

39

Tools

Meanwhile, the men were concerned with clearing land and building a permanent home. In the forested regions, the sound of the axe echoed through the stillness of the wilderness as trees were felled. The branches and limbs were cut for fuel, the brush piled up and burned, and stumps dug out of the earth with either a grub hoe or pickaxe. Henry Salzl, a farmer from St. Martin, Minnesota, said that one large oak stump often took all day to grub free. Progress was slow and painful; but once the blistered hands were calloused, they stayed that way forever. Forced to face the changing seasons, time was always in short supply. The settler often did not have money to buy the needed equipment, tools, and utensils. Fortunate indeed were the immigrants who brought these supplies with them.

The wide-faced (14″) broadaxe was used to cut flat surfaces on logs. Chisel-sharp, the head is twice as heavy as that on a felling axe. The wide, raised poll identifies this axe as American. *Jasper Bond, Mille Lacs County.*

Besides grubbing tools, a settler needed a felling axe, a pair of broadaxes, and an adze. For those who owned only a felling axe, the cutting and hewing were done with this tool alone. Smoother work, however, could more easily be accomplished with the broadaxe and adze. These tools were of

European origin. The gradual development of heavier polls and the curved, individually-fitted handles were an American refinement. Machine-made tool heads and commercially-produced curved tool handles were available during the central Minnesota settlement.[13] Because many immigrants were not accomplished in the art of hewn-log construction, cutting tools were not part of their baggage. However, some settlers thriftily brought tools in their emigrant chests, later to be augmented with homemade or blacksmith-crafted tools.

Materials

Fortunately, the materials required for building construction were close at hand. In central Minnesota the land was rich in timber and field-stone was almost too abundant everywhere. But while timber and stone were readily available for building purposes, the quantity was often a liability to the pioneer farmer who had to spend much of his time clearing land for planting. Stones heaped in large piles at the end of cultivated fields attest to the endless task of spring rock-picking.

The wood from adjacent forests was the primary building material for the earlier settlers. Tamarack, pine, oak, and poplar ("popple") were the common trees used for shelter construction. As a log shelter is essentially a walled box, larger logs were used for the "pen" (the four-wall enclosure) and smaller mill-sawn (sheeting boards) for vertical planking in the gable apexes. Doors, door and window framing, flooring, and shingles were usually of mill-sawn lumber. In most log buildings rafters were made from sapling pieces which were slightly hewn or left in the round. Ridgepoles were rarely used. The dimensions of individual timbers for barns and houses still standing are immense by modern standards. The oak timbers of the Poglajen-Petrich barn (1883), for example, are 32 feet long and 15 inches high with half-dovetail corner notches measuring 7½ inches by 7½ inches.

These logs, as are all others like them, are almost always heavily scored with axe marks, denoting handcrafted work; but most planking and shingling used in early construction appear to be mill-sawn.

All phases of a settler's life were influenced by wood. In Eric Sloane's words:

> (Wood) spanned rivers for men, it built his home and heated it in winter; man worked on wood, slept in it, sat on wooden chairs at wooden tables, drank and ate the fruit of trees from wooden cups and dishes. From cradle of wood to coffin of wood, the life of man was encircled by it.[14]

Fieldstone from glacial till was another abundant natural material; and in some areas, quarry granite. Random fieldstone was free, durable, and if properly mortared, impervious to the weather. Like wood when used in building, stone is beautiful to behold in its various sizes, shapes and colors. Stone was most widely used for foundations. Two methods of construction using stone were common: Pier construction, where buildings are supported at each corner by large, generally uncut, field boulders, and solid-wall foundations laid in heavy mortar. Coursed or uncoursed random-rubble have been observed; uncut, quarry-cut, and a mix of both were also widely used. Granite has always been readily available in Stearns County and most quarry-cut work was of that material. Fieldstone construction, however, was more common, especially in the earlier years of settlement. Although stone was readily available, no stone chimneys have been found or noted in the region. The availability of iron stoves, ranges and sheet iron stovepipe during the settlement period explains this phenomenon.

The wide use of stone construction meant that the early builder had to be not only a woodcraftsman, but a mason as well. A material, stone, that was a waste and a handicap was turned into a versatile medium of architectural expression under the hand of pioneer stonemasons.[15]

This claim shanty was built by the Funk family as temporary shelter to secure homestead rights. Originally, it had cheesecloth windows.

A larger, permanent structure utilizing more sophisticated techniques of construction represents a state of development above the claim shanty. The Kurtz-Ritter house stood in Avon Township, Stearns County.

The deep vertical marks on the wall of the Poglajen barn were made by a felling axe. The builder stood on top of the log to make vertical cuts along the chalk-marked barked surface. Spaces between cuts were then sliced out smoothly with a downward stroke of the broadaxe. An adze was used to finish the final planed surface.

Stone Structures

Three extant central Minnesota stone structures are excellent examples of the high degree of craftsmanship practiced among the early settlers. In Farming Township, Stearns County, Minnesota, Louis Lemke built a log house and stone barn in the 1860s. A German emigrant and Civil War veteran from Wisconsin, Lemke came to the area because of its abundant wildlife. As there were no roads to his chosen homestead, the Lemke family literally had to carve a cartway through the woods for several miles. They came equipped with only a grub-hoe and an axe with which to clear two to three acres of land a year. A small shanty housed them for a few years which then was replaced with a log house. The family prospered and built other shelters as they were needed and as time permitted.[16] The extant Lemke barn has walls that are constructed of multi-colored field boulders with log courses above. The west wall, a solid mass of stone masonry 15 feet high, is dramatic; and for the region, a rare form of stone design. Now standing on an abandoned farmsite, this once fine structure is in a state of partial ruin.

The Fred Christen barn, Farming Township, Minnesota, built in 1901, stands on land settled by Swiss pioneers who also emigrated from Wisconsin. Each person, including the women, homesteaded 160 acres. Traveling as a group, these settlers came because they heard that wild game was plentiful in the area. Upon reaching St. Cloud, Minnesota, several members went ahead to seek their homesteads. For a period after settling on their claimed land, they lived in temporary shelters. Later, members of this Swiss group helped one another erect "lofty homes."[17] In time as the families grew and the farms prospered they expanded their holdings by acquiring more land. Merylyn Gilk, a descendant of these early settlers, said that the Christens obtained large pieces of land as Civil War veterans who held military bounty land warrants. The Christen barn and a log smokehouse on the Gilk farm are the only remaining structures from the original settlement. The barn has walls of flat fieldstone of uncoursed random-rubble set in heavy mortar that are two feet thick and nine feet high. Standing on a hill in an open field, where it is still in use for storage, the barn is one of the more handsome old buildings in the region in terms of site, materials, and level of craftsmanship.

The Lemke barn, Farming Township, Stearns County, Minnesota (1860's). (above) This extraordinary log-and-stone barn has three walls that make use of heavy, multi-colored field boulders set in mortar. On the right is the interior wall of the animal shelter bay. Like the Lemke barn, the Christen barn (below), Farming Township, Minnesota (1901), utilizes stone for the ground floor walls. These extremely well-crafted and colorful walls were made of flat fieldstone pieces laid up in heavy mortar.

Bonding is uncoursed rubble. The incised lines probably represent the outline of individual stones—a method used to facilitate replacement of single pieces.

Near St. John's University, Collegeville, Minnesota, almost hidden by recent heavy growth, stand the walls of a fieldstone schoolhouse built in 1903. Because an 1894 cyclone destroyed the original wooden structure, the replacement building was built of stone and sited in a hollow. According to George Kline, an early resident, teams of horses were used to haul stone for the new school, and the lime for mortar was "cooked" in boxes. Stonemasons were paid $200.00 for the job and neighbors often came together to help the masons in the construction. The school had two doors, one to accommodate the girls, who sat on one side of the schoolroom, and another, opposite, for the boys who sat on the other side.[18] Although hardly visible today because only two triangular-shaped end-walls of heavy fieldstone and sections of brick side-walls remain hidden by heavy brush, this roofless, picturesque ruin is a reminder of a time when craftsmanship, practicality and building knowledge were fundamental principles for builders.

Log Structures

Log structures were by far the most widely used shelters in central Minnesota between 1850-1900. As a building type, the log house was introduced into America by the Swedes and the Finns who settled in New Sweden (later Delaware) in 1638. Log construction was spread by Germans and Scotch-Irish settlers throughout the eastern and southern frontier during the eighteenth and nineteenth centuries.[19] Although the log house was not indigenous, the settlers "Americanized" it through important adaptations throughout each succeeding stage of frontier development from east to west.

Many of the log structures in central Minnesota, however, were built by European emigrants in the tradition of their homelands. These central Minnesota shelters represent a transplanted European folk tradition which mirrors building types and forms, as well as the building techniques and materials used in medieval Europe. While the emigrant builders may have adapted their shelters to the environment in minor ways, essentially they changed very little from the European forms. Coming unexpectedly upon one of these buildings today is startling, and where a cluster of medieval buildings appears, one feels the presence of the European past deeply.

Our study of central Minnesota buildings included log structures built by emigrants from Yugoslavia, Germany, Czechoslovakia, and Sweden. These remaining shelters survived only when they stood outside the path of progress or when an adaptive use had been found. In many other cases, the original log walls have been clapboarded for insulation purposes, appearance, or as an outward sign of prosperity. Thus, unintentionally, many log shelters have been preserved for contemporary use—and study.

Characteristic types of log structures in central Minnesota are houses, barns, granaries, corncribs, blacksmith shops, and smokehouses. These are built of oak, tamarack, pine, or popple, and most have well-articulated half-dovetailed corners, vertical planking in the gable apexes, and stone foundations. Following the form of medieval folk building patterns (as in the case of the Anton Gogala farm), these buildings are also characterized by steeply-pitched gabled roofs, massive hewn-log walls and small windows.[20]

Individual aspects of log buildings, like door design, chinking techniques, and corner notching, reveal the esthetic quality of log construction. We have observed that door construction differs in style from one building to another and that craftsmanship is high. A fairly common type of construction is a door where strips of wood forming a "Z" are nailed to the door's vertical boards on the interior side for added strength. Often, vertical

Two "Z"-doors. A granary door (above) and corncrib door (right).

The configuration of the Gogala farm resembles the north-central European rural landscape. Slovenian emigrants literally transplanted their cultural and architectural-environment to mid-nineteenth century Stearns County, Minnesota.

Mid-nineteenth century European emigrants brought medieval building forms directly to the Midwest. The Gogala barn, St. Anthony, Stearns County, Minnesota (1860's), has the asymmetrical window and door placement that typifies rural European medieval building facades.

Hand-crafted metal hinge (above) and doorlatch (below).

exterior boards are clinched to horizontal interior boards to form a rigid door. However, a wide range of individual departures from this basic type is common, supporting Eric Sloane's contention that, like the young woman's hope chest, the man's contribution to the new home was an individually-fashioned door, designed and handcrafted with love and care.[21] Sometimes, the uniqueness of a door was enhanced by a piece of hand-forged hardware or a handcrafted wooden latch.

Like door design, materials and methods of chinking differ from structure to structure. Unfortunately, very few, if any, structures retain a fully preserved example of the original chinking material, though remnant pieces reveal some of the character of the wall surface as it was when new. The practice of leaving a space ("chink") between logs is attributed to German builders who settled in Pennsylvania in the 1700s. These craftsmen left gaps of one to six inches between logs to facilitate recaulking as the unseasoned log shrank.[22] This practice was widely used in central Minnesota for both caulked and uncaulked walls, though severe climate kept spaces tight. Traditional chink filler materials were mud, clay mixed with animal

Left: Thickly-applied mortar troweled flush with the log surface provides a beautiful wall. Only one section of this wall has been treated in this fashion. (Gogala blacksmith shop).

Below: Chinks in the Legatt upright log house were filled with round stones, blocks of wood, brick, and mud. John Skandar's work was so carefully crafted that when the walls were pushed over during demolition the chinking stayed in place. (Building razed, 1981).

manure, animal hair, moss, straw and grass, and mortar composed of lime and sand. Modern caulking is usually of cement, a product not recommended because of the damage it does to logs by encouraging moisture retention and rot. Other filler materials used included rock and brick fragments, pieces of split wood, and occasionally, gunny sacks, and, of course, a handy item for dating the building—newspapers.

A most craftsmanlike treatment of chink filling was noted at the Matthew Legatt site (treated in detail on pp. 60-61). Now destroyed, this rare, vertical, hewn-log house had wide chinks filled with bricks, wood blocks, small round fieldstones, and mud. This chinking had been carefully finished off with smooth mortar to the surface of the wall. The house was later clapboarded. Thickly applied mortar, troweled flush with the log surface, makes a most handsome wall surface as in the case of the Gogala blacksmith shop and the corncrib. In these examples equal amounts of log surface and mortar are exposed, forming an interesting study in line, color, texture, and pattern. Walls treated in this fashion resemble half-timber construction and reveal the highest degree of the log builder's art.

A detail of the Gogala log corncrib. Early builders first filled the spaces between logs with split cedar or stones and then covered them with clay, moss, and lime plaster. Cement chinking as shown below is a modern chinking material.

Although all central Minnesota log structures reveal their antecedent European forms and construction techniques, each structure to some degree was built to suit the needs of a new environment. Careful analysis of individual buildings shows that each frontier dwelling combined typical European features with concepts generated by immediate need. This mixture of the old and new processes produced an individuality and furthered the process of Americanization underlying the evolution of log construction. A good example of an "American log house" was built by a Czech craftsman named Heiziek in the late 1880s. Named for its first occupant, the Habas house still stands in an open field in Elmdale Township, Morrison County, Minnesota.

Handcrafted lath pieces, chunks of clay, and a coating of plaster constitute insulation for the Habas house. Nowhere else in central Minnesota was this kind of finished wall construction discovered.

Several unusual features distinguish the Habas house from other log buildings in central Minnesota. These features include a log (rather than stone) foundation and walls of round logs hewn flat at the ends and half-dovetailed. Another unusual feature is found in the construction of the interior walls, the mortar of which is held in place by pieces of handcrafted lath. Also, while most log houses are of one-and-a-half story height, the Habas house gains almost a full second story by the addition of two courses of log above floor level in

the attic story. Besides the protection provided by this insulation, living conditions must have been enhanced by light from tall, narrow windows that reach almost to the ground on the south and west. Finally, projecting eaves on the gable ends, which are very rare in central Minnesota, provide protection for the end-walls while adding to the esthetic beauty of the exterior. In floor plan, light source, and building technique, the Habas house shows an adaptability to the needs of the builder's family and hence breaks with traditional log-construction building patterns.[23]

At first glance the Habas house seems typical of common log construction; a closer look, however, reveals several unusual features. While most European and American log buildings follow fairly traditional patterns of form and techniques of construction, family needs and the builder's sense of design predominate here. An abundance of interior space, ample lighting, and well-insulated walls made this a unique frontier dwelling.

Notching

The most basic element of log construction is corner-notching. In the crafting of the corners, the builder often stated something about his ethnic origin, his ability as a craftsman, and his need to express the nature of wood construction. In appraising the beauty of a particular building, one should look first at the notch pattern formed at the corners.

Of the six methods of corner-notching described by authorities,[24] four have been observed in central Minnesota structures. Half-dovetailing, mixed half- and full-dovetailing, and mixed half-dovetail and square-notching are the most common types used in this region. Saddle, double, and

Left: Detail of the Justin forebay barn, St. Stephen, Stearns County, Minnesota. This section shows a rafter resting on a square-hewn plate with half-dovetailed bearing logs below.
Right: A half-dovetail notching detail.

square-notching occur occasionally. A carefully-crafted, tightly-fitted half-dovetail notch typifies most central Minnesota log construction. Even in smaller out-buildings, where square or saddle-notching was commonly employed elsewhere in the United States, craftsmen in this region chose to cut the more difficult dovetail joint. This choice is probably a reflection both of the practicality of this joint (rain is shed from the downward slanting plane) as well as the pride and skill of native Germans, Scandinavians, Swiss, Czech, and Slovenian builders.

A description of the four types of notches found in central Minnesota helps to understand the complexity of the craft as well as the ethnic sources underlying this region's past. The least common

type found is the square notch, thought to be a derivative of the "V" notch or the half-dovetail. Of Bohemian origin, the square-notch does not produce as strong a joint as the dovetail and thus is often nailed or pegged in place.[25] A barn constructed in 1883 by Matthew Justin, a Slovenian builder, near St. Stephen, Brockway Township, Stearns County, Minnesota, has a forebay constructed largely of square-notched logs uncommonly well-fitted and showing a high level of craftsmanship.[26]

The most ancient form of corner notching is the saddle-notch. Introduced to America by Germans and Swedes, the saddle-notch was easy to cut and hence popular among unskilled craftsmen along the frontier. This notch is made by hollowing out a saddle-shaped depression near the log's end, sometimes on the bottom alone ("single saddle"), or on both top and bottom ("double saddle"). This type is common to round log construction and was used for hog barns, smokehouses, corncribs, and other smaller service buildings. In most cases, the saddle-notched logs interlock beyond the corners, making an interesting pattern.[27]

A variant of the saddle is the double-notch, a saddle-notch with a square-shaped saddle. Double-notching originated in central or eastern Europe, spread to Scandinavia, and reached the wooded area of the upper midwest in the late nineteenth century by way of Finnish emigrants.[28] The Lind homesite in Sherburne County, Minnesota, constructed by Swedish emigrants in the 1870s, contains buildings with examples of both double- and saddle-notching (see family history). In the small corncrib, a square-notched sill sits on a stump foundation (an unusual method of support) and round saddle-notching appears on the courses above. On the larger Lind springhouse, particularly handsome double-notching is employed—the only example we have found in central Minnesota.

The Lind corncrib has a stump-pier foundation. Mixed half-notch and single saddle notches were used to join the corners.

LIGHT FROM THE HEARTH

The half-dovetail occurs in buildings throughout central Minnesota. Evolved from the full-dovetail with its two slanting planes, the single-plane half-dovetail originating in Czechoslovakia, was first found in North America in Virginia. It was a common log building technique used by skilled craftsmen across the United States. The half-dovetail is particularly useful for hardwoods and can be cut with only an axe. Usually the corner is sawn flush with the wall surface, making a neat box-like corner.[29]

The Lind springhouse corners (above) are an unusual mix of saddle and double notches. (The rounded log ends are saddle; the squared ends, double). Extending the logs beyond the corner of the walls was rare in central Minnesota. Full dovetail notching (below) is rare in central Minnesota. The center log (face to reader) was cut with two slanting planes in the fashion of cabinet-makers' corners. The concentric pattern on the log's face adds to the notch's beauty. (Hubbard County, Minnesota).

A log building's beauty stems from the color, texture, pattern and craftsmanship of the building's corner notching.

Primary Animal Shelters

While human shelter was of primary importance, it often competed with the simultaneous need to shelter animals. Since animals were a source of both food and power, they served as an integral part in daily pioneer life; hence their shelter was provided for when the clearing was made for individual homesteads. Immigrant literature often cites the proximity of animals and human beings. In fact, the earliest European shelters, like the English Saxon house, often housed the family and its animals under a single roof.[30]

In the earliest settlement years central Minnesota settlers used oxen as draft animals. Although slow and plodding, oxen were superior in strength to horses for breaking land and heavy hauling. Also, they needed only a homemade yoke in place of an expensive and easily breakable horse harness. To break virgin prairie turf, several yoke of oxen were needed. One person, often a woman, guided the oxen; and a second person sat on the beam of the plow to keep it in the ground. In wooded regions, oxen were used to help grub stumps that remained standing like rooted boulders after the trees were felled and cleared away.

The straw stable was one of the earliest primary animal shelters used by Minnesota frontier farmers to house oxen. According to Wiliam A. Marin, these were built of

> ... posts that are forked or crotched in the upper end; heavy poles were placed horizontally in the crotches so as to form a framework, and lighter poles are placed across these to hold up the roof. Following the harvest the grain is threshed near this framework and the straw from the carrier is used to supply a heavy cover for it. Frequently a thatch of heavy long prairie grass is placed over the straw to make the roof shed the rain.[31]

Three straw shelters similar to the late-nineteenth century one described above have been found in central Minnesota. Located in Stearns County, Minnesota, all three are still in use. On the Anton Gogala farm, St. Anthony, stands a dome-shaped pig shelter constructed of poles, planks, and rails nailed together to form a pen which is covered with meadow hay. The Gogalas use this and another such straw structure in seasonable weather to

shelter their pigs. Victor Lauer, another Stearns County farmer, utilizes a similar structure as a cattle shelter. In form and choice of materials both shelters are rooted in the primitive past, but trace their latest origins to late-nineteenth century temporary rural structures.

The form and use of the materials of these animal shelters are related to ancient, primitive building types. The earliest structures in ancient civilizations were of reeds and mud. The Gogala pighouse (above) and the Lauer cattle shelter (below)—both in Stearns County, Minnesota—are within that tradition.

Larger permanent log barns replaced primitive straw shelters as soon as pioneer builders found time to construct them. These were used to store feed, crops, tools, equipment, and often included a shop, where during long winter months, tools were made and equipment repaired. Often the barn provided solitude for the settler away from the crowded household, or a place where children learned the trades of their elders through quiet observation. Even today, in a log barn during milking time, amidst the smells of manure, hay, straw, hot animal breath, and warm milk, one can still sense the past. Inside a tightly-constructed log barn a small herd of cattle keeps the milkers warm, a daily experience on the Gogala farm.

Folk and Vernacular Barns in Central Minnesota: Log, Stone, and Frame

Folk and vernacular are useful terms to distinguish different barn types found in central Minnesota. A folk building is European in origin, one whose American adaptations are slight, of handcrafted materials—most often wood and stone. Traditional, unrecorded plans, passed down from one generation to the next by word of mouth, dictated the building's form. This form—the building's outline or silhouette—reveals its folk or non-folk origins. All unchanged log structures fall into the folk category.

A vernacular building shares a common heritage with a folk building wherever hand-crafted work and native materials have been employed. But, "vernacular" refers to a building that uses, at least in part, machine-made materials (mill-cut lumber, nails, paint) and whose form follows plans found in carpenters' handbooks or agricultural publications. These forms generally show the influence of *elite* architecture—the body of work produced by architects who follow accepted standards of design and style within the classical tradition. Most vernacular buildings are of frame construction and possess such elements of style as cupolas, multi-paned windows, and smoothly-painted surfaces. Although in barn construction these elements are generally integrally related to the total design so that practicality is rarely sacrificed, vernacular structures are more balanced and symmetrical and hence less practical looking.

In many cases, elements of folk and vernacular exist within a single building. This is especially true in areas where barns were put up by local craftsmen who knew the older techniques but made use of the latest technical developments in barn construction and design. In the Cater and MacDougall barns, for example, the form is "English style"—a type described in the handbooks. The influence of handbook design gives each barn's exterior the polished "classical" look and feeling of elite architecture. Both barns, however, have interior bracing of hand-hewn post-and-beam construction which tie them to the folk tradition as well.

The strongest influence of the folk tradition on the central Minnesota landscape can be seen in those structures built by Slovenian and German emigrants. A common form among barns constructed by these craftsmen is a single-bay, rectangular log barn with an animal shelter below and hay storage above. These barns are strongly medieval in appearance and feeling with their gabled roofs, windowless facades, and massive hewn-log walls. Four central Minnesota barns, all in Stearns County, follow this form. The first three were built by Slovenians, the last by a Pole. These are: the Justin barn, *c.* 1883, Brockway Township, the sole example of a forebay barn in the region,[32] the Poglajen-Petrich barn, 1883, a quarter-of-a-mile away; the Gogala barn *c.* 1868, St. Anthony, and the Pilarski barn, *c.* 1890, Holdingford Township. All have similar details—central doors on the gable ends, vertical planking in the apexes, and well-articulated corner notches. The latter two barns are still in active use as a part of farming operations.

Another strongly-European-influenced structure is the Grausam barn, Albany, Stearns County, Minnesota, originally a double-crib barn—a structure consisting of two bays connected by an open, central passageway. Built in the 1870s by a Bavarian emigrant, Martin Grausam, this handsome structure of massive hewn logs retains only its passageway and one of its two original bays.

The Justin forebay barn, *c.* 1883, St. Stephen, is the only one of its type in central Minnesota. The forebay is supported by four large cantilevered joists. The forebay keeps the door below free of straw when it is loaded into the barn or thrown down from above.

The Lemke barn, Stearns County, Minnesota, mentioned earlier, utilizes the shape of the site to create a distinctive form—the bank barn. This beautiful structure of fieldstone, log, and plank was built into the slope of a hill. The west wall, made entirely of large hewn logs, meets ground level at the crest of the hill. Below, the north, east, and south walls are of stone on ground level and log above. The bay on the south is open through two levels, forming a cathedral-like interior.

Another log and fieldstone barn stands in Brockway Township, Stearns County, Minnesota. Built c. 1879 by John Skandar, a Slovenian emigrant, and later purchased by another Slovene, Matthew Legatt, the barn had two adjoining bays. The south bay, used as a stable, was constructed of gigantic tamarack logs from a nearby swamp. The north (cattle) bay was enclosed by two-foot thick walls of fieldstone boulders set in heavy mortar. Both bays were covered with a web-like tamarack sapling pole roof of extremely well-crafted proportions and shingled with cedar. Today, the entire structure is a magnificent ruin. Commanding a view from a hilltop overlooking miles of gently rolling landscape, the Skandar-Legatt barn was once a fine example of the folk building tradition.

In Grove Township, Stearns County, Minnesota, stands the Herman Schweiters barn from the late 1860s. The Schweiters barn is a massive structure consisting of a hewn-log section

The Pilarski barn, c.1890, Holdingford Township, Stearns County, Minnesota, shelters horses which the owner still uses for plowing. The hay barn (background above) log walls utilized saddle-notching. The detail of the horse barn (below) shows ceiling joists that project through the outside wall to act as added support in the form of tie beam construction.

The Grausam barn, Albany, Minnesota, was originally twice the size of this present structure. Strongly medieval in form and mass, the barn represents the heritage of European building practices.

A detail of the Justin barn (left). The Poglajen-Petrich barn (right), c. 1883, St. Stephen, Stearns County, Minnesota.

(used as animal shelter and hayloft) to which is joined a framed lean-to shed. A dominant feature is the large sweeping tent-like roof that covers both sections.

Many folk buildings have disappeared from the central Minnesota landscape. Those few remaining still stand because they are useful; most are in ruins; and hundreds have vanished forever. In some cases farmers have covered their log barns with metal siding, as in the example of the Supan barn in Brockway Township, Stearns County, Minnesota. While this barn's folk form is still identifiable by its outline, its original materials and builder's techniques are hidden beneath modern materials.

Interior, Lemke barn. Materials include stone, hewn log, vertical planking, and hand-hewn rafters. This beautiful structure is still useful after 120 years.

many vernacular structures are closely related to the folk tradition. However, through the emerging use of machine-cut materials, drop-siding, and 2x4 studding, classical motifs like decorative cupolas and transom windows, and a growing dependence upon handbook designs, the folk tradition gradually

The log section of the Lemke barn, Farming, Stearns County, Minnesota, meets ground level on the west side. Log construction above and stone-boulder construction below make this bank barn a most distinctive log structure. The pedimented dormers constitute a touch of classical influence. The photograph below shows the stone walls on the south and east.

Now more of a picturesque ruin than an example of architecture, the Legatt barn once represented a fine example of folk craftsmanship. Tamarack-pole rafters, massive dovetailed logs, and field-boulder walls characterized this unique structure.

The vernacular barn is distinguishable from its folk predecessor by its form, details, and choice of materials. But since wood and stone were widely used for both and early framing for vernacular buildings was often of post-and-beam construction,

The Schwieters barn (top) Grove Township, Minnesota, utilized a large, tent-like roof to join the plank lean-to section to the log barn. A nearby granary (second) sits on stone-boulder piers. The wall reveals square-notching, deep axe marks, and a sill that has been notched to receive the floor joists. Crafted by Slovenian builders, the Supan barn (third) and the Poglajen-Petrich granary (bottom) represent the use of a traditional European form for rural buildings. Each structure has a two-level log bay to which a post-and-plank lean-to section has been added.

gave way to the vernacular. In the late decades of the nineteenth century and early decades of the twentieth, many examples of transitional structures bridging both traditions can be found. Because of their later construction and present use, many vernacular barns are in excellent condition, though these, too, are often threatened by needs of modernization.

Five excellent examples of transitional folk-to-vernacular barns were found in central Minnesota. Two are described in later chapters: the MacDougall barn (Morrison County) and the Cater barn (Sherburne County). The Ryberg barn (Morrison County), the Christen barn (Stearns County), and the Garner barn (Sherburne County) will be examined here. While these barns represent transitional types, each is also unique in form. The most traditional in form (although it is unusually tall because of its high stone foundation) is the Christen barn, 1901, which is rectangular in shape, gabled at two ends, and follows the general pattern of barns influenced by, but not directly copied from, carpenters' handbooks. Its uniqueness stems from the combination of hand-crafted interior bracing (a folk element) and exterior mill-sawn drop-siding (vernacular). The Ryberg barn combines a log bay (1900) and a frame bay (1915) in a unique, quasi-cruciform design. Most of the barn's materials have been hand-crafted, but the mill-sawn work has been carefully integrated with the structure's essential folk features. The Garner barn, 1915, is a frame barn, largely of machine-finished materials, octagonal in form, obviously influenced by early nineteenth century Shaker barn design. All three barns are excellent examples of the esthetic beauty of folk-vernacular architecture.

Careful examination of these three barns reveals their importance to the history of folk and vernacular architecture.

The original bay of the Ryberg barn was built of mixed round and slightly-hewn logs. These logs, forming walls eight courses high, are of a honey-

apart. A gabled roof covering this bay is cut into the log section joining the two bays and forming a spacious T-shaped haymow.

The mow has a most interesting and skillfully-crafted roof structure. Made of tamarack poles, only slightly hewn, the complexity of the interior roof

Two views of the Ryberg barn, Elmdale Township, Morrison County, Minnesota. Based on design of Scandinavian origin, this structure is roughly cruciform-shaped, the result of the addition of a wing (right, below) to the original barn. The east wall of the original barn bay (above) retains its log surface, while the west wall has been covered with the red-painted vertical plank siding.

Views of the elaborate rafter construction (above) and gable apex wall (below) in the Ryberg log barn section. Tamarack poles and rough-faced planking were crafted together to make a highly complicated roof system. The Ryberg barn fabric alone is a laboratory for those interested in the study of folk architecture.

colored hue and are still in excellent condition. The interior space of this bay measures 22 feet n/s by 28 feet e/w and includes seven horse stalls, a ladderway to the loft, and an aisle running between doors on the east and west. On the south side of the log bay is an open passageway ten feet across covered by a roof which connects the log bay with the frame addition. One passageway wall reveals the log bay's finely-cut hewn logs and exposed ceiling joists; the other wall is covered with mill-sawn drop-siding. Access to the 1915 addition is through a door in this wall.

The frame addition measures 18 feet e/w by 26 feet n/s and contains a large space for horses and a lean-to on the east for small animals. The horse area has round-log joists set close together and mixed round and hewn ceiling joists spaced two feet

fabric resembles the vaulting of Gothic church architecture. In the mow of the log bay is a three-course log wall on four sides. The rafter construction springs from this wall and forms a 15-foot high gable at the point where the two bays meet. With gables at both east and west ends of the log bay, this third gable helps form a complex and exciting space, the beauty of which is further enhanced by light rays entering the mow between the vertical boards in the gable apex to the east.

The east facade is of massive tamarack log construction with well-articulated half-dovetail corner notches and vertical plank sheeting, slightly projecting over the log wall, in the apex. A door and a small opening adjacent to it pierce the otherwise solid, blank wall. The massive log wall on the north closes off the barn from the weather entirely. Vertical planking of rough-surfaced, mill-cut lumber painted red covers the entire west facade. This facade has a window and a feed-door in the mow and a door and small opening at ground level. Much of the dignity and grace of this handsome barn is revealed in the form and texture of this wall. A 36-foot long wall of horizontal drop-siding covering the frame section is joined to this wall.

The joining of the log and frame bays of the Ryberg barn makes the entire structure roughly cruciform in shape. Whether intentional or not, the log bay resembles the transept, the frame bay, the nave. Coupled with the rafter vaulting and the delightful play of light streaming down from above, the correlation to church architecture is striking. In the craftsman's feeling for materials and the concept of design, the Ryberg barn stands as a masterpiece of folk-vernacular architecture.

The Christen barn, 1901, also represents the transition between the folk and vernacular tradi-tions. The folk characteristics are revealed through the use of stone, hewn-log walls in the lean-to, and handcrafted post/beam supports in the haymow. The use of drop-siding, machine-cut studding, and the barn's form, which is reminiscent of handbook design, are more related to the vernacular tradition. Of all the central Minnesota folk-vernacular barns, the Christen barn most successfully synthesizes the relationship between the rough, handmade quality of older, local building practices and the polished, machine-made nature of the best in modern building technology.

Sited on a gentle slope, the Christen barn stands alone in an open field. Measuring 26 feet, 9 inches e/w by 40 feet n/s with a 12-foot lean-to on the north, the barn has a 9-foot high, 18-inch thick foundation wall above ground level. Above this rigid ground-floor enclosure rises the frame section, a lofty, second-level space originally used for storage of hay. Two-inch by six-inch studding, covered by unpainted dropsiding weathered to a dark grey, form the walls of the frame section. In

the center of the cedar-shingled roof is a handmade cupola in the shape of the barn itself. The hewn log walls of the lean-to, which joins the north wall just below the gable ends, are covered with vertical siding.

As to the interior, the ground floor of the barn contains space for cattle and horses and in the lean-to a space for calves. Heavy 8-inch by 8-inch interior post/beam construction of hand-hewn tamarack supports the second story. An unhewn center beam, measuring 26 feet n/s, is supported by a pair of **∩**-shaped posts; 26-feet 9-inch tie beams spanning the width of the second floor support large struts. Broadaxe marks on all posts and beams reveal the work of hand-craftsmanship. The floor of this huge, second level expanse are covered with 1-inch by 8-inch tongue-and-groove boards.

The Christen barn is a synthesis of folk and vernacular materials and techniques. The view above shows the boulder walls and hewn-log lean-to; the detail below shows the drop siding and a cupola.

Huge timbers form the skeleton of the Christen barn (left). The tie beam measures 26' 9" in length. From the tie beams spring giant struts that support the roof system. (Farming Township, Stearns County, Minnesota)

Garner barn, Sherburne Co., Minnesota (1915) (above). The round or octagonal barn shape stems from religious and secular roots. The sacred circle, symbolizing eternal life, was appropriately used by the Shakers who believed that "every force has its form" and who demonstrated this belief in their famous Hancock, Massachusetts, barn (1824). A more practical reason for the use of round or octagonal barn (or house) shapes follows the theory that maximum floor space and minimum wall space result from non-rectangular designs. While a few of these attractive barns remain in central Minnesota, some in concrete form from the 1930's, their popularity was short-lived.

The lean-to is as interesting as the barn itself. The walls are made of square-hewn logs with deep broadaxe marks and some of the corner bracing has been pegged in place. The logs appear to be older than the timbers used in the main section and may have been part of another, earlier building. A sense of a more remote past is felt within its walls. The Christen barn is in better condition than either the Ryberg or Garner barns. Now used for storage of hay and lumber, the owners have taken pride in owning this fine example of rural architecture.

The Garner barn was built in 1915. Presently in a deteriorated condition, it stands alongside Highway 10 near Elk River in Sherburne County, Minnesota. Originally known as Bailey's, the farmsite was a favorite stopping place between St. Paul and St. Cloud for travelers during the 1840s and 1850s. The barn was built by Perry Garner, the owner of the farm in the early decades of the twentieth century. The barn is octagonal in shape, an unusual, although not rare form in central Minnesota. With roots in early nineteenth century Shaker architecture, this design often follows round, octagonal, or polygonal shapes.[33] Except for its field-boulder footings, the barn is largely the product of machine-design, and hence more vernacular than the Ryberg and Christen barns.

The core of the barn structure is a silo anchored in five feet of cement. Projecting upward from the concrete foundation to near the top of the silo is the rib-like internal structure over which the roof and siding are spread like the fabric of an umbrella. One of the eight sides forms a projecting gambrel roof beneath the peak of which is an

Views of the Garner barn showing its framework under construction (above) and its facade when new (below). Sash windows with pointed lintels are classical features that contrast sharply with the building's folk and vernacular origins and use. *Photos courtesy of Ralph Garner.*

opening for loading hay. Interesting details are the pointed lintels and the 4/4 sash windows. A high concrete foundation forms a base for the red-painted dropsided walls. Small square dormers with flat slanting roofs project from the main roof. The roof is slightly flared so as to protect the walls beneath.[34] Like the Ryberg and Christen barns, the Garner barn is a handsome addition to the central Minnesota rural landscape.

Outbuildings: Root Cellars, Smokehouses, and Corncribs

While barns are the dominant structures in the history and development of rural architecture, out-buildings also form an important chapter. Like the larger structures, out-buildings are rapidly disappearing since "the purpose for which they were originally built is now obsolete in today's economy and technology."[35] Scattered here and there throughout the central Minnesota landscape are excellent examples of out-buildings that reveal the characteristics of the folk and vernacular traditions.

A small above-ground root cellar of unknown date stands in Todd County, Minnesota. Built by a German emigrant, Joseph Brever, this rectangular structure is built of fieldstone and brick and is roofed with asphalt sheeting. Presently in a state approaching ruin, it will soon again form part of the natural landscape. A Mille Lacs County, Minnesota, springhouse displays the use of stone in

the form of round field boulders set into heavy mortar. This structure has a hipped roof which gives it the form of a classical building. This elite form is also found in a chicken barn built c. 1903 by the Thelen brothers in Farming Township, Stearns County, Minnesota. Standing on the original Anton Jonas farm, now owned by George and Arlene Winkels, this rectangular stone structure of coursed rubble has a hipped roof, deck, and a pedimented dormer surfaced with ornamental shingles. This unique building is plastered on the inside and calciminated pink.[36] It, too, is in poor structural condition.

Detail (above), dormer, Thelen chicken barn. A chicken barn (below), Stearns County, Minnesota, was built in classical form using local stone for its walls. The pedimented dormer facade is covered with ornamental shingles. This building demonstrates the influence of the academic architectural tradition (period styles) upon rural building practices.

More of a relic than a useful out-building, the Brever root cellar, Todd County, Minnesota, was built of fieldstone and brick. Boulders were split to form smooth quoin-like cornerstones. A Mille Lacs County, Minnesota, springhouse combines folk material (round fieldstone) with a classical form (rectangular walls topped with a hipped roof).

A small smokehouse on the Math Grausam farm, Albany, Minnesota, built in 1911, is a fine example of a structure influenced by classical architecture. The walls of this building are constructed of cement block manufactured to resemble stone. Each block was carefully chamfered and smoothly surfaced to create a finished appearance. A slightly flared, turret-like roof with thin shingles, ornate tin flashing, and a finial graces this unique structure. In sharp contrast to its classical form is a door of roughly-finished planks. The overall form of the Grausam smokehouse is decidedly elite, making it an unusual and important contribution to the rural architectural landscape.

Classical influence is also revealed in this handsome Stearns County, Minnesota, smokehouse. Cement block, manufactured to look like smooth-faced quarry stone. The turret roofed structure would be at home on an eighteenth century Georgian-styled English estate.

A tamarack-pole corncrib (above) in Stearns County, Minnesota. Though primitive in the use of material and form, the detailed framework of this corncrib reveals the patient skill of the craftsman. The beauty of this structure stems from the play of light and shadow through the frame and from the way in which the wind has shaped its form through time. (Moved, partially demolished). The drive-through corncrib (below) was a common sight on nineteenth century farms. The Cater corncrib, Sherburne County, Minnesota, is a particularly picturesque building in summer when it is half-covered with vines.

One of two known tamarack-pole corncribs was on the Otto Christen farm in Farming Township, Stearns County, Minnesota, until 1981. This unique structure was so simple in its construction, form, and use of materials that its historical importance and beauty were overlooked. Standing against the landscape, the corncrib appeared to have been shaped by the wind and its pattern of construction chosen to allow a play of light and shadow. Fortunately, Otto's son, Herb Christen, and Herb's wife Theresa, appreciated the beauty and usefulness of this structure. When they learned that it would be destroyed, they dismantled and reconstructed the corncrib on their own nearby farm where it is used as a cornpen. According to the Christens, the corncrib was built by Carl Lemke in 1870, and has been moved three times.[37]

A larger corncrib on the Sherburne County, Minnesota, farm of Joshua Cater is of the drive-in type. The unpainted board siding used throughout has been allowed to weather to varying shades of gray and brown. The Christen and Cater corncribs reveal the level of beauty attained through the use of common materials, simple shapes, and adherence to intended function.

A corncrib, a smokehouse, and a blacksmith shop on the Anton Gogala farm stand as examples

of durable log structures. The corncrib and smokehouse are still in use. All are constructed of hand-hewn poplar logs notched with well-crafted half-dovetail corners. Decidedly medieval in feeling, these buildings reveal the strong influence of the European past as it was transplanted to Central Minnesota by early Slovenian settlers. The Gogalas also make use of another disappearing rural structure—the wooden-stave silo. Constructed of vertically-set sawn planks of redwood, 6″ wide and 10′ in length, staggered in construction, and re-enforced by metal bands and cross-anchors, the silo resembles a giant barrel. Like the Lemke-Christen corncrib, the Gogala silo has been relocated from its original site to the Gogala farm site.

Even though small farm buildings are important historically and esthetically, they are

The wooden-stave silo is also a rural relic, although the Gogala brothers still make use of theirs. Redwood planks, 10' in length and vertically placed, re-enforced by metal bands and cross-anchors, constitute its construction. Often these silos were capped with a conical roof fabricated from ornamental metal plates.

being rapidly replaced by steel and aluminum shelters. Fortunately, alternative uses are often found for older out-buildings. Math Grausam uses his smokehouse to smoke fish while the Gogalas still smoke hams in theirs. The Gogalas use their stave silo to store silage while other farmers utilize granaries, corncribs, and other buildings for machinery and general storage. But because smaller buildings have lost their original function or lack the appearance thought to be symbolic of progressive farming, many are burned, bulldozed, or abandoned. In lamenting the changes that are taking place on the rural landscape, John Fraser Hart says: "(The barn) is a relict feature; the hayloft is obsolescent, the threshing floor is obsolete, and who needs stalls for horses?"[38]

Houses

Practicality dominated the underlying plan for primitive shelters, log houses, and out-buildings of the early settlers. After the initial period of settlement, however, a new sense of pride and accomplishment emerged as a result of the farmer's success over nature. This pride revealed itself in the form of white clapboarded or brick houses, the facades for which were copied from or influenced by carpenters' handbooks. With the arrival of the balloon frame, it was possible for the rural builder, armed with the handbooks, to build with "style." Therefore, in the latter decades of the nineteenth century houses were designed in a number of styles, including the earlier Georgian and Greek Revivals, but also in Gothic, Queen Anne, and other eclectic styles. To understand the evolution of domestic building history in central Minnesota we will examine various techniques of building construction and styles from the plank house and vertical log types to frame houses designed in the fashion of the late nineteenth century and early twentieth century.

The construction technique utilized in the Herbert Maximilian Fox House, 1876, is unique in Minnesota. Recently moved to Becker, Minnesota, from its original site near Santiago, Minnesota, the Fox House is a plank or girt house, a form of domestic building known to exist in North America as early as 1627 in what is now Plymouth, Massachusetts. From there the style spread throughout north-central New England where it became a common type of house construction until about 1860.[40]

The vertical plank construction of the Fox house (1876), Sherburne County, Minnesota, is unique to the region. These two views (bottom previous page and above) show carefully sawn planks running from sill to roof line. Recently moved, the Fox house is undergoing restoration.

The Fox House is constructed of 1½ inch x 8½ inch to 12½ inch solid planks of native oak set vertically from sill to roof-line. These planks are load-bearing and butted together to form corners in the place of corner posts. The only variation from the New England plank house is the use of nails in place of pegs where the planks are joined at the ground sill and at the roof line.[41] The Fox House was originally deeded to Ole Martinson, passed briefly to Samuel P. Glidden, and then to Fox and his wife, Eleanor. It is thought that Glidden may have been the builder. The house originally was a two-story structure, 16 feet by 23 feet, to which various additions were made through the years. Clapboard siding was used as sheathing from the beginning.[42]

Vertical *log* structures are rarely found today, although the technique was widely used in the eighteenth century by French colonists who settled the Mississippi Valley. These settlers utilized three variants of vertical log construction: *Poteaux-en-terre* (posts in the earth), *poteaux-sur-sole* (posts on the sill), or *colombage-sur-sole* (frame set on a foundation sill). Of unknown origin, all three were widely used from Arcadia west to the Great Lakes and south to and along the lands bordering the Mississippi. The first method utilizes upright cedar or cypress logs hewn flat on two or four faces, spaced a few inches apart, and set several feet into the ground. *Poteaux-sur-sole* is an improved method whereby a stone foundation is topped by a timber sill with the upright logs resting upon it. In both types log spaces are filled with a variety of materials, including *bouzillage*, a mixture of clay and grass or Spanish moss. Often these walls are left exposed in half-timber fashion.[43] *Colombage-sur-sole* resembles English framing in that the heavy squared posts are joined to the sill by mortise and tenon joints.[44]

In Brockway Township, one mile east of St. Stephen, Minnesota, a house framed with upright logs, hewn on four sides and spaced several inches apart, stood until it was destroyed in April, 1981. Built in the 1870s by John Skandar, a Slovenian carpenter, it became the home of another Slovenian family—the Matthew Legatts.[45] This structure was not only an example of the work of a skilled craftsman, but also a unique architectural

French construction techniques were utilized by a Slovenian builder in St. Stephen, Minnesota (1870s), for this rare upright log house.

60

monument. This house closely resembled *colombage-sur-sole* construction in its use of upright posts, filling material, and especially its mortise and tenon, post and sill construction. The Skandar-Legatt house may also have derived its framing technique from English or German half-timber construction as well.[46]

A close examination of the Skandar-Legatt house revealed frame-walls built of white and red oak logs set on a stone and mortar foundation. Each frame-wall had 12 "stud" posts, two corner posts, a girt, and a sill. The faces of the stud posts were hewn flat and rounded on the sides. The tops of each stud post were cut into beautifully-crafted tenons, 9 inches wide by 3 inches high by 1½ inches deep, and chamfered to securely fit into the girt and sill mortise holes. Each tenon had two one-inch diameter holes for pegs. Corner posts on the north

This detail shows beautifully crafted tenons which were originally pegged into mortise holes in the sill and plate.

and south walls had been notched 4 inches wide and 2½ inches deep to receive the rafters. The space between stud posts was filled with a variety of materials (small round stones, brick, wood blocks, mud, and clay) and finished off with mortar. The ground-floor interior walls had diagonally-nailed lath applied to the log surfaces and were finished in plaster. In the loft, however, the mortar was exposed in half-timber fashion.

Originally, the Skandar-Legatt house was a simple square structure with a loft. Later, Matthew Legatt added a frame "lean" along the north side

for a child's bedroom and a pantry. Matthew's son, Blaise, remembers that the lean was so poorly insulated that his mother would spend the whole night heating blankets and clothing on the stove to keep the children warm. The older children slept in the loft which was so cold that they would wake up with frost around their mouths. Also, one could see the stars through the roof cracks and the quilt would be covered with snow in the morning. The log section downstairs was divided into a living room, kitchen, and bedroom. A steep staircase led to the loft. A new kitchen "lean" was added in the 1920's.

The Skandar-Legatt house was an important folk monument. The scarcity of vertical log structures in Minnesota as well as the diminishing number of folk buildings throughout the United States makes its loss a cultural tragedy. Several questions concerning the Legatt structure remain unanswered: Why was a vertical log construction technique chosen? Upon what sources did builder Skandar draw? Did he have knowledge of French building practices, or, perhaps experience building with European half-timbering? All we know is what the building revealed to us—that Skandar was a highly developed craftsman-designer whose skills and talents led him to construct a unique building in central Minnesota.

At the time John Skandar was building his upright log house, other builders were making use of a technology that had already revolutionized building construction in America. This revolutionary technique, the balloon frame, was invented in 1833 by George Washington Snow, an early settler in Chicago who had been educated as a civil engineer and later worked as a surveyor, lumber dealer, building contractor, and city official.[47] The balloon frame, first used in the construction of St. Mary's Church, Chicago, substituted ". . . thin plates and studs—running the entire height of the building and held together only by nails—for the ancient and expensive method of construction with mortised and tenoned joints."[48] This new technique coincided with the improvement of sawmill machinery and mass production of nails, as well as the growing need for cheaper and more abundant housing on the western frontier. Balloon framing also had the merit of being able to be prefabricated. According to an 1872 publication:

> With the application of machinery, the labor of house building has been greatly lessened, and the western prairies are dotted over with houses which have been shipped there all made, and the various pieces numbered.[49]

The arrival of the balloon frame in central Minnesota marked the end of the tradition—if not the actual use—of log building. Hewn-log construction was persistent, however, especially where timber was readily available. Often, too, the arriving settlers from Europe, as in the case of the Slovenians who came to Stearns County, Minnesota, between 1865 and 1880, brought the folk tradition with them from their homelands. In another sense, log construction persisted when clapboard siding was nailed over a log building to give it the appearance of a frame structure. Because of this practice, countless central Minnesota farmhouses have solid hewn-log walls hidden beneath exterior siding.

The Gogala farmhouse was originally a log structure to which a frame wing was later added. Both log and frame wings are covered with clapboard. Following the influence of the Greek Revival style, the frame wing (right) represents the upright temple form.

The Anton Gogala farmhouse, St. Anthony, Minnesota, demonstrates a common evolutionary pattern for house construction on the central Minnesota frontier. The original house, built by a Slovenian emigrant, Anton Gogala, Jr., c. 1880, was a 1½-story log structure. As the family grew, more space was needed. In 1906, a two-story frame wing, forming an "L" to the original house, was constructed. This wing was designed in Greek Revival style, but bears only rudimentary (though handsome) elements of that style—a gabled roof,

corner boards resembling thin pilasters, and pedimented window moldings. In silhouette, this wing has the appearance of the Greek temple form. To unify the "L", the Gogalas clapboarded both wings and painted the building white, with eaves, window moldings, and door frames trimmed in green. Sited on a hill and oriented so as to provide a view of both wings from the driveway, the Gogala farmhouse is a fine example of the merging of folk, vernacular, and classical forms.

In the middle west during the latter decades of the nineteenth century builders could select from any number of architectural styles. Commonly, builders from those areas most remote from the settled eastern states often followed a style that was already out of fashion in the east. Those who could afford to, however, built in the current fashion;

often omitting more extravagant forms of ornament (heavy cornices, pilasters, ornate doorways) in their plans. Also, since late-nineteenth century buildings were highly derivative and styles were subject to periods of rapid change in fashion (in the wake of the post-Civil War search for *a* standard of taste) builders and clients often chose a style at random.

In this period of eclecticism, therefore, one could find houses in central Minnesota in the revival styles of Georgian, Greek, and Gothic, as well as those styles grouped under the general label "Victorian"—Italianate, Stick Style, Queen Anne, and Shingle Style. In some cases houses were "pure" in form; in others, a house would contain elements from several styles. Geographical distance from urban areas, absence of materials, scarcity (or lack of need for) architects, as well as practicality, common sense, and a generally high level of taste, led the westerner to a simpler and more appealing building idiom. While successful immigrants (now farmers) and their descendants might desire some "style" in a building, they continued to build outside of prescribed formal architectural *styles*, preferring in their place, local materials, hand-craftsmanship, and semi-professional builders. With the multiplicity of styles, materials, and building techniques available in the region, central Minnesota architecture is a synthesis of the folk, vernacular, and classical traditions.

One of the more handsome architectural styles is the Greek Revival, a style that played a strong role in the architectural history of central Minnesota. Historically, the style began as a reflection of America's sympathy for the Greek War of Independence from Turkey during the 1820s. In the Jacksonian West, the style was thought appropriate to an emerging democratic state. For the southern plantation owner, Greek architecture reflected the supposed ideal of the slave state. As Mary Mix Foley points out, educated Americans had been steeped in the classical tradition for over two centuries. When the Greek Revival began in 1820, a vocabulary was readily available for both builders and clients.

> The vocabulary of classical architecture—column, pediment, portico, entablature, cornice, frieze, architrave, modillion, dentil, and so on and on—had thus become the common property alike of the classical scholar, the merchant, the plantation owner, and the village carpenter. The one might have this knowledge in his head and the other in his fingers, but it was there.[50]

In the middle west, Greek Revival influence was felt beyond the time period which historians assign to it (1820-1860). As Foley shows, the Greek temple form was ideal for the gable-roofed house which was merely turned endwise so that the entrance served the street or road.[51] In villages and rural areas the temple was reduced to its simplest elements: The temple-form silhouette, a simple board frieze, corner boards (in place of columns or pilasters), pointed window and door lintels, and an occasional "hooked gable" (returning eave). Stripped of the more elaborate elements, Greek Revival farmhouses in central Minnesota possess the grace and dignity of classical lines and the beauty of simple design. Rarely found is the temple-form without additions either to the rear or to the sides. "T" or "L" plans, either original or added-on, are very common. A rare example of the temple-form without additions is the John Gasperlin farmhouse, St. Anthony, Stearns County, Minnesota. This house of unknown date has the rectangular shape and height of the Greek Revival temple-form, a pediment-shaped gabled roof, pointed window lintels, a frieze, corner boards, and a rarely-found transom window with small square panes over the entrance door. As often found in Greek Revival houses, the entrance door has been set to one side to allow wall space for the parlor. Now abandoned to face the elements, its once white-painted clapboard siding has turned a dingy gray.

The MacDougall farmhouse, *Riverside*, Morrison County, Minnesota, was built *c.* 1876 by a Canadian emigrant, Peter MacDougall, and combines features from the earlier Georgian style with those of the Greek Revival. In form, *Riverside* resembles a temple, but its entrance door is placed, not in the narrow end, but in the wide south wall. This facade is rigidly symmetrical, reminiscent of Georgian influence in its window and door placement and the relation of each to the available wall space. Although no classical door enframement appears, thin corner boards (capped with thin moldings on the north wall), cornice window heads, frieze boards, and sash windows reveal both Georgian and Greek sources. *Riverside*'s antecedents are the Canadian homestead of Peter MacDougall at Brucefield, Ontario, and Martha Gibson MacDougall's family home in Frederickton, New Brunswick.

The outline of the Canadian homesteads—the upright temple-form—was followed at *Riverside*. The end-walls, in particular, show this influence in

When Peter and Martha MacDougall built this farmhouse in Morrison County, they incorporated features from their respective Canadian parental homesteads. The rigid symmetry of the south facade is more typically Georgian, though the upright Greek Revival temple form is revealed in the outline of the west wall.

architectural forms, it was also an outward expression of the new machine technology. New inventions like the balloon frame and the scroll saw gave rise to curvilinear bargeboards, drip moldings, pinnacles, and other Gothic Revival elements, as well as the "picturesque asymmetries" of a building's form that mirrored another source of Gothic inspiration—the natural landscape.[53]

In central Minnesota, there are several excellent examples of Gothic revival farmhouses— many still extant because of the wide use of brick, a material often chosen for this style. (Central Minnesota builders utilized a yellow brick, manufactured from abundant supplies of clay in the region.) A farmhouse in Todd County, Minnesota, built by an Austrian emigrant, Joseph Brever, in the 1870s, has the asymmetrical outline of the Gothic Revival adapted to the "T" plan. The parlor-kitchen wing door and a door leading to the bedroom wing are placed at right angles to one another. This unusual arrangement reflects an intentional asymmetry, as does the placement of the gable in the parlor-kitchen wing. Hood moldings and label stops (executed in stone), ornamental brick panels beneath the windows in the bedroom wing, and bracketed porch canopies mark this handsome building's facade.

form and in the window placement, but the hooked gables of the Canadian houses were not retained. *Riverside* also lacks the fieldstone walls, Federal period doorway, double-stack twin chimneys, and 6 by 6 sash windows of the Gibson house. The expansive porch of the MacDougall's Ontario house, was omitted as well. *Riverside* symbolizes the richness of American vernacular architecture, influenced by the classical tradition by way of British and Canadian sources, as it is exemplified in a central Minnesota pioneer homestead.[52]

During the same period when the Greek Revival was a dominant building style, the Gothic Revival was also competing for attention. As an outgrowth of an emerging romantic spirit which began in the 1830s, the Gothic Revival, along with the Greek Revival, provided impetus for a variety of revival styles that span the Victorian era, 1837-1901. While the Gothic Revival's intention was to evoke nostalgic associations with the medieval past through

The "T"-shaped farmhouse could be adapted into any current style. The Brever-Grecula house, Todd County, Minnesota, is Gothic Revival. Constructed of yellow brick, it has the ornate window moldings, porch canopies, and asymmetrical massing common to the style.

The Joshua Otis Cater house, Sherburne County, Minnesota, was originally built in the style of the Gothic Revival. Built c.1870, the house had a veranda, paired lancet windows, and twin chimneys. Now largely remodeled, the Cater house combines features of the Georgian (hipped roof and balustraded deck) with the square, flat facade of the Federal Period.

The Gasperlin farmhouse (above), Stearns County, Minnesota, shows the upright temple form. The "widow's weep" and hipped roof are the only surviving elements of the original design of the white clapboard Cater farmhouse (below) in Sherburne County, Minnesota.

By the turn of the century, many rural builders had the means to erect larger frame houses for their growing families. An increased income and a style appropriate to it merged in the multi-roomed, gingerbread-clad Victorian farmhouse. As in the case of the Greek and Gothic Revival styles, the central Minnesota Victorian houses tended to be simplified versions of their Eastern prototypes. The middle western vernacularized farmhouse represents the style at its minimal decorative level, often expressed only by the projections and recessions of the Victorian silhouette. While towers and turrets, gingerbread on porches and gables,

and stained glass windows appear throughout the region, ostentatious treatment by use of these elements is rare. Wood continued to be the widely used construction material; but where brick was employed, local craftsmen composed ornamental bonds of high quality and originality. Two central Minnesota houses, will be described to reveal the range of interpretation found in the Victorian vernacular: The Simpson house, *c.* 1918, Mille Lacs County, Minnesota, and the James C. Cater house, 1898-1900, Sherburne County, Minnesota.

A simple, yet elegant, Victorian farmhouse in Mille Lacs County represents the vernacularized rural version of its more elaborate urban counterpart. The beauty of the Simpson house results in part from the retention of its original appearance.

The Simpson house shows how the builder's basic "L"-plan could be adapted to grander proportions without sacrificing practicality. The "L" consists of a parlor-bedroom wing in the form of the upright temple attached to the kitchen wing. Projecting above the upright wing is an asymmetrically-placed bay which terminates in a tent-roofed wall dormer. This handsome element not only gives visual interest to the building's form, but also allows ample light to enter the parlor and upstairs bedroom-study. The house sits on a fieldstone foundation, above which a wooden watertable board provides a well-proportioned base for the clapboarded walls above. The house is trimmed with capped corner boards, hooked gables, entablature, a projecting cornice and wide rake boards. This fully-developed classical enframement is rare in rural architecture. Well-scaled, handsomely decorated, and practically designed, the Simpson house is an outstanding Victorian building.

Between 1898-1900, a Sherburne County, Minnesota, builder named Wahl built a 10-room Victorian house for the James C. Cater family. Built of lumber from a Minneapolis sawmill transported by railroad to Cable, Minnesota, and by wagon to Haven township, Minnesota, the house sits on 8 foot high, granite-chunk foundation. Stone for the walls was quarried at the nearby State Reformatory. Essentially "T"-shaped, the house measures 30 feet e/w by 60 feet n/s and is graced on three sides by wide, one-story porches. Of a grander scale than most central Minnesota farmhouses, the Cater house combines elements from the Greek and Gothic Revival styles while carefully integrating its Victorian decorative features into the overall design.

The west facade reveals the Cater house's T-shape. Greek Revival influence is strongest in the design of this facade.

The pedimented gable of the Cater house (north facade) contains windows treated in Gothic Revival style.

The visual interest is strongest when looking at the east facade. This facade contains two bays, the north (top of the "T") projecting 7 feet eastward beyond the south bay (the leg of the "T"). The north bay contains a large bay window with a stained-glass panel and a row of dentils above. The whole is topped by a hipped roof surmounted by a capped chimney of yellow brick. Along the east wall of the south bay a porch with handsome scroll saw capitals atop ornate columns ties together the two bays as does a wide frieze board and connecting cornice. Hipped roofs on both bays meet at right angles.

The entrance (north) facade porch runs almost the full width of the house. Refined gingerbread trim and a small central pediment serve as decoration. Above the cornice is a pedimented gable dormer with Gothic style window treatment. The outline of the south facade resembles the upright temple-form. More plain in design, this facade meets the needs of a kitchen entry in a subdued, yet graceful way. Stylistically, the Cater house possesses the strong lines of classical architecture with a minimum of well-chosen decorative devices—used mainly in the porch design. In combination, these elements represent a Victorian standard of elegant refinement.

Ample living space was provided for in the interior. The downstairs has a parlor and living room in the north bay and a dining room, bedroom, and kitchen in the south bay. Maple and pine floors, white oak woodwork, and fir wainscoting—now restored to their original lustre—were utilized on the ground floor. Red carpeting originally covered

East and north facades of this Cater farmhouse. Several sources including Greek Revival, Gothic Revival, and Eastlake (porches) are combined in this handsome house.

these floors. Four bedrooms, a hired hand's room, and a "tramp" room for transients—all connected by a narrow hallway—constitute the upstairs floor plan. Transom windows and high, molded-baseboards are among the interesting upstairs details. The spacious attic area exposes a complicated system of roof supports made of high quality mill-sawn lumber.

The materials and craftsmanship used in the Cater house display the influence of the folk and vernacular traditions. After the Cater family moved from the house in 1914, the house deteriorated through sixty years of occupant renters until restoration was begun by its present owners in 1975. The owners, Jack and Penny Horton, have taken pains to restore the house to its original appearance. In spite of sixty years of neglect, its walls are still plumb—a tribute to its careful construction. True 2x10 floor joists and seven-layer wall construction (which precludes the use of modern insulation) attest to Cater's concern for and Wahl's pride in craftsmanship.[54]

The evolution of building history in central Minnesota is evident in this brief study of primitive and temporary dwellings through log to frame construction. The landscape of this region has been enriched not only by the variety of building forms—houses, barns, outbuildings—but also by the people who settled and built here. The viewer is impressed by the high level of

craftsmanship, integrity of design, and beauty of forms found throughout the region. And while pockets of common building types or elements—a barn form or a particular style of cupola—will appear within the scope of a few miles, one is always surprised to find individual structures and elements that fit no single pattern, plan, or style.

It is safe to say that all log buildings in central Minnesota can be classed as folk buildings. These buildings were constructed as they were needed according to the availability of materials and within the knowledge and skill of their builders. A hodgepodge of styles and types of construction can be found on any one given farmsite. Most rural buildings were built for practicality and are unpretentious in style. These structures seem to have an indefinable quality of endurance similar in character to their builders.

Unfortunately, most early central Minnesota log and stone structures are in a state of partial decay or ruin as can be said of the subsequent frame buildings on abandoned farms. The log and stone buildings that still exist reveal marks of craftsmanship and individuality; their natural structural materials, simple forms, and rustic beauty are vital remnants of our unrecorded folk and vernacular history.

1 An interesting literary treatment of frontier life in Minnesota based on true experiences is Ruben L. Parson, *Ever the Land* (Staples, Minnesota: Adventure Publications, 1978).

2 J.E. West, "Where the Pioneers Slept," in William Bell Mitchell, *The History of Stearns County Minnesota*, I (Chicago: Cooper and Company, 1915), p. 424.

3 Mitchell, p. 868.

4 Merrill E. Jarchow, *The Earth Brought Forth* (St. Paul: Minnesota Historical Society, 1949), p. 83.

5 Mary Mix Foley, *The American House* (New York: Harper & Row, 1980), p. 56.

6 Everett Dick, *The Sod-House Frontier* (New York: D. Appleton-Century Co., 1937), p. 113.

7 Jarchow, p. 83.

8 Jarchow, p. 48.

9 Della Tainter-Williams, "Reminiscences of Pioneer Life," in A.E. Tasker, *Early History of Lincoln County*, Lake Benton (MN) News Print, 1936, p. 190.

10 Earle R. Hubbard, *My Seventeen Years with the Pioneers, Thistles and Hay-Needles*, Raymond, S.D., (privately printed), 1950, p. 21.

11 Mitchell, I, p. 425.

12 Eugene Boe, "Norwegians on the Prairie," in Thomas C. Wheeler, ed., *The Immigrant Experience* (New York: Penguin Books, 1975), p. 60. The Boe family settled in Aastad near Fergus Falls, Minnesota, in 1868. They lived for ten years in a one-room hut built of dirt strips piled against the side of a hill.

13 An excellent technical explanation of pioneer tools is Ralph Hodgkinson, "Tools of the Woodworker: Axes, Adzes, and Hatchets," Technical Leaflet #28, *History News*, American Association for State and Local History, May, 1965.

14 Eric Sloane, *A Reverence for Wood* (New York: Funk & Wagnalls, 1955), p. 72.

15 For a discussion of stonework, see Richard W.E. Perrin, *The Architecture of Wisconsin* (Madison: The State Historical Society of Wisconsin, 1967), pp. 44-59.

16 Walter Haupt, "Frank A. Lemke," Genealogy Files, Stearns County Historical Society, 5 May 1932.

17 _____, "Fred Christen," Genealogy Files, Stearns County Historical Society, 7 February 1938.

18 Mitchell, II, p. 1360. George Klein, 95, remembers that log houses in the St. John's University area were "filled out (chinked) with warm, wet yellow clay, both inside and out." Personal interview, 30 March 1981.

19 Carl W. Condit, *American Buildings: Materials and Techniques from the First Colonial Settlement to the Present* (Chicago: University of Chicago Press, 1968), pp. 20-21.

20 For a discussion of the medieval roots of American architecture the best source is Hugh Morrison, *Early American Architecture* (New York: Oxford University Press), pp. 20-21.

21 Sloane, pp. 29-33. One-, two-, and three-batten doors are cited and illustrated by Sloane. Doors were often built of apple, cherry, or mahogany. Critics disclaim Sloane for his romanticism, but he is still the chief source for hundreds of previously undocumented (and beautifully illustrated) pieces of Americana.

22 Terry G. Jordan, *Texas Log Buildings: A Folk Architecture* (Austin: University of Texas Press, 1970), pp. 43-46. Jordan says that in Europe chinks occur only in Czechoslovakia and the German provinces of Bohemia, Moravia, and Silesia. Craftsmen from these regions brought the method to Pennsylvania where it spread to succeeding frontiers.

23 Field work observation, 1981-1982.

24 Fred Kniffen and Henry Glassie, "Building in Wood in the Eastern United States, A Time-Place Perspective," *The Geographical Review* 56, 1966, pp. 40-66. The authors cite saddle, "V", diamond, square, half, and full dovetailing as the predominant eastern U.S. types.

25 Jordan, pp. 65-71.

26 This barn is in good condition because the present owner stores hay in it. The name of the craftsman was obtained from Anna Petrich.

27 Jordan, pp. 58-65.

28 Jordan, p. 71. The popularity of the double-notch was spread by "Lincoln Logs," a toy that introduced log construction to several generations.

29 Jordan, pp. 54-58. Jordan says that the art of half-dovetailing is "almost forgotten everywhere in America." p. 54.

30 (Families in) the very ancient . . . Saxon house lived in the same space and under the same roof as the animals. The family enjoyed restricted quarters by the hearth; threshing took place in the central space or nave, which was flanked by cows on one side and women's quarters above and horses on the other with menservants above." Eric Arthur and Dudley Witney, *The Barn: A Vanishing Landmark in North America* (Ontario: M.F. Feheley Arts, 1972), pp. 38-39.

31 William A. Marin, "Sod Houses and Prairie Schooners," *Minnesota History*, Vol. XII, June 1931, p. 137.

32 Sources for the forebay barn are difficult to track down. Jordan attributes the form to Swiss emigrants who migrated to Pennsylvania in the eighteenth century. The typical Pennsylvania forebay is often called the "Switzer" barn. Terry G. Jordan, "Alpine, Alemannic, and American Log Architecture," *Annals of the Association of American Geographers*, Vol. 90, #2 June 1980, pp. 154-180. Jordan concludes that American log barn forms originated in eastern Switzerland, Upper Bavaria, and Salzburg Province (p. 165). The Justin barn fits Jordan's "Pennsylvanian and Midland American" barn category.

33 The Shakers built their monumental round stone barn in 1825 at Hancock, Massachusetts. At the turn of the nineteenth century, the agricultural press praised round forms for their maximum floor space combined with minimum wall space. They have not been a popular type among owners. For an excellent discussion of rural architecture, see John Fraser Hart, *The Look of the Land* (Englewood Cliffs, N.J.: Prentice Hall, Inc., 1975), pp. 123-136.

34 Information on the Garner barn was provided by Alva Moses, 87, a Garner neighbor, phone interview, 9 March 1982, and a phone interview with Ralph Garner, Perry's son, 7 June 1982. Moses described the interior as having cattle stanchions and wall gutters. This plan was considered practical, but the lack of room for hay offset it. Mr. Garner was a young boy when the barn was being built. He remembered his father as a "good carpenter."

35 Charles Klampkin, *Barns: Their History, Preservation, and Restoration* (New York: Hawthorn Books, Inc., 1973), p. 1.

36 Agnes Rausch, Personal interview, March 1981.

37 Theresa Christen, Personal interview, March 1982.

38 Hart, p. 136.

39 Minneapolis restoration architect, Foster Dunwiddie, is in charge of restoring the Fox house, now permanently located on the grounds of the Sherburne County Historical Society, Becker, Minnesota.

40 Condit, p. 20. According to Condit, two-inch planking provides a "rigid and durable structure while at the same time offering considerable insulation against heat loss."

41 Morgan's measurements, April 1981. The planks are of milled lumber from an island in the St. Francis River.

42 Jon Michael Fox, "The Fox House: Alternative for an Historic Structure in the Sherburne National Wildlife

Refuge: Sherburne County, Minnesota," private report, 6 June 1978, pp. 6-7. A copy with an attached memorandum from Will Dunwiddie and National Register Nomination Forms are available at the Sherburne County Historical Society.

43 Morrison, pp. 256-257. See also Kniffen and Glassie, "Building in Wood in the Eastern United States," pp. 43-48. Some scholars distinguish between *poteaux* as squared and *pieux* as round posts. According to Morrison, *colombage* designates "widely spaced, normally braced, vertical, squared timbers," while the two *poteaux* terms refer to "closely set, unbraced vertical timbers." (257).

44 Condit, p. 18. Condit cites possible Huron and Iroquois sources for *poteaux-sur-sole* construction. A description of the Church of the Holy Family at Cahokia, Illinois, built in *poteaux-sur-sole* construction, summarizes the technique well: ". . . massive timber sills, laid directly on levelled ground, support heavy, hewn timber posts about ten to twelve inches wide and about nine inches apart. Diagonal braces at the corners support the structure. The spaces between the posts are filled with a mixture of rubble stone and lime (*pierrotage*). Channels cut into the posts help hold the filling in place." John De Visser and Harold Kalman, *Pioneer Churches* (New York: W.W. Norton & Co., 1976), pp. 20-21.

45 Several on-site visits were made during 1980-1981. A few days before the house was razed, Blaise Legatt, Matthew's son, gave us a tour. Blaise, who was born in the house in 1901, did not know of its special construction until several years ago when the clapboard siding was stripped off the west wall. The roof had also been removed in recent years. The house had been vacant since 1950.

46 The Minnesota Historical Society has recorded six vertical log structures, not including the Skandar-Legatt site. According to their documentation, French Canadians who settled in the St. Croix River Valley and along the fur trade route from Grand Portage to Baudette built upright log structures. Five are in the Baudette area; the one in the St. Croix Valley is a "curious composition of French and Scandinavian log construction." Loren C. Johnson, "Louis J. Moser Homestead," *National Register of Historical Places Inventory-Nomination Form*, 21 Dec. 1978, p. 5. An important upright log house, moved from Chisago City to Almelund, Minnesota, sits in a farmer's field awaiting possible restoration. In this fine folk structure, 10 inch-wide hewn logs were placed tightly together in an upright position, 17 logs to a wall. Horizontal strips were notched into the face of the wall to receive vertical plank siding. Craftsmanship throughout this building is superior. Morgan and Jasper Bond, Field-study, 6 June 1982.

47 Sigfried Giedion, *Space, Time and Architecture* (Cambridge: Harvard University Press, 1954), pp. 345-353.

48 Giedion, p. 345.

49 Giedion, p. 349.

50 Foley, p. 135. Another view states: "What the average builder needed was a vocabulary simple enough to be spoken by the unlearned, flexible enough to take a character from the local dialect, and above all, transla-table into wood. Given these, the remotest Michigan settlement could pass in a few months from the log house to the frame dwelling . . ." Oliver W. Larkin, *Art and Life in America* (New York: Rinehart & Co., 1956), p. 155. According to Larkin, Asher Benjamin's *Practical House Carpenter*, a popular handbook for builders, ran to 14 editions between 1830-1857. (p. 156).

51 Foley, p. 149.

52 Much of this information was gathered in a personal interview with Clement and Katherine Du Frene, Cottage Grove, Minnesota, 2 June 1982. Mrs. Du Frene is Peter MacDougall's granddaughter. Photographs, deeds, tools, and furniture from the MacDougall homestead are in the Du Frene's possession.

53 Foley, p. 150.

54 Personal interview, Jack and Penny Horton, 21 June 1982.

III.
Central Minnesota
Living Pioneer Family Histories

The Anton Gogala Farm

Nestled among progressive, modern farms one mile south of the village of St. Anthony, Stearns County, Minnesota, is the Anton Gogala farm. Established in 1865 by Slovenian immigrant, Anton Gogala, the farm is operated today by three great-grandsons, Joseph, Andrew, and Anthony (Tony).

Joe, Tony, and Andrew Gogala in their rural St. Anthony, Minnesota, home.

The Gogala farm is significant because of the values held by the brothers: Pride, familial attachment to the values of previous generations, and a willingness to preserve continuity through the use of pioneer buildings—particularly revered folk structures of hewn log construction.[1]

The Gogala family emigrated to the United States in 1865 from Ljubljana, now the Republic of Slovenia, Yugoslavia, but then under Austrian rule. They learned of central Minnesota through the influence of a Slovenian Catholic Missionary priest, Father Francis X. Pierz.[2] Disillusioned with the class divisions in Slovenia, they, along with five other families, decided to emigrate to America, leaving Bremerhoff in the spring of 1865. Their journey lasted from 15 May to 15 August.

The first generation of Gogalas in America were Anton senior and Agnes (Marat) and their five children: Anton junior, Johanna, Mary, Theresa, and Agnes. The senior Anton was fifty-one years old; the younger Anton twenty-two. Both had been blacksmiths in Europe. Having been told that a gun was a necessity in the new wilderness, the father traded their prized anvil for a double-barreled, muzzle-loading musket, handcrafted for them by a local blacksmith and finished the night before the family sailed. The musket is unique as it has hexagon-shaped barrels, one for buckshot, the other for bullets. The stock has an ornate metal inlay with a hawk engraved on the side. This handsome artifact, proudly displayed by the brothers, is a prized family possession.

Because Anton, Sr., had been a local mayor, the family had some money for the journey. Unfortunately, they were robbed of all their money while in New York City. Joseph said:

> In New York they got jobs and when they went around in the city, they marked the corners of buildings with chalk so they would for sure get back to the ship because they didn't speak the language.[3]

Upon reaching Minnesota in the fall of 1865, Anton, Sr., and his son took jobs in the sawmills of St. Anthony to earn money and to pick up trade and craft information useful for establishing their homestead.

In the spring of 1866, the Gogalas traveled to central Minnesota. They had planned to establish themselves in St. Stephen, Brockway Township, where a settlement of Slovenians was already established. Finding the soil too sandy, they continued on about seventeen more miles to section 32 of Krain Township, Stearns County, Minnesota, the site of another Slovenian settlement, where Anton, Sr., and Anton, Jr., each took deeds to 160-acre homesteads.

The Gogala family reached their destination with all of their belongings packed in two trunks. They lived with neighbors until their first house was built. The entire area was a wooded wilderness. The young Anton Gogala took a job in a brewery in Sauk Centre and worked there a number of years until enough land was cleared to make a living from farming. Andrew said:

> When grandfather worked in the brewery, he did not dare drink water, only beer. When he quit working there, he would dream of beer because he had gotten so used to it. If there had been a bar in St. Anthony he would have become an alcoholic.

With only a felling axe and a grub axe the Gogalas cleared the land and built their first house. (Joe said, "If they would have had a bulldozer, they would have got rich much faster. This way it was a lifetime job!") After a short time, Anton, Jr., also built a house.

Wild animals roaming about in the wilderness were a constant threat to the early settlers. The buildings were placed in proximity to each other because bears dragged away whole hogs, foxes killed chickens, and skunks raided the nests for eggs. In the distance wolves howled at night. However, wild animals were also a main source of food. Many times even bear was eaten, but deer was the settlers' main meat food, Joe said. The brothers have a favorite story about a deer. They were very plentiful in the area. "In fact," Andrew Gogala said, "Grandfather once had a deer so tame it came up to him and ate tobacco out of his hand."

Religion has always been a major value in the family life of the Gogalas. Agnes, a sister, talked about the importance of their Catholic faith.

> In the very early days [she said] they walked to St. Joe to go to Mass. They'd start out late Saturday night and they didn't have a watch. They judged the time by the moon and they were back by Sunday night before dark. What faith they had!

Because young Anton Gogala had built a large house by the standards of that time, it was used as a church once a month when the visiting missionary priest passed through. Generally, a messenger let the family know when the priest was to arrive and the men of the family would walk all night to inform the neighbors that there would be mass the next morning.

On the day of the mass the priest would sit in one corner to hear confessions while the men sat in another to smoke and visit. "They had to be quiet," Joe added. The priest performed baptisms, marriages, and burial services on this day and then a mass would follow. During the mass, "Grandma cooked for all the people," Agnes said. Ordinarily, women did not attend these masses because they were expected to stay home to care for the smaller children.

As the area became more heavily populated with Catholic families, the neighbors decided that a church must be built. Anton, Sr., donated forty acres of his land for this purpose. The new log church was dedicated on 13 June 1874, and named St. Anthony, as was the town later, in honor of the saint and recognition of Anton Gogala's generosity.[4] Joe said:

> They were going to build the cemetery around the first church and then they changed that. Dad always said

that one of his brothers is buried there close to the priest's doorway. Three of them died as infants. They died of croup or whooping cough. There was nothing they could do. There was no doctor around.

When Anton, Jr., married Gertrude Slivinick they walked to St. Cloud for the ceremony with only twenty-five cents in their pockets, Agnes said. This marriage produced ten children: Johanna, Mary, Helen, Anna, John, Mike, Tony, and three other children who died in infancy. As the children came along, a larger house was needed. The main section of the present house was built of logs in the 1880's and the old log house became a summer kitchen and wash-house. Later it was torn down and its logs were used on Joe's farm for a granary.

The Gogala farmhouse. This L-shaped vernacular building was originally a log structure to which a two-story frame bedroom wing was added. The log section (left, foreground) was built in the 1880's. The bedroom wing (background) was built in 1906. The porch (right, foreground) is a later addition.

The present house is vernacular Greek Revival in style. The original log section, now a 1½-story kitchen wing, joins a two-story frame bedroom wing added in 1906. The two wings form an "L" which has been clapboarded and painted white. Dark green corner boards resembling thin pilasters, window moldings, and overhangs at the gable ends give the house its classical appearance. The house sits on a heavy granite-boulder foundation with 15-inch-high corner blocks hewn on site by Anton, Jr. Sited on a slightly rising hill, the house presents a strong visual picture as one approaches the farm.

A bedroom loft in the log section of the house once served as quarters for an itinerant missionary who shared the room with family members. The bedroom wing contains ample space for large, rectangular rooms. A doorway from the kitchen enters a hall to the bedroom wing which contains a sitting room and two bedrooms below and two bedrooms above. Ornate hardwood moldings are used throughout the house. In choice of style, siting, and use of interior space, Anton Gogala provided a handsome and comfortable dwelling for his growing family.

The earliest animal shelter was probably a crude pole structure used to house oxen. In the late 1880's a log barn was constructed to hold newly-purchased dairy cattle. Still in use, this

The Gogala dairy barn. The buildings were placed close together to provide protection from wild animals.

barn is an excellent example of medieval folk architecture. Constructed of hewn oak and tamarack logs, its facade is 23' 9" wide. The 17"-high foundation is of granite-boulder construction set in heavy mortar. Resting on the foundation and running nearly the building's width is a massive oak sill which bears deep broadaxe marks. The wall, ten log courses high, has individual logs which vary in height from 7" to 12". A mixture of half-dovetail, full-dovetail, and saddle notching appears. The west (front) facade is pierced by a 6'-high vertical-plank door and two windows—one small four-pane window below and a larger hayloft window with a shutter-door above. The windows and door form a rough triangle—an asymmetrical plan which is strongly medieval in feeling. Vertical plank siding of uneven widths and lengths cover the gable on this side. Clapboard siding has been used on the north and corrugated metal siding on the east. The various types of siding indicate the

evolutionary stages through which the structure has passed.

A single large room forms the ground floor of the barn's interior. Three round center posts and a 7"-thick hewn beam support the hayloft. Natural heat from a small dairy herd keeps the room warm. Joe feels that "log barns are better because they are naturally warmer."

At the south side of the barn is a wooden silo 12' in diameter and 24' high. Constructed of vertically-set, tongue-and-groove planks of redwood, 6" wide and 10' in length, the silo is reenforced by metal bands and cross-anchors. Resembling a giant barrel, it was moved to its present site in 1952.[5] The silo is attached to the dairy barn by a silo shed, 7' 4" high.

The silo-shed-barn configuration, the various textures of materials and the siting are striking. The barn itself is one of the best surviving examples of medieval architecture in central Minnesota.

Since the Gogalas had raised sheep in Slovenia, they soon acquired a flock here too. Most of their clothing was made from sheep's wool. The brothers remember caps, mittens, scarfs, wristlets, and stockings handmade by their mother and grandmother. They also remember the women carding wool that was used inside their homemade quilts.

A sheep barn was built soon after the dairy barn was built. The sheep were raised for wool and for sale. They processed their own wool, washing it with "nice white homemade lye soap," according to Joe. The family did not eat mutton. (Joe said no one in the family liked mutton and when he was in the army in Australia he tasted it and found out they were right! "But those little lambs were nice.") The Gogalas stopped raising sheep when store-bought or peddler-purchased fabric became plentiful. The logs from the sheep barn were then used in building a horse barn. The Gogalas have always believed in natural methods of farming including recycling, using or reusing anything that was still useful.

The Gogalas always kept four or five draft horses for their own use and for breeding. No horses have been raised by the Gogala family for twenty years now. Originally, a lean-to on the east side of the horse barn was used for raising chickens. The eggs were traded for supplies in town, as was wheat and barley. Joe said, "Grandfather often said that they carried 100 pounds of flour home on their backs all the way from St. Joe." Today the horse barn is used for calves and young stock. The building measures 18' 6" north/south and 46' 9" on the west. Utilizing red-painted drop-siding, this structure is part of the modern group of farm shelters on the Gogala farm.

One of the few primitive-like structures that can be observed in central Minnesota is the Gogala's pig shelter. In form, use of materials, and method of construction, this dome-shaped mass more closely resembles primitive than folk antecedents, though a similar structure described by Byron D. Halsted, an early authority on farm buildings, shows the use of this type of structure in the nineteenth century.[6]

The pig shelter is roughly square in shape, measuring 6' 10" on each side. The roof is covered with meadow hay and its over-top dimension is approximately 20'. A six-foot high pen, constructed of poles, planks, and rails nailed to vertical logs which are cut in a triangular pattern, form its sides. Narrow openings on two sides allow animals to enter a yard that is enclosed by pole fences. The pig shelter is important because it links an architectural form from the ancient past to the needs of contemporary farmers.

Because of its use of materials, the hog barn is an excellent indicator of the architectural changes that have taken place on the farm. Measuring roughly 18' east/west by 11' 7" north/south, the barn is a frame-and-log structure, gabled, with weathered red siding. The south wall is of frame construction and is clapboard-sheathed in the gable apex. The east wall is of exposed log construction with half-dovetail corners. The west wall has been covered with drop-siding. Although the hog barn has limited esthetic appeal, it does have value as a symbol of the farm's evolution from log to frame construction.

Another interesting log building is the smokehouse which is nestled among tall, stately black walnut trees just west of the main house. Built to smoke, cure, and salt meat, the smokehouse is still being used for that purpose today. The form of this log structure is strongly medieval. Constructed of smoothly-adzed poplar logs, eight courses high, this structure has half-dovetailed

The Gogala brothers still make use of the smokehouse that stands in a walnut grove on the family farm.

joinery of excellent craftsmanship. A lean-to of double-notched round logs, 6' 5" in length, is attached to the back. This unique addition was built by the brothers as children to be used as a playhouse. Joe said:

> Those were nice times. We played Drop the Hankie, Hide and Seek, Hide the Thimble, Ante, Ante Over, and Tag. We had to make up our own games. We had homemade sleds in winter.

The gable on the south (entrance) side of the smokehouse has 7" drop-siding; a vertical plank door serves as an opening to the smoking area. The east side still retains the original cedar shingles—these are weathered thin, lending themselves to the character of the structure. Overall dimensions of the major unit are 9' on the south and 11' 6" on the east.

Thirty-five yards south of the farmhouse, stands a blacksmith shop. Around 1900, great-grandfather Anton sold his farm in St. Anthony to become a full-time smith, his trade in the old country. This building became his shop. According to Joe Gogala:

> He was actually smarter than any welder. He had to hand-forge everything. One time some people from Albany needed a plow shear sharpened. They didn't have a wrench to take it off the plow so this person carried a whole walking plow on his shoulders to have it sharpened. I sure couldn't do that. He was sure strong.

The west facade of the blacksmith shop is most picturesque as much of the surface is of exposed hewn poplar log construction, eight courses high, of varying shades of brown and gray. With its steeply pitched roof and weathered surfaces, it closely resembles its medieval source. Measuring 10' (west) by 16' (south), the structure rests on corner piers of stone. The heavily-mortared chinks form a strong pattern against the half-dovetail joinery. The gable apex is covered with handsome weathered pine and clapboard siding. The roof angle is unusually steep for an out-building in this region. ("Shingles last longer on a steep roof," Tony says.) Cedar shingles are used on the south; asbestos on the north. The shop contains many original tools, including an anvil, a bench, and the chimney for Anton's forge. The Gogalas use the shop for repair work and tool storage today.

Now used for storage, the shop was once used for blacksmith work.

Andrew Gogala said that many times people would come into the blacksmith shop to ask his great-grandfather for medical advice because he had also been a doctor's apprentice in Slovenia as a young man. He was called on to set bones and to heal wounds with herbs and homemade medicines. One concoction that seemingly worked was a poultice mixture of cattail roots pounded out for oil, mixed with tallow and turpentine. He had a special wire to pull teeth. Andrew relates:

> One guy—he had an infection in his toe and he said to great-grandfather, 'I think you'll have to cut this off' and he (great-grandfather) blew the dust off the anvil and he said, 'lay it on!' The other guy backed off!

Along with the dairy barn, smokehouse, and blacksmith shop, the corncrib completes the group of folk buildings. This crib is the only building where square nails were used. Standing about 15½' high, the structure measures 7' 1" on the east by 11' 10" on the north. It is gabled east/west and constructed of 4" to 6½" high "popple" logs, nine courses high, and clapboarded in the gables.

Chinking has been eliminated to allow air circulation. Finely-crafted full- and half-dovetailed corners are used. Windows pierce the gable ends 5½' from the ground and there is a 2' 4" door on the east; 7½" sawn purlins and butted rafters appear in the interior gable area. Older shingles and a small handmade hardware latch add to the weathered beauty of this attractive structure.

Tony Gogala beside the log corncrib.

A most interesting structure, situated at the end of the driveway below the main house, is a temporary corncrib. Its elongated rectangular form and domed roof of meadow hay resemble the primitive shape of the pig house. The crib pew, however, is constructed of a modern material, corn-cribbing wire, which is baler-twined to the same kind of triangular wooden posts used in the older structure. Approximately 16' 4" high, it measures 5' 7" in width by 22' 5" in length. Storage of corn in late fall makes this a colorful addition to the farm scene.

The Gogalas also have several frame and clapboard structures that postdate the folk buildings. One of these is a granary, rebuilt in the 1960s from an earlier granary. This pleasing white-painted building is rectangular (15' 3" by 24') and gabled north/south. Machine-sawn 9" to 11" oak sheathing from the original granary and rough-sawn oak boards used for pens and dividers form an attractive interior. These boards have been worn smooth from grains sliding and rubbing against them over the years. They are pleasant to behold and feel like naturally-polished, fine wood.

The granary, a garage, a feed shed, a machine shed, and a storage shed constitute several modern buildings of a later development in the architectural history of the Gogala farm. Although these structures may not be as interesting as the folk buildings, they are functional and esthetically pleasing. As in the case of the granary, materials have been used from earlier structures. Most of the modern buildings employ drop-siding or clapboard and are painted red or white. While this phase of building history seems to stand in stark contrast to the pioneer era, the newer structures attest to the Gogala's desire to link the past with the future.

The layout of the Gogala farm is interesting as it is made up of triangles: Farmhouse-blacksmith shop-horse barn; horse barn-hog barn-corncrib; farmhouse-pump-smokehouse; storage shed-pump-temporary corncrib. The primary working area lies along a lane between the horse barn and dairy barn on the east and the hog barn, feed shed, and corncrib on the west—a hub around which the wheel of farm activity moves. All of the folk structures play a major role in the farm's daily operation. The newer structures indicate the Gogala brothers' desire to modernize the farm.

The desire to modernize probably grew out of necessity because the farm was split into two eighty-acre parcels when the third generation of Gogalas, John and Frances (Geisendorf) Gogala and their children, took over one parcel and John's brothers, Mike and Tony Gogala, the other. Progress and economics demanded beneficial additions and changes. Today, John and Frances' three oldest sons, who never married, farm the land. Andrew and Anthony live on the home eighty acres and Joe lives on the eighty acres formerly owned by Mike and Tony. Joe tells the following story about his uncle:

> I remember Uncle Mike. You know he grew up in this house where it was cold upstairs. They all lived here at first, you know, until they split up the place. In the bedroom upstairs it could be thirty below and he had the window open. You had to be hardy. In the old house there was snow on the quilts in the mornings. They just shook the quilts and swept up the snow. It was that cold!

Joe says that he goes over to the main house now to keep house and "cook up a little hash for myself and Andrew and Tony since mother died."

This fourth generation of Gogalas has many fond memories of the past and present times. At Christmas time they always had a tree with candles. Agnes said, "Father would light them very carefully and let them burn only while gifts were being opened." They remember all the good smells in the house from the many traditional Slovenian foods their mother baked. They remember that mass was first celebrated in Slovenian, and then in German, and by custom the men would sit on one side of the church and the women on the other. In 1947 Father Preusser came to St. Anthony's as pastor. According to Joe, the priest changed this custom:

> 'Why are you still doing this? You live together all week and then you come to church and we go there and you go over there.' He mixed them up and had no problems.

The Gogalas had telephone service for as long as they can remember. Their grandfather Anton never learned to speak English, but he would answer the phone with *kiner da heim* (No one is home). They got electricity in 1939 and they milk the dairy cows with electric milking equipment in their log barn. They use gas engines to pump water.

When asked if their forefathers ever considered their life too hard or if they ever considered going back to Slovenia, Andrew said:

> No, they came here to be free. They never wanted to go back. When World War I came and they lost the war they said of Franz Joseph 'That's what he had coming.' They didn't speak up for him. They didn't have any regrets.

The Gogala brothers possess the hospitality and good manners for which the Slovenian people are noted. Although they cling to many old customs and traditions, they blend well into the mainstream of the area.

The young Gogalas did not lose interest and move away when the old people died. The farm has been declared a Century Farm by the Stearns County Historical Society and is listed on the National Register of Historic Places. The brothers hope the farm will stay in the family. They love their farm and are very proud of it and their heritage. Very likely, one day the fifth generation of Gogalas in America will be farming it.

1 The authors visited the Gogala Farm on 1 August, 14 August, 18 September, 25 September, and 15 December, 1980. We wish to thank the Gogala brothers for their assistance and willingness to take time from a busy harvest season to talk to us. We also wish to thank Thomas Harvey of the Minnesota Historical Society, for his on-site assistance.

2 William P. Furlan, *In Charity Unfeigned* (Paterson, New Jersey: St. Anthony Guild Press, 1952), p. 195. Pierz is proudly referred to by central Minnesota Catholics as the "Father of the Diocese of St. Cloud." He is traditionally credited with procuring the Benedictine monks and sisters who eventually founded St. John's Seminary and St. Benedict's Convent in the area. He is also responsible for bringing a seemingly endless stream of German immigrants into central Minnesota between 1854-1864.

3 Interview with Joseph, Andrew and Agnes Gogala by Marilyn S. Brinkman, 25 September 1980. All further quotes, unless so indicated, are from that interview.

4 *St. Anthony Centennial* booklet, St. Anthony (Minn.) Parish, privately published, 1974.

5 Tony Gogala, 25 September 1980.

6 Byron D. Halsted, *Barns, Sheds, and Outbuildings* (New York: Grange Ludd, 1881), pp.68-69. Henry Glassie documented a central New York thatched corncrib constructed, according to local tradition, by a "Yugoslav or Pole." The few "roughly thatched open sheds" Glassie cites in Piedmont Virginia and the Ohio valley are pigsties. Henry Glassie, *Pattern in the Material Folk Culture of the Eastern United States* (Philadelphia: University of Pennsylvania Press, 1968), pp. 208-212.

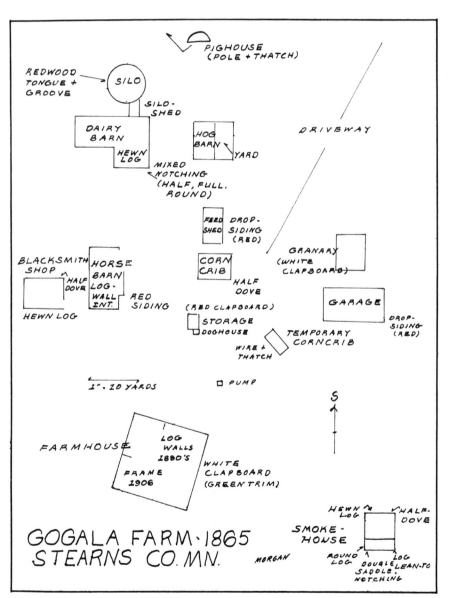

Steve and Frances Supan

Steve and Frances (Schumer) Supan live in a lovely, gray, naturally-weathered, two-story hewn-log house surrounded by a bed of colorful petunias, new sidewalks, and a carefully manicured lawn. The house stands in Section 19, Brockway Township, Stearns County, near the town of St. Stephen. Standing on a fieldstone foundation, the 30' by 40' house has one of the best preserved hewn-log walls in central Minnesota. This wall (south) is constructed entirely of massive oak logs, 13" to 15" high and some as long as 27 feet, set in courses 10 logs high. Each log has been carefully adzed and heavy broadaxe marks appear throughout. The wall is heavily chinked with smooth yellow mortar troweled flush with the log surface. The corners are half-dovetailed. One square joist end which projects through the wall appears above the door.

Like many folk structures that have undergone change through the years, each wall of the house is different. The south is log; the east, clapboard and vertical plank; the north, horizontal plank in the gable apex and vertical plank below; on the west, stone and clapboard. The stone is

Steve and Francis Supan in front of their two-story hewn-log house built in 1890 by Slovenian builder Mathew Justin. *Photo by Jeff Harrington.*

particularly attractive, being made up of quarry pieces and fieldstone set in smooth mortar. The elements of time and weather have been kind to the exterior of this house; in contrast, progress has changed the interior to suit modern needs. To walk inside is to leave one hundred years behind.

Blaise and Mae Legatt, Steve and Francis Supan, and Marilyn Brinkman stand near the front entrance of the Supan's log house. Constructed of massive oak logs, the Supans have lived here for 48 years.

Steve and Frances are a lively, happy couple who have lived in this house the entire forty-eight years of their married life. They are of Slovenian descent, and like most Slovenians are traditionally conservative and frugal. Why discard buildings that are "still in pretty good shape" expresses their architectural philosophy.[1]

The history of the house is etched in the memories of Steve and Frances. It was built in 1888 by Mathew Justin, an early Slovenian builder who homesteaded the farm. Steve said the massive oak logs were purchased from friends and neighbors and were paid for with blackberries. "They got them for nothing, but gave them blackberries just to be good." Other blackberries they took to town and sold and "that's how they paid for those logs," he said.

As fieldstone was plentiful in the area, a stone addition was built in 1890 to serve as a kitchen with a root cellar beneath. The walls are a full two feet thick. Frances says the kitchen is very difficult to clean and dust because she is very short and not able to reach beyond the thick walls to the windows. Also, the stone walls were plastered over on the inside for increased light, however, paint does not

hold because in winter there is frost in the corners. A recently enclosed porch on the west end of the kitchen holds the Supan's washer, dryer, and freezer. Over this door on a sandstone block Mathew Justin proudly etched his initials and the date—"M.J. 1890."

Slovenian builder, Mathew Justin, carved the date and his initials (hidden beneath the door frame) when he constructed the stone addition to the log house.

Steve has lived on this farm and in this house for seventy-two of his eighty-five years. Prior to their marriage in 1934, a portion of the exterior was clapboarded over and allowed to weather naturally. Evidently, this did not agree with Frances. She said:

> So then when I got here, well, you couldn't paint it anymore then either because the boards were warped then already. So then we just let it go too; and then, well, as the boards got rotten, we tore them off, one here and one there and so this last summer, our son Lawrence and I, we took everything off on the outside there. We won't paint the logs as someone suggested because, my God, think of all the paint those old logs would take. At my age: Never!

In recent years, another log building, the barn, has been covered over with tin "to make it a little bit nicer," but it retains its log-building form. A picturesque white "S" decorates the brown gable end which faces the driveway. It is not known when the barn was built as, "they didn't put a date on the barn," Steve said, in his mild, folksy manner.

Mathew Justin also built a fieldstone chicken barn. Built into a hill, it deteriorated quickly and vanished years ago. Frances still shivers when she talks about the chicken barn:

> That was so cold. I don't see how the chickens ever lived there. Then we had an old shed, and a chicken coop was built onto the shed. That's where I kept my chickens. Oh, that was nice! We went through about the same hard times as my mother and dad did. During the thirties—that's when we got married—in thirty-

four. Boy, oh boy! Eggs were sold for six cents a dozen, or sometimes twelve cents a dozen!

The Supans raised seven children on their farm. "We were not big farmers—only fifty-six acres," Frances said. Times were hard. They planted corn and oats and milked fifteen cows. There was always work to be done. Frances remembers one event especially. One of the younger children started a fire in the house by sticking paper into the chimney of a kerosene lamp. Steve and Frances were in the barn milking cows. The barking of their dog told them that something was wrong in the house. Fortunately, the older children had known enough about fires to put it out with a blanket, and there wasn't much damage.

Frances indicated times have changed greatly since she and Steve first started out. "There aren't many of us Slovenians left anymore," she said. The generation of their children do not speak Slovenian anymore and for this reason they are no longer considered true Slovenians. "Also," she said, "the ethnic pride is gone in the new generations." The farms in the area "most always" stay in the families and the names stay the same, but other people move in among them, and often the old traditions, as well as the old buildings, must give way to change. "The old people, however, do tend to hang on to their traditions through their faith and the church," she said.

General changes in the St. Stephen area came very slowly and cautiously. For example, until World War I sermons were preached in Slovenian, and in time also in German. Then, during that war sermons in German were prohibited in American churches. Frances recalls the struggle to maintain their own ways and ideas:

> I remember so well. I was quite small yet, but Father Trobec was our priest, and he said in church that before he was going to preach a sermon in English the river would have to run backwards! I'll never forget that. I remember that so well!

The St. Stephen parish church itself has not undergone the extensive architectural changes that many older Catholic churches have. Although some of the frescoes have been painted over, the old statues are still present. Frances and Steve feel strongly about so-called improvements. On the other hand, necessary changes such as adding a door for a fire escape, a bathroom, and general

repairs and improvements are approved. The Supans feel those things are necessary but believe the main church will stay as it is as long as there are Slovenians as church trustees.

The Supan's log house is a different story, however. They modernized their log house with electricity in 1952. About 15 years ago a porch was enclosed on the west side to make a utility room, when indoor plumbing was installed. About ten years ago the Supan children remodeled the entire house: The kitchen was insulated, plaster-boarded, and paneled as was the log-section living room. At this time the floors were also carpeted.

Even with these changes, however, some of the older amenities of log-house living have been retained. The entire house has its original chinking, wood-burning stoves are used for heat (in the kitchen they have an electric stove), and the house has the strength and durability of log and stone construction. As Frances says:

> We don't have to be afraid of the house falling anyplace because the stringers are right on the ground. The floor has log stringers with rough sawed lumber for flooring under the carpeting.

A son, Lawrence, still lives with Frances and Steve. Another son, Donald, now owns the farm and lives in a trailer home adjacent to the log house—a common practice on many farms. Donald farms the land and supplements his income by driving a school bus. When he was married a few years ago, Frances said a party was held in the log house and about fifty people came for lunch and dancing. It was just one of many good times the family has enjoyed in their wonderful home. The Supans are a close family who are very proud of their home and lifestyle.

Supan house, 1982.

Frances says that Donald will probably keep the house after they are gone because "it would be a shame to tear it down after we fixed it up so much." Hopefully it will stand as a reminder for future generations of the Slovenian pioneers who settled the area, people who put their faith and trust in God!

1   Personal interview with Frances and Steve Supan, 9 October 1980.

The Supan log barn has been covered with metal siding. Its original form is still discernible.

Original Supan settlers in front of their log house.

Cyril and Olivia Schwieters

Cyril and Olivia Schwieters are friendly, progressive farmers who live in rural New Munich, Grove Township, Stearns County, central Minnesota. Their family farm was originally homesteaded in 1862 by Cyril's German immigrant grandfather, Herman Schwieters. A Stearns County Historical Society plaque proclaiming it a Century Farm stands proudly in the lawn near the driveway of the farm.

Olivia and Cyril Schwieters. New Munich, Minnesota.

Immediately visible from the dirt road leading to the Schwieters' driveway are two large, well-weathered log buildings still in use and in very good condition. They are nestled among a mass of modern buildings: A large horseshoe style barn with an unusual lean-to addition; two steel pole sheds, used as shelters for cattle; a corncrib, two machine sheds, two grain bins, a storage shed, a smokehouse, a four-car garage, the main house, and a trailer house. Clearly these contemporary buildings of concrete, steel, and milled lumber depict the progress of the farm through time whereas the log structures depict a deep sense of pride in the pioneer past. The Schwieters have utilized the past through their buildings in a meaningful way.

Cyril and Olivia are kept busy today with farm work, hobbies, and community events. Eleven children, one still at home, and many grandchildren also keep them busy. The Schwieters have a unique family history with documents dating back to the 1860s that are kept in a fireproof safe in Cyril's office. Unfortunately most of these letters, deeds, and cards are written in German and they are fragile and difficult to decipher. Most of the family background that Cyril and Olivia remember comes from their memory of stories told by Cyril's father, Joseph, an only son, who was born in a log house on the farm in 1883.

Cyril said that Herman and Gertrude (Blenker) Schwieters emigrated from Germany in 1862 to the heavily wooded area of New Munich because other German Catholics were already established there. They homesteaded 160 acres for which five years later they secured a patent. (1867 is the date on the Century Farm plaque). Since the land around New Munich was rich farmland, the area was quickly settled by fellow countrymen. Cyril says the entire area has always been heavily German Catholic. Until the last decade, there were no other nationalities or denominations represented in New Munich. They are proud of their German pioneer heritage; in fact, in the last few years the town has begun an annual celebration similar to Oktoberfest in Germany. It involves a beer garden, food, music, a parade, and a wooden wheel derby, in which all contestants must race a vehicle with wooden wheels.

After the pioneering Schwieters arrived at their destination, the first structure they built was the house, followed by a number of barns and outbuildings. Two of these are the log buildings still found on the farm today. The walls are gray-weathered oak and tamarack with the original plaster chinking. These structures have been moved to new locations on the farm and their use has changed: The granary is now used as both a granary and as a storage shed and the sheep barn is used as a hog barn/machine shed with straw stored in the haymow. They are strong structures and, according to Cyril, the logs won't move.[1]

The combination hog barn and machine shed is one of the largest structures of its kind in central Minnesota. Particularly impressive from an esthetic viewpoint is the tent-like roof which sweeps down from the ridge to about six feet from the ground on the north. This feature provides both a pleasing silhouette as well as protection from winter winds.

Construction of the hog barn is hewn-log and plank. These materials have been treated in a robust and straightforward way which gives the barn its massive appearance. Two walls are of particular interest. On the south where the barn opens onto the hogyard is a wall 14 logs high containing exposed joist-ends and a mixture of square and half-dovetailed joints. At one time this wall was chinked with mortar, but much of this material is missing. The east wall contains hewn-log construction below and extremely wide (15″ to 18″) vertical planking in the gable apex. The logs show deep axe marks and the use of mortar chinking. Like the Gogala barn, the door/window configuration is asymmetrical, a plan that, along with the heavy lines and grayish color, gives the building its medieval appearance.

The Schwieters' combination hog barn and machine shed is one of the largest structures of its kind in central Minnesota.

The granary is also an impressive log structure, one of the best examples of its kind in the area. Four-square and forthright in conception, the granary sits on a stone-boulder pier foundation and has huge hewn logs heavily chinked with mortar. Pattern, line, form, and texture make this a fine example of the esthetics of hewn-log construction in central Minnesota.

The first crops grown on the Schwieters' farm were wheat and potatoes. Horses were used for most of the fieldwork. For this reason they were considered more important than the cattle. Only five or six cows were kept to supply the family with meat

and milk. The horses and cattle were housed together in one barn and the sheep, raised for their wool, in another. Cyril said his father often spoke of the days when wolves roamed about in the woods and many times they would run off with sheep. "Then all of a sudden they were gone," he said. "I never saw any myself."

Chickens, ducks, geese, and pigs were other sources of food. A frame smokehouse, still in use today, was built to cure and smoke and store pork, as the family would butcher four or five hogs each year. This was supplemented by one or two beef a year which were canned and stored in a root cellar, Olivia said:

> You canned the beef, put it in jars, with salt and pepper on it, then cold pack it on the stove. Some people browned it first and then you get a nice brown gravy, but we always canned it raw in jars.

In 1888, when Joseph was five years old, the old log house was moved and a new frame house, the one still on the farm, was built. It has since been remodeled.

In 1908, Joseph Schwieters married Catherine Hallermann, a German girl who had emigrated to New Munich in 1893 when she was eight years old. They took over the family farm when grandfather Herman died in 1910.

Cyril remembers his father as an early riser who believed in keeping busy. In the mornings before it was time to start the daily chores he often busied himself with work traditionally considered women's work. He helped to get the day started in this way. According to Cyril:

> He always got up in the mornings at about five o'clock and lit up the stove. You know at that time it wasn't so warm. The house wasn't insulated. So in winter time he started the stove and then he'd sit down and spin awhile, and by six o'clock he'd call us. But we could always hear him—you know, the whirr of the spinning wheel.

Cyril's mother must have appreciated being able to wake up in a warm house and have some yarn spun for her too, as she did all of the knitting for the family. She made many pairs of mittens and some stockings. She didn't have much time for anything else. She always had a large garden and did a lot of canning and preserving. "She worked hard," Cyril said.

Like many central Minnesota pioneers, Joseph

took advantage of the rewards of living in a wooded area rich in wildlife and fish. He trapped and hunted muskrat, mink, raccoons, and other fur-bearing animals. In good times a large, thick mink pelt brought $50.00. Joseph had a cattle dog that could not only sniff out mink, but could tell the difference between a mink and a muskrat trapped under water. Cyril added, however, that "the dog was never any good for cattle." Joseph skinned and stretched the pelts and then stored and dried them "in the old kitchen, now torn off." He also enjoyed fishing, and gladly walked the mile to the nearest lake. In fact, he went fishing just a few days before he died at age 71.

Cyril Schwieters was born in 1921, one of nine children. He graduated from a one-room local school. He said he started at age five because he could go along with his bigger brothers and sisters. However, his attendance was not always faithful because he had to stay home many days to help with the farmwork. Times were especially hard in 1927 when they lost most of their possessions in a barn fire. The barn burned on August 2, a very hot day. The fire was caused by a type of combustion involving wet hay and heat—a door flew open, causing the hay to ignite. Cyril said the New Munich fire department was called. They dropped a firehose into the well but it couldn't pump water fast enough to put out the fire. Cyril added that they did manage to save a horse with a colt.

Before the barn burned, there had been a horse in there. It had a colt. We just left them both out that morning or they would have burned. You know, it was born that weekend and the barn burned on Monday morning.

Cyril and Olivia Schwieters with children, left to right, back row: Mark, Joe, Patrick, Norman. Kneeling: Dave, Irene, Alice, Karen, Ruth, Rueben and Joyce in front.

The barn had held about twenty milk cows, some young calves, and horses. To finance building a new barn, Joseph sold twenty acres of land. Cyril said, "They sold the land to get money to pay for a new barn. Luckily, a neighbor wanted the land."

When grandfather Herman came to the area, it was covered with trees. He began farming the land as it was cleared of trees. Joseph continued to clear land and he also bought more as time passed. At one time the farm totaled 305 acres. Gradually, parts of the farm were sold. Today the farm totals 225 acres. Cyril said: "In those days they did a lot of land transferring, especially during the Depression."

Cyril added, however, that the Depression, as most people know it, was not as much a factor for the central Minnesota farmer as was the drought that occurred at this same time—this is what caused the Depression for the farmer. Nothing grew. There were no crops to sell or to feed to the livestock; therefore, there was no money. Pigs sold for two cents per pound. Gas cost ten cents a gallon. There was plenty available, but no money to pay for it. Cyril recalled:

> I worked a lot of days for fifty cents per day at my uncle's place doing farm work—$15.00 per month. It was a lot of money in those days. Nowadays kids wouldn't work for that. Seven years I worked out like that before I was married.

In 1934, the lake behind the Schwieters' property dried up. It has never happened since. They had to build a fence across the lake to keep the horses home. Some people cut the hay or wild grasses over the lake bed to use as bedding or feed for the livestock. They cut it over the ice with horses.

The Schwieters' didn't have much hay in the drought years, but they did raise corn by this time. The corn grew, but it did not have many ears. Therefore they decided to build a silo and fill it with the stalks and few ears to use as feed. It was cheaper to go into the ground than up, so with horses and a scraper they dug a hole seven feet deep and fourteen feet around. Then a silo company erected a cement stave silo over the hole. It took a week to build, during which time the building crew stayed on the farm, eating and sleeping with the family. The silo was built thirty feet above ground. This feed kept the cows in production until times got better. Milk was separated and the cream was hauled to the creamery at New Munich. The skim milk from it was mixed with ground barley and oats and fed to the hogs.

Cyril, like his father, also married a local girl, Olivia Pundsack, a farm girl from New Munich. She attended school in New Munich as a young girl and was taught by Benedictine teaching nuns. Whereas Cyril received catechism instructions on Saturdays, Olivia had religion classes each morning after attending mass. The parish priest also came to school every Tuesday to teach more catechism and every Wednesday for Bible classes. "Things were stricter years ago than nowadays," Olivia added.

Cyril, like his father and grandfather before him, also cleared more land, a total of forty acres. In Cyril's time the work was simplified, but still difficult.

> It wasn't real heavy woods. It was pasture. I cleared it, but there were real heavy trees on it. I bulldozed it—about twenty years ago. Well, there still was a lot of work to it yet, you know. You clean it up and then all of the rocks are on it yet that have to be picked up.

The family farm has provided a good life for three generations of Schwieters. The fourth generation is now in the process of taking over the farm. Cyril and Olivia's son, Patrick, is married and lives in a trailer house near the main house and controls the operation of the farm. His parents will remain in the house for some time yet, as the youngest daughter is still in high school. Cyril has lived on the farm all of his life, farming it with his younger brother since taking over completely shortly after his marriage. His brother died a few years ago and Cyril wants to keep the farm in the family. After he retires he would like to remain active by helping on the farm. He also enjoys driving a cattle truck and going to farm auctions; and he and Olivia like to travel and attend horse and dog races. "I just don't want to work for someone else," Cyril stated adamantly.

Clearly, Cyril and Olivia are very proud of their heritage and lifestyle.

1   Personal interview with Cyril and Olivia Schwieters at their home, 6 March 1981.

Fred Swan

Although he was born and raised in Benton County, Fred Swan also lived in southern Minnesota; he served in France during World War I, and he endured a portion of the Great Depression in Sioux Falls, South Dakota. He came back to his farming roots in Glendorado Township in 1933 because, as he said, "There was no work in Sioux Falls and I wanted to get out of working for someone else all the rest of my life."[1]

Fred is eighty-six years old and lives in a tidy aluminum trailer house just fourteen feet from the remodeled Queen Anne farmhouse in which his son and family live. He prepares his own breakfast and dinner but takes his supper with the family in the main house. "It gets kinda lonesome livin' alone, but I can make it and I don't wanna go to a nursing home," he says.

Fred Swan at his rural Benton County farm.

Fred is a tall, easy-going Swede who enjoys the outdoors and is happiest when working on the farm. He gets up each morning at 5:00 a.m. to feed his baby calves and in the afternoon he helps to feed the cattle and his calves again. He calls them "his" calves because he is in complete charge of them;

and one gets the feeling he truly loves them, as he does all of the farm animals. When he walks from his trailer to the barn, his steps become faster and easier, and his manner changes to one of optimism and joy. He teases and jokes and playfully fondles the calves, and they respond to his attentions.

Fred remembers the past and tells about his heritage. He said the Swan family emigrated from Stockholm, Sweden, in the 1860's. His father, Ulrich, came to America as a young man with his parents and brothers and sisters. They settled originally in Sherburne County because—

> There were some more people from the old country settled down there. There was a whole colony down there, about in the middle of the county. Most of them were farmers there. It was timberland and a little open here and there. They cleared a lot of land in them days. Farms were 40 to 80 acres in all.

Fred's mother was also of Swedish origin. She was born in Becker Township, Sherburne County, where she and Ulrich married. They lived in Princeton, Mille Lacs County, for some time, and then moved to Benton County where they homesteaded eighty acres in Glendorado Township, about one mile from the present Swan farmsite. Originally, the area was covered with hardwood timbers—oak, ash, elm, and basswood. Fred remembers living in a log cabin when "timber came right up to the house. It was like living in the little house in the big woods." In time, they bought eighty more acres adjoining the homestead because there were eleven children in the family and they all needed work to do and the family had to be fed. Fred said he was the oldest "of the whole tribe!"

The Swans spoke Swedish at home, but by the time the children were old enough to start school they had also learned English. Fred began grammar school at age seven in School District 13 near his home. However, after a number of years that school became too crowded with forty or fifty children in one room with one teacher; therefore, another district was formed and Fred completed his education in School District 48. This old, white frame building still stands, neglected and forgotten, about one mile from the Swan farm.

Fred said the Glendorado area was primarily settled by Norwegians and a few Swedes. Most of the families were quite large and there was tension between the different nationalities and religious denominations. According to Fred the children also became involved in the tension. He said:

> Oh, Ya! You know, kids are what kids are. I don't care whose they are. We got into arguments and scraps. I didn't very much; I was big for my age. That took care of that! I remember my brother next to me. He was always in it. See, Sweden and Norway fought and Norway lost. Then they split. There's always been hard feelings. It's hard to understand. I never could see that. Some people are selfish. They think they're better than the next one. Heck! I never felt that. I figured that if you were born and was in company you should not be so jealous. I always got along. There was a Polish family in the area, and when they started school they were made fun of. The Norwegians taught them to say things that weren't very nice and they didn't know it. In those days the Catholics hardly talked to you. The Catholics didn't mix with the Lutherans.
>
> And then, you always got a bunch of smart-alecks. Worst part of it was we had three boys that came from St. Paul. They was always trouble-makers. Well, they got into arguments and fights and stuff and we had strict orders from home not to fight. It didn't bother me. I could take it. I laughed about it.

Fred attended school on an irregular basis because of farmwork, as did most farm children in those days, and he graduated at thirteen or fourteen years of age, because children were not graded according to chronological age. After completing the required number of books and taking the eighth grade examination, he was graduated.

The Swan family attended religious services at the Glendorado Lutheran Church. On May seventeenth of each year a joyous spring festival was held, involving a big celebration and dinner. This has since been discontinued because "some pastors want it and some don't," he said. Fred, however, proudly displays a commemorative plate on his living room wall from one of these celebrations.

In his youth Fred went hunting and fishing to pass time. He also loved to go dancing at dance halls and in homes. He and his brothers and sisters would go together and once in a while his parents would go along. They usually got there by walking—a mile or two was nothing—at night, in mud, or in snowstorms. Music was provided by boys from the neighborhood playing guitars, fiddles, or mandolins. Fred liked the mandolin best. Often one room was cleared of furniture and made into a dance floor, with the girls providing a potluck lunch. Fred met his future wife at one of these dances. Dancing became a favorite form of entertainment all during their married life. Fred said he did not drink much liquor in those days because his church was against it, nor was there much free money to throw around. On the other hand, moonshine was available in the area; in fact, a wholesaler lived on the farm Fred now owns.

As a young man Fred did road construction work and also rented land adjoining his family farm. Then, in 1916, he was drafted into the army. He served as a machine gunner in France for thirteen months, until the Armistice when he was shipped back to the states. "They turned us loose again!" he said, smiling.

Upon returning from the war, Fred went into carpentry work for his brother. For some time he worked in southern Minnesota. In January, 1922, he married Julia Thompson, in Rock County. Four of their seven children were born while they lived in Sioux Falls, South Dakota. Fred liked doing carpentry work; but when the Depression came along, work was difficult to find. He did some work with the WPA, and Julia raised much of their food in a large family garden and sewed all of the family clothes. Unfortunately, conditions did not improve during the thirties. Fred said,

> That was during the Depression and we've got another one coming. You darn right, and that's gonna be rough. I know. I went through the other one. And conditions are like that now. There was hardly any work then. I was lucky. I always had work then, but you didn't get nothing for it—$4.00 per day for ten hours of work doing anything you could put your hands on.

By this time Fred and Julia had spent fifteen years outside central Minnesota. They longed for the familiarity of their homes. They packed up their family and came back to Benton County to the land and to their roots, as did many people during the Depression. They wanted to begin anew. The Swans rented a farm from the Federal Land Bank for two years before buying it. Fortunately, the land was productive and good, Fred said. When asked why some people stayed on very poor land, Fred replied that many times these people settled for what they could get at the time; and once they were established, they hated to pull up their roots. People tended to "stay put even though the land was poor." The Depression had taught the people to hang onto what they had. Land, especially, was precious. Fred highly valued what he had found again. Since his land had trees on it, he could cut his own wood for heating and cooking and didn't have to go to town for coal. He made a new beginning and was confident and proud of it.

The Swan granary has a belltower—an unusual feature for a rural building. The bell was rung at mealtime to summon fieldhands during the early days on the farm.

Fred is also very proud of his wife and credits her for much of their success. He said when the family moved back to Benton County, they brought along over 500 quarts of canned goods, half a wagon-box full that Julia had preserved while in Sioux Falls. The first few years on the farm were still difficult, especially for Julia. Since they did not have a smokehouse, she canned much of their meat, including chickens. She pre-fried their fresh side-pork and put it in jars in fat. She raised a large garden and canned and preserved a great deal of vegetables and produce from it. No matter how hard the work was, she always managed to get something on the table to eat, even when they were short of everything, Fred stated proudly. She continued to sew the family clothing, and helped milk the dairy cows until 1943, when Fred purchased electric milking equipment. Furthermore, she also helped out in the fields "when they were in a pinch or something."

In 1943, Fred bought another eighty acres adjoining his farm and moved to their present site. He said he had four sons and they needed something to do and eighty acres wasn't enough land to make a good living. "It ain't like it was 40, 50, or 60 years before when you could raise eight to ten kids on forty acres," he says.

A house, barn, and granary, all constructed about 1904 were on the farm when the Swans moved there. A picturesque granary has an unusual feature: a belltower (or belvedere) in the center of the roof. Fred's son Tom said that this bell was rung at mealtime to summon the menfolk home from the fields, and that it could be heard from a great distance. The granary has the lines of Greek Revival style though in a very simple and minimal way. These lines are discernible along the rake boards. The belltower is particularly interesting and unique as it features four small pediments and tiny bargeboards—very unusual elements in rural architecture. Of frame and clapboard construction, the building is greatly in need of repair.

The barn that has now vanished but was on the farm when the Swans bought it was very large by the standards of the day—fifty-five feet wide, with a haymow in the center and a lean-to on each side for cattle. The Swans milked eighty to ninety cows by hand for many years in these two lean-tos. After their horsebarn burned, they also kept five or six horses there. It had been constructed of local lumber sawed at a nearby sawmill. In 1968 the roof of the haymow caved and the barn was razed. A new horseshoe-style barn was built by local contractors to replace it.

The Swan homestead is a remodeled Queen Anne style farmhouse.

The Swan house was completely gutted and remodeled two years ago when Fred's son, Tom, moved into it with his family. The house is Queen Anne, a late-nineteenth century style. Unfortunately, the use of modern siding hides the textural richness essential to the integrity of that style. The silhouette with its hipped roof, projecting gables, returning eaves, and richly detailed veranda retains some of the flavor of the original structure.

Next to the main house is the trailer house, a machine shed, the granary, a two-bay corncrib, a hog barn, a red brick chicken barn, the new barn, a red brick silo and cement stave silo, a steel pole shed, and a steel grain bin. In the far distant pasture are the remains of a portion of the roof of a round barn. This barn was built by Ole Stay, a local lumber salesman and contractor, according to Fred. Unfortunately, it had to be moved from its original site to make room for a road coming through the area. Today the remains are a reminder of a once unique structure.

Two years ago Fred sold his farm to his son Tom. "I can't take it with me anyhow and this was his home too," Fred says. Tom has lived there and worked the farm with his father for twenty-three years. The farm will stay in the family and Fred will always have a home. A trailer house near the main house is a very common site in central Minnesota. When the young people take over the home farms, the old people do not care to leave; and this seems to be a very amicable solution to the problem.

Fred says he does not regret anything that has happened to him during his life. In the old days he had to be more careful with money, but money went further; things have changed a great deal, but work is easier now, he feels. People are just as good as they were years ago, and they get along better now, he says. Fred is content with the way his life has turned out; and although he has been lonesome since Julia's death, he says he is happy. He gets along on his social security and has earned the rewards of old age because, he says, "there ain't a man in two shoes who worked harder than I did, and my boy thinks the same!"

1   Personal interview with Fred Swan at his home, 3 March 1981.

John and Anna Petrich

John and Anna Petrich still live in a log house. They live much as their ancestors did at the turn of the century, without benefit of electricity, running water or indoor plumbing. They have been married sixty-nine years, and still climb steep wooden stairs to the loft where they sleep. Although John has suffered a minor stroke he still insists on carrying out such chores as pumping water and carrying it into the house for use in drinking and cooking. He also gathers kindling for the large kitchen range and the potbellied stove in the living room. The wood is brought by wheelbarrow to the kitchen door several times a day.

The Petriches live simply in the manner they

John and Anna Petrich sit in their living room which is heated by the woodburning stove in the foreground. *Photo Mike Nelson.*

have been accustomed to all of their lives. Although their children have urged them to leave the farm, and offered to house them, Anna says their roots are on the farm and that neither would be happy in strange surroundings. The only modern convenience they have is a telephone, which was installed after John's stroke.

Anna is a small, energetic woman with a quick wit, very much in tune with the times. She reads widely and writes a weekly column for her church newspaper. In the spring she plants a large

garden and cultivates and harvests it herself. She still drives her Chevrolet to town for groceries and cooks and bakes and cares for her ailing husband. It is obvious that life is hard for the Petriches, but Anna's spirit, humor, and her religious beliefs help her to accept life as it is. She says, "The good Lord wants John and me to look after each other a while longer because we haven't earned heaven yet."[1]

Each year Anna Petrich plants, cultivates and harvests from her large garden. She also raises flowers for the altar of the St. Stephen parish church.

Anna's maiden name was Poglajen. Her family came to America about 1883 from the mountainous region of Veldes, Ljubljana, Republic of Slovenia, Yugoslavia. They came to the St. Stephen area of central Minnesota in Stearns County, Brockway Township, section 34, because they longed for freedom and ownership of land. This area appealed to them because fellow countrymen were there and people from similar nationalities usually settled together. This settlement had evolved through the efforts of Father Francis X. Pierz who was eager to have fellow countrymen settle this area.

Anna said her mother told her that their people came in groups from Slovenia, and their group was one of the largest and last to come to the area. She said, "If I were ever to travel again, I wouldn't want to be in such a big crowd." They traveled to New York by ship, to central Minnesota by railroad, and to their St. Stephen homestead on foot.

Although Anna's father often spoke affectionately of the beautiful hill country that was their homeland, where bells could be heard ringing through the hills several miles away, they never regretted emigrating because their lives in Slovenia had been difficult and advancement and improvement were almost impossible. Also, "none of them were rich, otherwise they would have stayed where they were, I guess," Anna added. They brought only their clothes with them because people had told them they could buy everything in America, the Land of Plenty. Anna says they knew of one family that lived southwest of St. Stephen, however, who were more frugal and forward looking. She said,

> They were real saving people. They brought everything: Axes, shovels, and my mother said, 'How useful it would have been if we had taken some things. We came here and we haven't got anything.'

John is a slight man with a distinctive twinkle in his eyes, very patient and serene. He was born in the plains area of Slovenia, a one-mile walk from the area of Ljubljana where Anna's family lived.

John Petrich still insists on carrying out daily chores. *Photo by Sister Nancy Bauer, St. Cloud Visitor.*

He put the fact of their emigration in much the same way. He said, "If my country where I was born had been so great, we wouldn't have come to America!"

John's father came to America and worked in the iron mines of Eveleth, Minnesota, to earn money to send for the rest of his family. He sent money for one son; the two of them saved for a second

son, and later the oldest daughter came. By the time of her arrival, the two sons were already planning to marry. Anna says, "Their mother stayed in Ljublajna selling milk. They had it hard. It was a hard kind of life."

After three years had passed, John and his mother finally came. John was eleven years old. By this time the family had established a homestead in Northome, Minnesota, but times were still hard, especially for John's mother. She could not speak English and often wrapped up barley or other things she did not know the name of and showed people what she meant. According to Anna,

> They walked ten to twelve miles to sell butter and bring back flour in trade. John said his Ma carried the flour and he carried kerosene and that was hard because the handle cut into his hand and he had to carry a gun on his shoulder. There were bears and wolves all over. It was just a trail.

Meanwhile, Anna's family came directly to St. Stephen, then called Brockway. Her father said of the land in the area, "All you could see was the sky up between the trees—you had to clear it first." Her parents lived with friends until enough land was cleared of timber for a house. The timbers were hewn and used to build the log house, and when completed, the family could move into their own home. The house was followed by a log barn to shelter the oxen and cows that were purchased from friends and neighbors.

The Petrich farmsite represents the most important example of folk culture in Stearns County because John and Anna Petrich still live in pioneer conditions and utilize buildings common to the late-nineteenth century Minnesota frontier. Also, the site contains more buildings that can be identified as folk architecture than any other site observed in central Minnesota. (By folk is meant a type of structure influenced by European antecedents, particularly of medieval origin, designed, built, and used by immigrant craftsmen). The Petrich barn, house, and granary are good examples of the folk tradition, while four other outbuildings reflect vernacular building materials and design. In these latter buildings, frame rather than log construction predominates, and the level of craftsmanship and originality of design fall short of the folk structures.

The house built by John Poglajen in 1883 is constructed of round logs, but its log construction is hidden beneath clapboard siding. The sharply-pitched gables, brick chimney, shed-door, and small windows give it its medieval appearance.

The interior is quite comfortable and homey. The shed-door on the south opens into a large kitchen which is illuminated by a small stationary window on the west, deeply set in the log walls, and sash windows on the north and south. Chinks are filled with wood and cement which Anna and her friends repair yearly. (Creosote and whitewash are used—a treatment that makes the room lighter.) A large Monarch kitchen range, where Anna cooks and bakes, heats this room. A dry sink is fed by pails of well water. The room is furnished with cupboards and a table. Anna and John receive guests in both the kitchen and the parlor. A small lean-to off the parlor on the north is a bedroom. An enclosed sun-porch extends along the east front. The second story is an unfinished loft with exposed rafters which serves as sleeping quarters. The loft is reached by a steeply-pitched, narrow open staircase.

The Petrich log house, now clapboarded, was built by Anna's father in 1883. A sense of timelessness pervades the Petrich homestead.

The Petrich barn was also handcrafted by Anna's father. Completed in 1883, this structure is the best preserved folk building on the site. The barn is made of hand-hewn oak logs on the ground floor with vertical plank construction in the gable apexes. It is a single-bay structure with a haymow above. Three unenclosed sections are divided by post-and-beam construction. These posts have been left round and are crudely notched to receive the beams. The beams are spiked rather than pegged in place. Eight of these round posts support three 32′ half-round and half-hewn ceiling joists. Doors open at the gabled ends (north/south) and into the haymow on the north and west.

Oak log construction has been used throughout. The barn logs are particularly enormous even for this region—most of them measuring 10½″ to 13″ in height and 25′ in length. These logs have been notched in half-dovetail style with most of the notched surfaces measuring 8″ by 8¾″. All of the log surfaces reveal deeply-cut broadaxe marks and thick wood-and-mortar chinking—much of it original. Large fieldstone-boulder piers and some sections of solid stone-and-mortar construction were used for the foundation.

The barn walls are of particular interest for each wall reveals in a unique way the richness of the folk tradition, considered in terms both esthetic and structural. Like most folk buildings that have served continual use, materials have been applied to the log surfaces down through the years. Each wall hence becomes a history of the stages through which the building has passed. (The application of tin pieces and cement chinking reveals this change.) The Petrich buildings also reveal another characteristic of folk architecture—the individuality of each structure as well as the uniqueness of each wall surface on a particular building.

The individuality of each wall can be understood by a close study of the Petrich barn. The north (entrance) wall is 13 logs high, each log measuring between 13″ and 15″ in height. Vertical planks appear in the gable apex. A plank door with horizontal boards outside and vertical within is clenched with heavy nails and hinged with handmade hardware. The surface texture of this wall is enriched by this picturesque door, the weathering process, and the patterns formed by the thin, gray, serrated vertical boards above.

The west wall is 13 logs high with pronounced half-dovetail joints. This is the most beautifully articulated wall because of its long lines, deep axe marks, and grayish-brown surface. Deep open spaces where mortar has fallen out appear between courses. Eave brackets and the ends of the cedar shingles cast shadows along the wall surface.

94

The Petrich granary is also an excellent example of folk architecture. It appears to be of the same period as the barn and is presently in use as tool storage. The granary is a single-crib structure 13′ 6″ wide with a 12½′ wide lean-to shed used for tractor storage attached on the east. Log construction was used for the granary section, pole-and-plank construction for the shed. A large, sweeping, cedar-shingled roof covers both sections.

The south wall of the granary section contains a multitude of materials which results in an interesting overall pattern. Constructed of logs below and vertical planks and slats above, the wall has been covered in places with corrugated tin and flattened coffee tins. Chinking is wood-and-mortar. This section rests on granite-boulder piers, round sills, and its walls are eight courses high of deeply-marked, half-dovetailed hewn logs.

The west wall is 17′ 7″ wide, sits on a round sill, and is constructed of hewn logs, 8″ to 12″ in height, 13 courses high. This wall is patched with horizontal and vertical planks, nailed on helter-skelter, making a rich textural pattern. The north wall uses thin clapboards in the gable apex, has ten courses of 9″ to 12″ high hewn logs below, and board/batten construction in the lean-to wall. The lean-to wall (east) is five feet high and is of post-and-plank construction.

To the south of the granary stands a 5′ 9″ by 16′ 3″ keystone corncrib constructed of sapling poles and planks. Of a type rapidly disappearing from the rural landscape, these crude cribs are interesting because of their structural design and esthetically pleasing because of the shadows cast by the horizontal poles. A vertical-plank door and a horizontal-plank gable apex mark the south wall. The building has weathered to a gray tone and is in a poor state of repair. The granary was built when Anna was three or four years old. She remembers it as a happy time, and says:

> It was so nice to watch my father build it. With strings they marked the hewn logs. The shingles were home-split. Oak splits real nice. Even now when John splits oak for wood there comes a piece that just reminds me of the old shingles from that building.

A storage shed stands adjacent to the barn. Also, keystone-shaped, this shed is primarily of pole-and plank construction. A 2″ x 4″ frame, set

The Petrich barn was built by John Poglajen, Anna's father, in 1883. At the time of its construction the St. Stephen area was heavily wooded. The barn is constructed of heavy oak timbers.

outside the wall surface, makes this structure unique. The combination woodshed and pighouse is also a crude shelter. It is a frame building, covered with clapboard, painted red, and measures 7′ 6″ east/west by 31′ north/south and is 6′ 6″ in height. The front entrance has two doors and a window. Attached to the west is an unusual pighouse, the front wall of which has a truck window mounted in the wall as a light source.

A garage, housing Anna's Chevy, measures 19′ east/west by 20′ 8″ north/south. It is constructed of planks covered with drop-siding. The south wall is of particular interest. Covered with tarpaper, held in place with horizontal and vertical boards and lath, this wall presents a pattern of unusual lines and forms.

The layout of the Petrich farm is circular, allowing for relatively simple access to the garden, pump, and outbuildings. To the east are Anna's garden, a small storage shed, and the privy. Running clockwise from the house in a north-to-south direction are the barn, storage shed, woodshed, garage, and granary-tractor shed. The major avenues of use are mainly for water and wood. The pump is located in the middle of the farmyard.

Initially, the people in the St. Stephen area were all farmers. Their first crop was wheat and sometimes corn. The first seeds were bought from neighbors. Butter, cordwood, and eggs were traded for supplies and garden seeds in St. Joseph, ten miles distant. Once seed was procured, enough was saved from the crop for the following year's seed. Garden produce was stored in a root cellar over winter and some was kept for seed the following spring.

> They didn't have a big variety of food stuff. One lady took eggs in a basket and carried it on her head on a round little pillow to about one and a quarter mile around a little turn. She came there and tripped and there went all of her eggs. You know to this day it hurts me to think that's what she was going to buy something with. She must have walked almost fourteen miles with those eggs! [Anna winces when she tells this story. You can almost see the hurt she still feels for the woman.]

Corn was shelled by hand, and sacksful were taken to nearby mills to be ground into cornmeal. Husks were used as mattress stuffing; the hard outer leaves were discarded in favor of the soft inner ones. These made a fairly soft bed, "but everyone could hear you if you turned around in one of those beds!" Anna laughed. She said they had to be fluffed up every morning.

Local craftsmen, known as tradesmen, made furniture. Anna remembers stories about a particular one who made real nice beds. He made the crib that she slept in as a child.

Tools such as axes, grub hoes, shovels, and forks were purchased at local stores. Wooden forks and rakes were used for hay and straw. These were homemade by men who were good in woodcrafts. John recently made a beautiful handle out of a tamarack pole for a tool Anna uses to rake grass and leaves.

Candles were made from tallow, in forms. Soap was always homemade. Anna says she still makes it today but follows the directions on a lye can. "If mixed just right, it turns out real good," she says.

The Petriches never had sheep of their own so they bought wool from friends and neighbors to be spun into yarn. Anna says:

> Some ladies made a lot of money that way. The choicest wool could be made into such nice yarn. Ladies could knit many pairs of mittens and stockings to sell where people worked in logging camps, and in stores.

Besides work, school was an important part of Anna's childhood. She spoke the Slovenian language as a child and learned to read it before she went to school because she was an only child and loved books. She walked to school alone, three and one

quarter miles every day, usually leaving the house an hour early to get there on time. When there was work to be done on the farm, like hauling hay, she, like most farm children, was expected to stay home and help. She said:

> Well, you just stayed home, but there were tears. I read a lot. I can read as fast as anybody. You know, I had no one to play with. I read everything I could get my hands on. For $1.00 or $1.25 once a year you got six books from Europe: One was always a religious book, a calendar, a history, some on herbs and poisons, and so on. The Germans read *Der Nordstern*. The Slovenians had a newspaper published in the Iron Range. Sometimes we had that.

In school penmanship was stressed, and Anna learned arithmetic, spelling, language, grammar, geography, history, drawing, and simple things like sewing if the teacher was a woman. Sewing was considered basic because all young girls learned it as soon as they could handle a needle and thread. Anna always had a woman teacher who taught all eight grades in one room.

> We learned enough, but you had to be quiet. I was never very smart. Father Vogel says that the Lord made some perfect heads and the others he covered with hair, and mine had hair!

All of the children in the school were Catholic. Sometimes they attended Mass in the mornings before school. A prayer started the school day, followed by a few songs. The parish priest who came to the school to teach catechism wore a path from the church to the school. At Christmas-time they held simple religious programs for their parents and friends.

Anna and John Petrich met when the Petrich family exchanged timber from their homestead in Northome for 120 acres near the Poglajen homestead. Anna's father was sickly. "It was so hard for him to work," she said. And both he and her mother approved of John, so they encouraged her marriage to him at age seventeen. Anna says of her marriage,

> I know I was young, so sometimes I just say they wouldn't issue any more marriage license after that!

There was no hopechest for Anna:

> If there were a number of boys in a family you could get further ahead money-wise. They would buy the sons a farm and the girls would get a cow and a few hundred dollars or so, but I was an only child. There wasn't much money.

John and Anna lived on the Iron Range for a short time after their marriage. Anna said their hardest times were around 1916 when money was tight. John worked for 14 cents an hour. They were used to buying canvas shoes for everyday use at $1.00 or $1.25 a pair. When they needed money, they waited until they had a whole canful of cream to sell for "maybe $6.00," and then they bought shoes. "It was hard," Anna said.

In time they moved onto the Poglajen farm because her father had died and her mother was alone on the farm. Here they again started from scratch. The children walked almost in stocking feet. They had very little money. However, Anna's intense faith helped them through the bad times. She says, "but all went well. Sometimes they say that when people have it too easy they can't take much." Anna felt she was strong enough to take anything.

Together John and Anna made a success of the farm and Anna, like most farm women, did her share. She sewed all of the family clothes with cloth purchased in St. Cloud and she copied dress patterns from pictures in magazines. And some things were ordered from mail order catalogs—Sears, Wards, and Savage. This, however, did not always turn out well—

> Once Joe picked out a pair of shoes in a catalog much like men's shoes. When they came they were too big, and how Joe cried because he couldn't wear them.

Anna also helped with the chores around the farm. Her mother had raised chickens and she did too:

> I always had chickens. I liked chickens. Oh that was always my money afterwards when we came here. The egg money was mine! Raising chickens wasn't hard but it took time and care and the men didn't have time for such stuff. The men took off for the fields early and were gone all day. The cows were never milked without me if I could stand on my feet. Women worked hard and always helped wherever there was work. They didn't have as many cattle as now. We all grew up with cows—and horses. The horse is a patient animal if you are kind to him. I helped with the horses and horse machinery. I never disliked work, and it had to be done.

When people were sick they did the best they could without the aid of a doctor. "How in the world could a doctor come out into the woods?" Anna asked. They just helped each other. "Sometimes

things were done the way they shouldn't have been but most of 'em survived." Broken bones were often left unset. People used certain homemade remedies for known ailments. Certain soups were good for upset stomachs. A sick person could not be hauled by oxen or horses, so in most cases they were treated at home. Their simple faith helped people through difficult times. Anna, like most Catholics, felt better when a priest was present if a sickness or an accident warranted calling one:

> One lady had a sick husband and her biggest worry was—would the priest get there in time to give him the last sacraments? The times were hard. They had to go on horseback. Priests came from St. John's. They took care of the Slovenians and Germans together. They didn't come every Sunday for services.

Anna says people lived more simply in the old days. They were more satisfied and stayed in one place, and each lived his own life. The church was the most important thing in their lives. There was less explanation of the faith and the simple things that they knew they believed and lived. She added,

> Of course, they were human; they made mistakes, but it seems to me that now all the explanation that the church gives us, well, don't you think we could be better? I think we could be better. Today people have money and want to change this and that. That isn't always the best.

In St. Stephen, Slovenians and Germans mixed in church because, as Anna says, "the Lord created all nationalities." Many of the Slovenian men learned to speak the German language because they had served in the army. Here, there were more Slovenians than Germans so the Sunday sermons were preached in Slovenian two Sundays out of three. Announcements and catechism instructions, however, were in both languages. The children soon learned to speak both languages, as children adapt easily to change. The women, however, did not have that opportunity. Anna said,

> They just stuck to their own language. You know, the ladies, they had to stay home so much. There was always work to do and children to care for. Everything was homemade and they couldn't talk much—except Slovenian.

Just as national groups settled together, so did religious ones. There were no other denominations in the St. Stephen area until 1925, according to Anna. Anna's unyielding faith is revealed when she says that although she accepts other faiths, her own

Catholic faith has never faltered.

About the future, John and Anna say they do not intend to leave their home as long as they can take care of themselves. Anna says

> Life is like roses, beautiful but there are thorns. I much prefer to dig in the garden and work around than sit someplace and wonder what it's gonna be for dinner. If I had to leave here I suppose I'd feel bad but nobody stays forever. You have to live someplace, and well, maybe it's selfish but I can do what I can do and get into my old Chevy and go to mass and if I have to go to town, my old Chevy takes me. I have a driver's license. It comes in handy now. You can't always depend on other people, but they are always willing, but you have to consider them too—neighbors.

John and Anna Petrich have succeeded in adhering to many of their traditional Slovenian cultural and religious ideals; yet they have managed to blend comfortably into the mainstream of life around them. They are respected and loved by the citizens of St. Stephen. Furthermore, they are now celebrities in central Minnesota because of their unique lifestyle. Today, people from all over the region come to visit them in their log house.

1   Personal interview with John and Anna Petrich, 17 June 1980.

Vincent and Clara Symanietz

Vincent and Clara Symanietz live in Brockway Township, Stearns County, in a white clapboarded house built in 1906, facing a dirt road that winds through the hilly country of St. Stephen, Minnesota. Their farmstead nestles on a slight rise to the south, beyond which lies a tamarack swamp several hundred yards behind the buildings. A tamarack rail fence and a picturesque stone building, once used as a barn, can be seen from the road.

Clara and Vincent on their 65th wedding anniversary.

This stone building, now used as a garage is an interesting structure. Three thick walls are constructed of heavy boulders of red and gray mica-dotted granite set in mortar. The west wall is dominated by double doors of vertically-set 8″ to 9½″ wide planks below and richly weathered black, tan and brown 5½″ to 6″ planks above. The gambrel roof is covered with corrugated tin.

The north and south walls of the garage are entirely of stone, 5½′ high, with the north penetrated by three small windows. On the south several trees have punctured through the projecting tin, forming an interesting visual effect. The building is sited on a slightly rising hill. In selection of site, form, color and choice of materials the Symanietz barn-garage is a fine example of folk art.

Originally a barn, the Symanietz garage with its heavy granite-boulder walls is a fine folk building.

Just beyond this stone building is a tamarack rail fence constructed of rails and posts of rough construction and joined in some places by corner notching. It has held together over the years due to the fine craftsmanship of the builder, Vincent Symanietz.

In his younger days Vincent was an agile, handsome man who married Clara in 1916, at age twenty-eight, when she was seventeen. They have lived on this small farm all of their married life. Kind neighbors now look in on them and do outside chores such as bringing in wood and water and shoveling snow. Clara says they haven't moved to town because they love their farm and, "it would hurt Vince so if he had to leave here."[1]

Clara is a small woman. She says she has never weighed more than 110 pounds and has never been very strong. However, her gentle will and ardent determination are qualities that have sustained her throughout her difficult lifetime and have marked her as an extraordinary woman. She is very open and direct and honest when she speaks of herself and her past.

Clara was one of the 100,000 Orphan Train children sent west between 1854 and 1904 by the

New York Children's Aid Society, a group founded in 1853 to help neglected and destitute children find homes in rural America. Clara was a year old when the Orphan Train brought her to central Minnesota in 1900. Valentine and Agnes Wentland of Holdingford, Minnesota, gave Clara a home. The Wentlands, however, did not officially adopt Clara or her step-brother, as this was not required in those days. Clara painfully remembers her childhood as one of hard work and little love or affection. She said:

> I was fed enough but I was abused and called names. People made fun of me. If I needed clothes, I had to wear whatever they gave me—sometimes they had holes. You weren't loved as much as the orphans are now, I notice that. A lot of work we had to do. I think they adopted children more for help than because they loved the kid. When I was nine years old, I was working out on farms, taking care of mothers that had little babies and herding cattle and doing chores. One time I couldn't use my arm at all. You see there was a strain on it, so then I came home and I told them about it and they didn't want to believe me. They took me to a doctor, and the doctor said it was a strain from too much work for an age like I was. I had to husk corn sitting on a stack of corn at one place where they sent me in a blizzard where you couldn't see the world hardly, and I had to sit on that corn stack and husk corn so they had something to feed the pigs. They had pigs and one horse. In the evening I had to sleep upstairs and there was a window-pane out, sleeping under a horse robe. You know years ago when a horse died they skinned it and made it into a robe. That's what they had on my bed. Or sitting in the basement (pause)—Oh, what do you call it yet? It is so hard for me to talk in English real good—grading potatoes. You see, they didn't get to dig potatoes early in fall and so then half of them were frozen and then I had to sort them out. You see, or they would get rotten and they wouldn't keep. So that's the way life was. I tell you I worked!

Clara's adoptive parents were of Polish descent. They came from Poznan, Poland. In 1860, two Wentland brothers and their families had emigrated to America. During an arduous journey by ship, a child was born. On shipboard, potatoes baked in ashes were their only food, but nursing mothers could also get goat's milk to drink. Unfortunately, this was not enough nourishment for both mother and child. The infant died and had to be buried at sea and the mother was left weak and discouraged. The families traveled on to Michigan

where one brother settled. Agnes did not recover from her loss so they traveled back to Poland, but returned again when her father sold land to finance a second trip. When they were unable to locate their brother in Michigan, they journeyed on to Silver Lake, Minnesota, where they had other relatives and friends. They found this land unsuited for farming, however, so they sold it and bought eighty acres of open land in Holdingford, Stearns County, Minnesota.

Vincent's parents, Thomas and Agnes Symanietz, also of Polish descent, came to America in the 1870s. Thomas decided to emigrate to escape military punishment for a minor offense committed during a drinking spree. He and Agnes came with two small children and another child was born during the trip across the ocean.

The Symanietz family homesteaded in St. Anna, Minnesota, near Holdingford, along Two Rivers Lake. Upon arriving there, they found Indian huts everywhere, but the Indians were friendly. In fact, Clara said they even brought the immigrants food when they first arrived there.

In time, the Symanietzes had ten children— six boys and four girls. Vincent's older brother had married into the Wentland family, and Clara had been courted by another brother a few times. She knew Vincent about a month when:

> He came over with his mother on a Sunday afternoon, and his mother said, 'Clara, you're such a good worker and a good girl, why don't you marry Vince?' He didn't say anything and what was I gonna say? And she said he was a good worker and a saver, so then I said Yes. I thought it can't be any worse than the life I have. I'll try it for better or worse and I hit it for better and I thank the Lord.

Before Clara could be married, however, she had to have a birth certificate. Her parish priest wrote to the orphanage in New York and obtained it for her. This was when she discovered her real name was LaDue. Unfortunately, nothing else was learned about her origin. Clara lamented—

> Sometimes I think it would be nice to really know my background. It should have been done years back already but there was no money. I had a good home and a good husband, and so I didn't worry about it. I didn't care then.

Clara's adoptive family did not give her a wedding so she and Vince went off quietly and were married. Later, one day friends and neighbors came over for a chivaree—a noisy serenade for newly-weds:

> Because it was such a fast wedding, they thought we should have had a celebration. It was noisy and got out of hand. That's the way some people are. They just make a horse out of a fly. I felt awfully bad, but what are you gonna do?

After a while, those people left and Vince's family and close friends came over for a bridal dance. This was held in their granary. The floor was cleared and the men danced with the bride. After each dance Clara took the men to a table filled with a stack of plates. Each man would throw a silver dollar into a plate and try to break it. If the plate broke, the bride could keep the dollar. After a while the men "got smart" and hit the plate with their fists as they threw in the coin. In this manner Clara received about $30.00, but, Clara says, they broke a lot of plates!

After the wedding Vince and Clara made their home on Vince's farm which he had purchased two years earlier for $3,900. The house, granary, stone barn and blacksmith shop were there already. Her wedding day was the first time Clara saw the farm. She grew to love it and has lived there ever since.

Vince had grown up in a loving family and had received $1,000 from his family when he bought the farm because up to that time he had given all of his money to his parents. Clara got nothing from her family. Upon arriving at their farm, Clara took over cleaning the house and Vince took a load of cordwood to town to sell—their wedding day.

The Symanietz farm was originally all wooded and one had to grub to make fields. The cordwood from the woods was hauled to St. Cloud and sold for $3.00 to $5.00 per cord to pay the taxes, pay off the mortgage, and even to buy new machinery. Sometimes the weather was so bad "you couldn't see the world," according to Clara. Many men stayed in town but Vince always came home, Clara said. At times, in winter, the snowbanks were so big that the horses couldn't make it over them. They got so used to it, however, that Vince would tie the reins over the rack and let the horses find their own way. "They knew easier where they could get through," Clara remembers.

Clara said she was lonely on the farm. There were no other Polish families in the St. Stephen area and other nationalities kept to their own kind. She and Vince walked to St. Wendel to attend church with other Polish people, rather than to St. Stephen with the Slovenians and Germans.

Clara helped Vince grub the land. Vince would cut the trees and let the stumps rot in the ground for a few years. Then he would place dynamite under six stumps at one time. Clara was called upon to light three fuses and Vince would light the other three so they would all go off at one time. "Boy, was that scary! I would ran as fast as I could to the house and still a couple of pieces would fall on me," Clara recalls.

An even more terrifying chore that fell to Clara was lowering and raising Vince out of their well when it filled up with quicksand. With a roller and crank she had to roll him down and then up again with a bucket of sand. She said,

> Sometimes I just cried because it was so hard, and if I slipped he would have gone right down and been killed, or I could get killed by the crank and roller. I was 110 pounds and Vince was 130 and I had to get him and a bucket of sand out. It was hard! I still have the roller and crank. In time we put in cement curbings, and by that time the kids were big enough to help and then I got out of that work.

On their new farm there was always work to do. Once the land was cleared, Vince and Clara planted oats and corn. They bought their animals from neighbors to get started. Horses were always older because these were cheaper, but then they didn't last as long because of all those long trips to St. Cloud with cordwood. Clara helped with all the work. Milking was her main job, she said. When potato-digging season was at hand, she put her baby in a soda cracker box in the field beside her while she picked up potatoes. During the time Vince hauled one load to town, she picked another. As the children got older, they were put on blankets; and later they also helped with the work.

Clara and Vince also raised turkeys, chickens, ducks, and sheep. Clara spun her own wool and sewed all of the family clothes on a sewing machine purchased in 1925 for $100. All of the work around the buildings was done by Clara with the help of the children because Vince was out in the fields most of the day in summer and in the woods in the winter. "I don't think he could have drove a post in the ground without me," Clara said. "There was no other way. You had to do it," she said.

Vincent Symanietz built this tamarack-pole fence many years ago. This view, looking south, shows a rise in the land beyond which is a heavily-wooded tamarack swamp.

Because Clara was young and healthy, she never minded the work; in fact, she wanted to work. Things got easier for her when the children could help. She planted a large garden. To supplement their income during hard times, Vince would work for $5.00 per day grading roads for the township or county.

In 1923 life became very difficult. Their barn burned, but since the foundation and walls were constructed of fieldstone, that part of the building was saved and only the roof had to be replaced. For this, tin was used. They built a new barn in 1925. They also bought forty more acres of land, increasing their acreage to 120.

When each of their four boys and two girls were born, Vince traveled to Opole, a distance of about ten miles, for a midwife. Already in labor, Clara stayed at home alone during this time. When her first child was born, the midwife examined Clara and said to her, "My lands! Another five minutes and we couldn't have saved you anymore." The midwife had to turn the baby for it to be delivered safely. Everything turned out well, fortunately. Clara had great confidence in midwives. She said:

Midwives were so good. If doctors knew midwives were there they wouldn't come out at all. The midwives

were better. They didn't harm you as much as a doctor does. You see, birth, then, it was all natural. Any praying helped too. I think the good Lord was the biggest help of all. It was hard but I was healthy. I could take everything. This was the happy part about it. I didn't regret it. I didn't cry. And the good Lord suffered too and he didn't do anything wrong. He shouldn't have had to suffer. It was meant that way. We all have to go through some kind of cross. And Vince was a good man. And it was much better than when I was with my foster parents. I was always stepped on then and always looked down on, so that's hard, especially when you come to age sixteen and seventeen. I had to be in by 9 o'clock or the door was locked, but not for their own children.

Although Clara has had a difficult life, she has maintained a distinctive sense of humor. Her humor becomes apparent when she speaks of the muzzleloader Vince's father gave him when he bought the farm. It was his father's in the old country when he was a soldier. Clara still keeps it as a family heirloom. She said that every New Year's Eve Vince would shoot off the gun. He loaded it himself, kneeling on one knee, filling it with gravel and paper. "It took so long to load it," Clara says, "Why, it took almost half a Sears Roebuck catalog to fill the thing!" Once Vince shot a rabbit near the barn. "What a noise! Oh, brother, there was just a cloud of smoke! and the rabbit never moved!" With a sly smile she said, "How could they have used that gun in the army?"

Life on their farm has always been hard, but Clara and Vincent are satisfied with their results. They raised six children, sending two through college, and giving them all some money. In 1953 they held a farm auction and sold their personal property, but they couldn't get the price for the land they were asking so they decided to stay on it. Clara then wanted to get a job in town but Vince did not want her to work away from home so she turned to gardening and made her bread and butter that way. She raised a large garden and sold some of the produce from it to earn extra money.

In 1979 they finally sold the land, but they are allowed to rent the house and live there as long as they wish. About the past, Clara says people were more helpful and trusting in the old days. Once a friend gave Vince $500 with only Vince's word as collateral. Nowadays, she feels, people live more for themselves and they don't like to be bothered with other people's needs. Years ago, Clara said

> People sooner helped each other out. If you needed help you got together and helped each other out. Even when I had little babies, I went from neighbor to neighbor shocking and husking corn. It was like that all over. I never learned about my own background, but my kids tell me it doesn't matter. I got old and I have my family. The good Lord takes care of us. I'm happy for my children. They all married good and all stayed in the church. My daughter in Atwater (Minnesota) even distributes communion in her church. I only wish they were closer. But you have to go where you can make your bread.

Vincent is a frail man now and Clara takes care of him and their home. He is a bit hard of hearing. During one interview when we asked Clara who adopted her, a sparkle came into Vince's eyes. He looked directly at us, and said: "I did!"

1   Personal interviews with Vincent and Clara Symanietz, 13 November 1980 and 11 February 1981.

Voronyak-Habas

Many Russian Orthodox and Czechoslovakian traditions are still practiced in the Upsala area of Morrison County, by Ed and Irene Voronyak. They can still speak the language. although there are few people left with whom to speak it. Irene paints Ukranian eggs with a kiska—a tool used to make designs on eggs with beeswax. She also sews, knits, and crochets numerous items of fancy work for herself, friends, and family; and, as a family, the Voronyaks always celebrate "Little Christmas"—a traditional holiday twelve days after Christmas marking the visit of the three wise men to the Christ child. A traditional meal consisting of seven dishes to symbolize the seven days of the week is served.[1]

The Little Christmas celebration gives Irene a chance to practice her favorite Czechoslovakian recipes. Her mother taught her many hearty, peasant-style recipes and she is an excellent cook. She loves to make the traditional proeghi and bibolki, as well as cottage cheese rolls, poppyseed bread, and kolache. She likes to serve mushrooms in brown gravy and sweetened navy beans. She said these dishes used to be cooked all day on the back of the big wood-burning stove. Today, however, she uses a crockpot or a low temperature on her electric range to give them the mellow, rich flavor that makes them special.[2]

Ed and Irene Voronyak, Slovakian descendants living in rural Upsala, Minnesota.

Both Irene's and Ed's families emigrated to America from Puste Chermerni, in southwest Czechoslovakia, in the early 1860s. They came with a small group of people who were all equally dissastisfied with their lives in their native land. Irene said:

> Landed gentry controlled most of the land and the people who worked for them. They had a little plot of their own land and four days a week they worked for the lord and one day a week they worked for themselves. So that's why they left—for better opportunities—to better themselves.

The first Slovakians to come to America settled in Pennsylvania where they worked in the steel foundries. However, between 1886 and 1888, a panic and depression hit the United States and many people lost their jobs. For this reason many of the Slovakians decided to take advantage of the Homestead Act and journey to an area of central Minnesota where land was available. They had been farming people in the old country and loved the land. Further, they had heard from newspapers and advertisements sent to them by an established community of Czechoslovakians in Minneapolis, that this was a wooded area, a part of the legendary Big Woods of America. The vast supply of wood and lumber in the central Minnesota area lured them. Irene said:

> Most of the immigrants remembered having to gather twigs and sticks for fuel. To them wood was a priority. They all highly valued the wooded homesteads in the South Elmdale area of Morrison County, where quite a settlement of Slovaks settled together. First one came and then others followed.

Irene's mother, Helen Cherub, had come to Pennsylvania at age nine, and her father, George Chuba, came as a young man with his mother. His father had been killed in a railroad accident in Europe. Eventually, George and Helen met in Pennsylvania, fell in love, and were married. After their marriage they decided to travel to Minnesota to try farming. They traveled by train to the railroad juction in Royalton, Minnesota, arriving in wintertime. The date, "February 10, 1888," was painted on their trunk. (Irene still has the trunk and regrets having painted over the date some years ago.) From Royalton they journeyed to South Elmdale Township by sled. Irene said her mother told her this trip was a most difficult one. She said:

Mother always said it was the coldest day of the year and they were dressed in their fancy clothes, with light coats; and they nearly froze because it was in the middle of winter. She said they rode on a sled in the cold. Then when they got here they had to soak their feet in cold water. She often talked about how cold they were.

George and Helen's adaptation to their new environment was similar to that of numerous other pioneers in the area at that time. Upon arriving in South Elmdale, they moved in with a family already living in an established log cabin. During this period they set themselves to the task of clearing an area of trees and building a log cabin of their own. In those early, difficult years neighbors were a godsend. Irene said, "Everybody got together and helped each other out." There were other Slovaks in the area, a Yankee named Stewart, and an Irish family named Kieley. All these neighbors helped them build their house. As neighbors, these families soon became good, true friends. In fact, Irene said, although they were of different nationalities and religions, they fostered a bond of friendship by getting together on Sunday afternoons for Sunday socials, sharing mutual lifestyles, food and drink. Each Sunday they visited at a different home and all brought food. This was topped off with a keg of beer purchased at Royalton.

Because cash money was necessary for staples, supplies, and equipment, the early Elmdale pioneers cut and sold railroad ties in winter. These were hauled to Royalton once a week. Here again, the neighbors needed each other, as the ties had to be hauled up a high hill. There were no roads so people traveled on trails in the woods. According to Irene, "they would gang up together and help each other over the hill." The ties were sold for $3.00 per load.

After George and Helen had their log house built, they also needed furniture and utensils. Most of this was homemade by George from trees he cut himself. Among other things, he made a rolling pin out of one length of maple which Irene still has. He also made a table out of one very large tree. The table top was a four-inch thick slab of lumber placed on the stump of the tree. It wasn't very stable, however, Irene said:

If mother wasn't careful when she put a pitcher of milk

on that table, dad would take a glass of milk and then set it too close to the end and it would spill. I wonder how many pitchers of milk they spilled that way?

As with most early pioneers, life in a log cabin in the woods often presented difficulties. Women were often left alone while the men went off to work in the fields or the woods. Indians roaming about in the area frequently frightened them. Helen told Irene of one of her most frightening experiences: One fall when she was making her delicious cottage cheese rolls two Indians came into her house. She was just taking a pan full of rolls out of the oven. They were very hot and she set them on the table to cool. ("She was never so scared in her life!"). She tried to tell them they were still hot; however, they didn't seem to mind and picked some up, blew on them, and then ate the whole pan full and asked for more. They motioned to another pan of unbaked rolls on the table. While Helen baked these, the Indians just stood around, and although she was very frightened and afraid they would kill her, she "acted like they were good friends." Eventually they left quietly, and three days later, upon hearing a noise outside the door, George opened it to find a big hunk of venison. Irene said:

The Indians repaid but you never knew because there was still hard feelings among the Indians. I think they were Sioux. They were passing through.

George and Helen never retired from the farm. They lived with their youngest son on the farm until George died at age eighty-two. Helen died in a nursing home many years later, at age ninety-nine.

Irene was the second youngest child in a family of nine. The family worshipped at St. Mary's Russian Orthodox Church in South Elmdale. For fun and pastime they attended house parties in the neighborhood. "No one went to nightclubs in those days," she said. Storytelling was also a common pastime and Irene remembers many of the stories her mother told her on long winter nights.

Irene attended grammar school at a local one-room country school, high school in Holdingford, Minnesota, and college at St. Cloud State, Minnesota.

After obtaining a teaching degree at St. Cloud, Irene taught school in a number of rural schools and later in the Upsala elementary school. She taught fourth grade. Irene said,

I really liked teaching in rural schools. It was really nice. I think we lost something when we went to bigger school systems. Kids were more independent in rural schools. They learned to work on their own better and there was more family and more people were interested in what their kids were doing. There was better discipline. We had real nice rural schools. In rural schools kids helped each other more.

When the rural schools went in about 1967, I just hated to see them go. It seems like part of our life, our independence, went; and you know, kids had more respect then. Of course, the whole country has changed. So much of it comes from the home. Some parents don't do enough disciplining. You can just pick those kids out. Of course, the pendulum is swinging back again. Parents are finding out. It's not just the school. You can't teach the kids manners and things that they aren't taught at home. You can impose on them but that doesn't stay because they don't have to do it at home.

Irene taught school for many years and feels that an education is essential. Each of her four children graduated from college.

Irene married Ed Voronyak on June 17, 1935. They are now seventy-one and seventy-four years old respectively, and just as Irene is spirited and interesting, so Ed is carefree and direct. They have retired to a modern home in Upsala where Irene enjoys her crafts and hobbies and Ed returns to the farm to work and pass the time.

After Ed and Irene were married, they rented a farm in the Upsala area until a Federal land bank loan made it possible for them to buy a farm in South Elmdale. "There wasn't much money in those days," Irene said. Their farm consisted of 160 acres. Then a number of years later, they added eighty more acres adjoining their farm, and, in 1954 they purchased the John Habas farm, also adjoining their farm.

The Habas' were also Russian Orthodox Czechoslovakians. Their beginnings were similar to the other Slovaks in the area. They had come in the late 1880s and homesteaded on section 10 in South Elmdale Township. They built a log house and log barn and a little corncrib. Later they added a lean-to to the barn and a frame house was built. By this time, Irene said, there were specially skilled craftsmen adept at individual trades in the area. Often, these craftsmen shared their skills with other builders in moving from one project to another. Irene remembers a mason named Orvatz "who could take a trowel and just cut the rocks

straight down. A man by the name of Heisiek was the builder. They were good at building together." Unfortunately, the frame house burned a number of years ago and only the cement steps and porch are left amid the charred ruins—a deep hole filled with yellow chimney bricks, debris and cinders, and trees and thickets that are trying to reclaim the site.

The Habas family lived on this farmsite until John died in 1948. His widow then sold the land and moved away from the area. In 1954, when the Voronyaks bought the land, the buildings had stood vacant too long and were in a state of disrepair. Today the corncrib is completely gone and the log barn has collapsed into a heap of logs and rafters. The original log house, however, is still standing in a clearing by itself—a structure that is in fairly good condition.

The Habas log house, built in 1888, was constructed of round oak logs mixed with a few hewn tamarack logs. The large living room/kitchen

Standing alone in a pasture clearing, the Habas-Voronyak log house in rural Upsala (Morrison County) evokes feelings of the solitude pioneers must have felt when they arrived in central Minnesota.

has seven hewn tamarack joists at head level which project through the walls on the east and west. The second floor is reached by a stairway. This level is amply lighted from windows in the gable ends. Two log courses project above the floor level to receive the rafters. Tamarack poles and 2 × 4's were used for rafters and roof-boards are of 12″ to 14″-wide mill-sawn planks.

A unique feature of the Habas house, one not found elsewhere in central Minnesota, is the use of hand-cut, diagonally-set lathing for the first floor wall construction. Individual laths are shaven smooth on the front and back sides and left barked on the edges. Each lath is 20″ long, 1½″ wide, approximately ½″ thick, and tapered and notched at both ends to hold the mortar. The use of handwork construction is visible throughout the Habas house.

Unusual lathwork was used in the Habas-Voronyak house. Hand-crafted lath pieces were notched at either end to hold the mortar in place. Folk material of this type is rarely found in the architecture of central Minnesota.

Irene Voronyak says she would like to restore the house and use it occasionally. She says she wants to sleep in it one night just to find out what it may have been like when the pioneers slept there. Furthermore, although none of their children want to farm the land, they would like to have the land stay in the family.

The Habas log house stands alone amid piles of chopped wood, tall trees, piled up boulders, and cattle mulling and eating grass near a rotting tamarack pole fence. One can almost imagine the pioneers coming to this site, standing in the clearing, listening to the birds, insects, and wild animals, and eagerly planning their future. Here they envisioned a new beginning in a strange land where many of the things they held dear in the old country could be taken for granted and used as one saw fit. Surely central Minnesota would become the paradise they longed for if they were willing to sacrifice and work for it!

1   Personal interview with Irene and Ed Voronyak, 19 May 1981.
2   Mary Lahr, "There's No Rush During Slovaks' Little Christmas," *St. Cloud Daily Times*, 7 Jan. 1981, sec. B, p. 1, cols. 1-3.

Math Grausam

In 1888 Martin and Maria (Mader) Grausam and their five-year-old daughter Julia left their homeland because they were very poor.[1] They emigrated from Fieltach, Bavaria, then part of the Austro-Hungarian Empire to Albany, Stearns County, central Minnesota, where relatives and other German Catholics were living. Originally, Martin came by himself. He found land and opportunity in central Minnesota and returned to Bavaria to bring his family.

After only a few years in America, the Grausams had established the beginnings of a prosperous homestead. Today, their son, Math, lives alone on the family farm in a large, rambling yellow brick house amidst a cluster of old log buildings, a modern barn and silo, and memories and mementoes of a life long past.

Math is a jolly eighty-three year old man who enjoys the farm and the outdoors. He has a wry

Math Grausam, Albany.

smile that lights his face when he talks about his younger days. He looks directly into a person's eyes and watches for a reaction when he makes a comment or remark about the old days. He enjoys life but says he does get lonely:

> I don't like it very good living alone. I go fishing a lot with friends and neighbors. I'm still single. It would be nicer if I had a family though. I wish I had one. It gets lonesome.

While Math cooks the fish he catches, or when he sits on his front porch or in his large kitchen with the woodstove burning nearby, he forgets his loneliness and talks about his family and his life.

According to Math, the Grausam family brought all their belongings to America in two trunks. These are still in his possession. One with the Grausam name still printed very boldly on it sits on the side porch of his house.

The journey from Bavaria to America must have been a trying one for the small family as Maria gave birth to a child that died on the ship, during the journey. Math tells the chilling story of that ordeal. The parents could not bear to give the infant to the sea, as was the custom if people died aboard ship. Instead:

> They wrapped him up in vinegar and put him in that and brought him here and buried him in Albany when they got here. The vinegar made the body stay together.

The only tool they brought was a felling axe, as Martin knew the entire area was tree-covered and had to be cleared before they could farm the land. There were basswood, elm, birch, and some oak trees which were used for the first buildings. The first year the family lived with Martin's brother, Hubert, in Albany. Albany was just a hamlet then.

Their land was purchased from the railroad, 60 to 80 acres at a time, until the farm totaled 140 acres. Money to pay for the land was earned by working for the railroad, grubbing land for future rail lines. Even as young boys, everyone pitched in, Math said.

The Grausams were devout Catholics and worshipped in a log house belonging to an already established family named Schwinghammer. This house served as the church in those early days. Math says,

> Right here were German Catholics and toward Holdingford were Lutherans. During threshing time we all worked together. The Lutherans were nice

people too. I couldn't see nothing wrong with them. In those days things were more strict than now. We didn't mix so much then. Anything goes now.

Eventually six more children were born to Martin and Maria, one of whom also died in infancy. In those days there were no doctors in town, Math said. Math was born in 1898, one of five surviving children.

The still remaining log house was their first shelter. It consisted of two rooms with a door between and a loft for the children to sleep in. The kitchen had a cookstove and the second room had a box stove. The loft was terribly cold, according to Math. Snow came in through the roof and often they woke up with a blanket of snow over them in the mornings. They slept on straw mattresses with homemade quilts and "nice down feather" pillows, he said. Usually they took a hot water bottle to bed with them to keep their feet warm. Most of the furniture was purchased in Albany; Math's dad, however, made wooden benches for them. Math added:

> Life wasn't so bad. We always had plenty to eat. I liked beef soup but beef didn't keep in summer so mother prepared mostly pork then. We all ate together.

The remnant section of the log house on the Grausam farm is an excellent example of an unpretentious log structure commonly used by pioneers in the early years of settlement. In size and type it represents a step above the log shanty. Like most log structures in central Minnesota, each wall surface of the Grausam house has evolved into a different pattern through addition of various materials which makes for a rich textural composition.

A closer look at the house suggests its importance to the folk history of the region. The house rests on stone-boulder piers and measures 12′ 4″ north/south and 19′ 7″ east and west. The entrance side (east) has two doors and reveals its hewn log construction, 10 courses high, notched with square and half-dovetail joints. Each log is massive, measuring 10″ to 12″ in height. A lean-to porch roof, possibly original, adds an unusual touch. The use of a porch and a two-door facade are unique for log construction in central Minnesota.

The west wall, opened by two windows, is made up of 14″ hewn logs with a smaller 6½″ sill. This construction appears to be original. Seven joist

The Grausam house, a fine example of an unpretentious log house in Central Minnesota—two rooms and a loft.

ends are exposed on this side. Eight-inch corner boards, an unusual log feature, appear on the west as well.

Clapboard siding hides the log construction on the north and south walls. A small window appears on the north. The gable area had been allowed to weather; and white paint, now grayed, was once applied to the lower walls. A capped yellow-brick chimney graces the roof.

In its use of ornamentation the interior also departs substantially from log houses observed elsewhere in central Minnesota, though many of its features may have been later additions. In the living room, factory-processed window trim of about 1870 vintage has been used as has beaded wainscoting. The walls above are of plaster and lath construction. Although the crude pole-raftered loft probably reveals the true character of the original, the ground floor interior appointments, if original, suggest an elegance more closely related to elite architecture.

Math's mother always had a big garden where she raised potatoes, cabbage, cucumbers, onions, and garlic for sausage. Math says he made many a batch of sausage. The neighbors helped each other when butchering and making sausage. Often six hogs and a beef were butchered in one day, and a few days later sausage was made. Nothing was ever wasted—even the intestines were used as casings for sausage. The sausage was smoked in the smokehouse, using sawdust because Martin believed sawdust made better smoke. Today, Math still uses the smokehouse to smoke sausage and fish though he uses maple wood for fuel.

The Grausam smokehouse is a unique structure on the central Minnesota landscape as its design is essentially classical. Measuring 8′ north/south by 10′ 3″ east/west, it is constructed of ten courses of cement block. These blocks were made to look like stone—in some cases smooth-surfaced and others quarry-faced. All joints are sealed with raised mortar. Above the square mass formed by the wall is a flared, turret-like roof with a deep overhang. This roof, with its thin shingles, ornate tin flashing, finial, and its graceful shape, is unusually classical for rural architecture. The door, made of narrow rough vertical boards, is a sharp contrast in material use and feeling to the overall design. Incised into the window lintel on the west is the date 1911.

The Grausam garden produce was kept in a root cellar. Sauerkraut was made in thirty-gallon crocks. They picked wild fruit and berries; from these Maria made jellies: Raspberries, gooseberries, strawberries, and chokecherries—"I didn't like them," said Math chuckling.

In summer the food was better and more plentiful than in winter when chickens and geese did not lay eggs and were fed corn and oats just to keep them alive for eggs in spring and summer. In winter dairy cattle went dry and were fed cornstraw and meadow hay to keep them alive until spring when they calved and were put on pasture and all summer milk, cream, and butter again became available. Turkeys, however, were a different matter. According to Math:

> Turkeys were tough. They stayed outside all winter—sat way up in the trees. In those days there was money in turkeys, seven cents a pound. We had fifty at one time. They ran loose in the yard. Then they got sick and we lost them, so we quit turkeys.

Math's mother made her own lye which she used with tallow from beef to make soap used for laundry and hand-washing. She also spun and carded her own wool, obtained from the sheep they raised, for mittens and stockings.

The Grausams never owned oxen, as far as Math remembers. He said they plowed the land by hand and with horses. Their first crops were corn

and wheat. They kept part of each crop for the following year's seed. They sold some of the wheat to the elevator at Albany and had some ground into flour for their own use.

Clothes and staple groceries such as sugar, salt, and vinegar were bought in Albany. Often they traded cordwood for these items. A load of soft wood sold for $3.00 and oak for $4.00 a cord. Some days Martin hauled one load in the forenoon and another one in the afternoon.

A rail fence held together with pegs, one on top of the other, kept the animals out of the yard and garden as most of the animals roamed around freely. The cattle wore bells around their necks and each farmer had different bells so each could distinguish his own cattle. The cows didn't milk well in those days—maybe an eight-gallon canful from twenty cows. Math remembers the rigors of milking cows and doing other farm chores as a boy:

> Milking cows, helping in the barn, making hay; everything. In those days you had to do it all by hand. Oh, man! Nowadays there's no work to it. We dug our own wells by hand!

Modified form of an early connected barn. One side housed horses and the other cattle. Only one side remains.

The log barn, still standing in modified form, was built soon after the house was completed. It was a connected barn, housing horses on one side and cattle on the other with a driveway through the center from which hay could be unloaded into either side. It was built of trees felled and hewn on site. A unique facet of this barn are the numerous tiny pigeonholes, similar to the pigeonholes in an old-fashioned secretary desk, cut into the wall with a handsaw for a pigeon roost. Math said:

The pigeons messed up the barn, but boy, they were good! The young ones. Old ones, they're no good. They made good soup. We took the young ones out of the nests before they could fly. That was good. They stayed all winter.

The Grausam barn is an important landmark in central Minnesota. Like the Anton Gogala barn, Grausam's is essentially medieval in origin, though the two tiny windows and a door on the south wall are more formally balanced than is commonly found in buildings of that time. The barn sits on a fieldstone foundation and is rectangular with three-fourths of its surface enclosed. On the east side is a large drive-in area used to shelter machinery.

The south wall contains massive smoothly-adzed logs 16 high and of a weathered gray tone. Half-dovetail joints appear at the corners and exposed joints extend through this wall.

The inside east shelter wall opens into the haymow. The wall below is constructed of 10″ to 11″ logs, 19 high, partially covered with drop siding. Pole rafters in the mow can be seen. The exterior west wall has been covered with tin and the north shelter wall has tin below and horizontal plank siding above.

The north wall has 15 courses of hewn logs and a massive plate. Strong broadaxe marks are seen. Like the south wall, this one has half-dovetail joints and exposed joints. The west wall is of log, contains a small window in the loft, and has drop siding in the gable.

The Grausam farm layout is more strongly linear than any observed in central Minnesota. While most farms make use of a cluster plan, Grausam's outbuildings march in line from east to west and in a line north of the yellow brick house. Although many of the buildings have been moved, this is an interesting and surprisingly pleasing pattern esthetically. Separate buildings from east to west are: A rainbow roof dairy barn and silo of contemporary origin; the log barn and a hen house to the rear; a corncrib and an ice house, both of red clapboard; a privy; the log house; a granary and a garage, both utilizing drop siding; the smokehouse and a modern machine shed.

The ice house, still partially filled with sawdust obtained (many years ago) from local sawmills was once used to cool the family's dairy products—milk, cream, and butter. The ice was chopped in winter from nearby lakes and hauled home on sleds pulled by horses.

The log house is badly in need of new shingles. Math would reshingle it but wants to use wooden cedar shingles, and he said they cost too much. The smokehouse was built by Math's brother, John; and when asked why he built it with the graceful, steeply pitched roof, Math replied, "I don't know why. I guess maybe because it looks nice!" John also built most of the other newer buildings on the farm. He worked as an apprentice carpenter for some years before starting his own business. He built the yellow brick house that became the family home in 1910. The brick was obtained in St. Cloud, but Math says it is not well insulated and the house gets very cold in the winter.

Near the smokehouse is another unique addition to the farm—a swillpit, dated 1923. It is a deeply-rounded cement hole that looks like a large cooking pot embedded in the ground. It was used to cook mash for the hogs. Potatoes, water, and ground corn and oats were all dumped into a huge kettle and set on scrapwood in the pit to cook. Math said the pit was practical as well as useful because,

Cement keeps the heat all in. Otherwise, in the open, it takes much more wood. This was better and that was good feed. It was poured into troughs we built ourselves out of planks.

The Grausam family spoke only German at home but the children soon learned to speak English in school. On the school playground, however, everyone still spoke German as all the children there were of German ancestry. The school was a one-room country school with up to ninety-two students for one teacher, usually also of German heritage. "Teachers came and went," Math said with a chuckle, "but we learned more than the kids do now." Math completed his readers by age fourteen and then stayed home to help with the farmwork. He said, however, that he often missed days of school in the spring and fall because he had to stay home to help with farm work. Math and his brothers and sisters always walked to school and carried dry bread with lard and syrup in their lunch pails.

When times were very difficult for the Grausam family, Math's father traveled to the

Dakotas to work in the wheat harvest fields to earn money. Sometimes he was gone from home the entire months of August and September. He traveled by train when tickets cost only two or three cents a mile. During the time Martin was gone, Maria and the children ran the farm.

Math feels that in those days people were tougher. He says he liked hard work and pitched hay by hand and put it in stacks. Corn was chopped off by hand and shocked and husked by hand and put in the corncrib to dry. Their crib held twenty boxes of corn and, "I husked a box a day," he said.

Whereas Math talks about the hard times and the work, he often abruptly changes the conversation to the good times and the fun he enjoyed as a young man. He remembers:

> When I was younger, up to thirty years old, you know yourself what kind of fun you have at that age, there were good neighbor parties here. We danced and had fun. Sometimes we went to dances in Holdingford and Albany in the city halls. Sometimes we walked there. We danced mostly waltzes. We had moonshine. I never made it myself. Some was pretty good stuff. Neighbors made it in a still. It was cheap—$2.00 or $3.00 a gallon. We had fun!

As Math's two sisters became old enough to work, they left home and found outside employment. His brother Carl was a drayman who hauled freight from the depot in Albany to the local stores. Math and his brother Christ ran the farm. In 1937 they built the rainbow barn and the contemporary silo which Math calls a triple silo because it has wooden staves on the inside, paper in the center, and redwood siding on the exterior. They milked twenty-five cows at this time and farmed 140 acres. Then, in 1948 Christ became ill, so they held a farm auction and retired from farming, renting out the land to neighbors until 1975 when Lloyd and Mary Schiffler bought the farm. Math has the privilege of living in the brick house for the duration of his life. Fortunately, the Schifflers and Math intend to preserve the old log buildings.

Math worked in a locker plant in Albany for ten years after he retired from farming where some of his knowledge of butchering and smoking meat was put to good use. He tried living in town for three years after he retired but moved back to the farm in 1951 because he didn't like living in town.

Math added, with an abrupt though melancholy change in his voice:

> Life wasn't so bad. We always had enough to eat. My parents never wanted to go back to the old country. Here they had meat to eat. Over there they had only soup.

1   Personal interview with Math Grausam, 6 August 1980.

112

Ryberg

I n a family history that Ida Ryberg wrote, she says, "We live in a fast-changing and speed-conscious world, vastly differing from the beginnings of this century."[1] Certainly this is also true of Ida herself. From humble beginnings in a log cabin in South Dakota, Ida's life has progressed with the times. She undertook a successful and exciting career in nursing and teaching; she has always been an active church member; she is head archivist at Gethsemane Lutheran church in Upsala; she has traveled to numerous parts of the world and she still writes a weekly column for a local newspaper. Clearly, age has not diminished her interest and activity in the changing world around her. She celebrated her ninetieth birthday on August 18, 1980.

Ida Ryberg in her apartment in Upsala, Morrison County.

Ida is a small person with a large heart and an open mind. She has written a warm and sincere family history that she calls "The Ryberg Saga." In it she records the lives of her parents, the first Rybergs in America, her own life and the lives of her nieces and nephews who hold the future of the Rybergs in America. Her mind is a living archive; yet, she is always receptive to new ideas and people.

She said, "I'm old but I learn things all the time."[2]

The Ryberg saga began in 1888 when Johan and Anna Mari (Johnson) Ryberg emigrated from Hinneryd, Smaland, Sweden.

> Things were difficult in Sweden in the 1870s and 1880s [Ida said]. Dad always said if he came to America his children would have a chance to get further. In Sweden they couldn't improve themselves. They just had to stay where they were. He wanted them to get their own way of doing things. In Sweden if you were poor you stayed poor; if you were rich you were above everybody else. There was this class distinction; and, therefore, an awful lot of Swedish folks left.

Johan and Anna Mari left their homeland with three small children, Anna Mari's aged mother, and three of her brother's children. They had a difficult and troublesome journey by ship to America. Food was scarce and unappetizing, and storms and seasickness caused Anna Mari to declare, "If I ever get on land again I'll never go out on water." She kept her word.[3]

After reaching America, the Rybergs traveled to South Dakota by train where Anna Mari had two sisters and a brother living. They had left Sweden earlier and were farming in the Graton-Clermont, South Dakota, area. However, when Johan and Anna Mari reached their destination they found—

> It was all prairie, as far as you could see. There was nothing to see excepting just wheat fields, and my dad wasn't used to that. He was used to woods from Sweden.

For two years the family lived there in a tiny log cabin. Johan had been in the Swedish Army and had saved a small sum of money. He also worked as a tailor's apprentice and Anna Mari took in washing and helped in homes to earn money in South Dakota. When Ida was born, the minister who baptized her remarked, "This is the smallest baby I ever baptized." She weighed only three pounds; yet, in three months' time the family embarked on another journey. Ida's father had heard about a Swedish settlement in central Minnesota where "he could get wood for the stove— so to Upsala we came!" Ida said.

The Rybergs first winter in Upsala was spent in a log cabin which had been recently vacated by a family that had lost several members to tuberculosis. They were very poor. Johan had $96.00 to his name. Ida said:

Christmas was coming and in their beloved Sweden that meant going out in the woods to cut a tree for the home. Necessity never lacks ingenuity so the ten-year-old brother brought in a thorn bush. A candle or two and a couple of trinkets and there was the first Christmas tree in the new country.[4]

The following spring Johan set out to locate a farm. As he had little money, he bought an eighty-acre farm four miles south of Upsala in Elmdale Township for $3.00 per acre. It was wild, swampy, and tree-covered but it was the best they could afford. The week between Christmas and New Year's Day they moved into their own log cabin. The ends of logs protruded at every corner and Ida's earliest recollections of it was seeing grass growing on the thatched roof. As in Sweden, Johan had covered the roof with birchbark and a layer of sod which held together as the grass roots and weeds grew. It had two small windows and a door with a latch and string. A small, four-hole cookstove provided heat and cooking, and their trunk served as the table. Beds were homemade and tree stumps served as chairs. Ida's uncle Otto had helped to fell the trees for the cabin and he loved to tell this story:

The hurriedly-cut logs were fresh, so by the warmth in the cabin began to sprout and grow leaves. An exceptionally large one was sent to his friend in South Dakota with the words: 'Now you see how leaves are growing here this winter.'

Ida grew up in a home filled with love and strict discipline. Their first crop was rye, as they had been used to rye from Sweden. From that they made a type of porridge called "Grot" which was served with milk and set in the middle of the table every night for supper. Ida said she often pouted about that and her dad always straightened her out with this remark in Swedish, " 'If you don't want to eat what's on the table you go hungry.' I tell you, Ida was quiet then!"

An ox was the Ryberg's first and only animal for some years. It was used to break the land. As soon as they had a little spot cleared a garden was planted. Potatoes were planted near the stumps around the house. Johan went back to South Dakota and worked in the harvest fields to make a little extra money. He also worked for a neighbor to earn the yoke of oxen and later a cow. Their first wagon had to be taken to a slough and soaked in water so

it wouldn't fall apart in the ruts and stumps. Anna Mari roasted barley for coffee. Homemade bread was their "staff of life," and they picked wild berries. There was always an endless round of work. Clothes were handmade from wool and calico bought for a few cents a yard. Melted snow or creek water was carried in for washing clothes.

In time a lean-to was added to the small log house to shelter the cow. After a larger barn was built, this lean-to was converted to a bedroom for Ida and her sister. The walls were covered with newspapers, which at times, according to Ida, "made interesting reading." The barn "started out small and grew," she said, as more cows were added as well as horses to replace the slow, plodding oxen. The barn began as a log structure in about 1900; a bay for horses was added about 1910. It had a drive-through from which to load hay into the barn. ("We had a lot of fun in that haymow!" Ida said.) About 1915, a wagon shed lean-to was added.

A new log house was built around 1900. Ida recalls, it was "very grand" with two rooms and a pantry, and two bedrooms upstairs. Later, two more bedrooms, a summer kitchen, a cream separator room, and a front porch were added. Johan planted trees around the house and they had a lovely, prosperous farm in their new adopted country. They were improving themselves.

In years to come they added a granary and a car/wagon shed. Ida's brother, Albert, helped his father establish the homestead and farmed the land until he and Ida moved from it to Upsala in 1958. In 1965 Ida sold the farm after it had been in the Ryberg family for seventy-five years. Today the buildings are deteriorating, but they are fine examples of Swedish folk architecture in central Minnesota.

Ida and her brother and sisters attended a one-room rural grammar school. Instead of being in grades, they merely went through their McGuffy readers. Ida said that if they were in grade five, it meant that they were in the fifth reader. They also studied standard subjects such as grammar, geography, history, spelling, arithmetic, and physiology. For most of them, school was their first experience with the English language, as Swedish

The Ryberg barn is an excellent example of the esthetic beauty of folk architecture in central Minnesota.

was generally spoken in the homes. The Ryberg children walked two miles to school. Oftentimes when they reached the school on cold winter mornings the food in their lunch pails was frozen and had to be placed near the stove to thaw out. A pail of water with a dipper supplied their drinking water.

Ida's father believed in education. "He wanted everybody to go on to school, including the girls," she said. He had only gone to school a few days in Sweden before he went into the army. Anna Mari, Ida's mother, never attended school. Ida's sisters, Hulda and Otelia, went to Duluth and Little Falls respectively to continue their educations. They both became rural school teachers and eventually married and raised families.

Ida also wanted to try teaching: She said,
There was nothing else for girls to do in those days, except to go to Minneapolis or someplace else to do housework. I didn't care to do that. I wanted to go to school someplace.

Ida followed the example of her sisters and went to Little Falls to continue her education and become a teacher; however, she became very homesick and returned home to Upsala after only a

very short time. "I always tell people—be real good and homesick once and then you're cured for life. That's the worst sickness there is."

Back in Upsala, Ida was kept very busy. She said "People always had me do things I had never learned before because no one else wanted to do it." Besides helping on the farm, Ida became a very active member in her church.

Our Lutheran church was practically everything in our lives. I always was interested and my dad was pretty strict about that and I'm glad he was. Somehow young folks now don't do so much. You have to do so much for them.

By this time Ida's sister was teaching and earning $30.00 per month. She bought a "little old organ" and taught Ida how to play it. From those lessons she became the church organist. (In 1910 Ida bought a piano for $100.00 for herself.) She received $50.00 per year as organist. In summer she taught Swedish school—

I did some funny things ... The old people wanted the children to keep on with their Swedish speech so our church sponsored a Swedish school every summer for five summers so the people could keep their Swedish, not talk only English in America and forget Swedish. I got $50.00 a month for that.

During the years Ida stayed at home, school was still on her mind. She dreamed of becoming a missionary. So, from 1919 to 1921 she attended Lutheran Bible Institute in St. Paul and taught church summer bible school in St. Paul. From there she traveled on to Omaha, Nebraska, to attend the Immanual Deaconess Institute. A missionary course there appealed to her; however, a course for nurses opened up and Ida joined that group. "These were busy and happy years which I would never, never regret," she said. She graduated as a registered nurse in 1925. Wherever Ida went she worked for her board and room. Once when she had only two cents left, she wrote to her brother who sent her $5.00. "That's all I ever got to help me through my schooling," she said.

After graduation Ida returned home to Upsala to seek work. By the end of the summer, however, she was called back to Omaha to serve as assistant to the superintendent and be a full-time teacher at the nursing school. She spent fourteen years at this job and loved it and made many lasting friends. "I never liked any other work as well as I did teaching those nurses. I loved it," she said.

Ida returned to Upsala after those fourteen years to care for her aging parents. "In Sweden it was the thing for younger folks to take care of the older folks, if necessary," she said. Ida stayed home then for another fourteen years. She again resumed her church work, Luther League work, and some rural nursing. She added:

I always tell people I never married because I never had time! That was always a good excuse, but I really am glad I never did. I'm really happy. I've had an interesting life and I've always had good health. Well, of course, everybody thinks about getting married but I never found anyone I really cared to marry. I could have. I refused a few. But I really have been happy. Teaching those nurses, that was everything.

In 1945, Ida's nursing career led her away from Upsala again. She was offered a job in Big Fork, Minnesota—in deep logging country. Here again, Ida found her work rewarding. She became hospital superintendent, charge nurse, surgery and obstetrical nurse, anesthetist, and business manager.

The hospital in Big Fork had been in existence only three years when Ida got there and it was in debt. When Ida came before the hospital board she said:

I know if a hospital is run the way it should be it'll hold itself, and they said, 'Well, Miss Ryberg, you can do whatever you want,' and I did. I got them out of debt and we added beds and added doctor's offices and we never once, not once, went into debt again. I collected bills, I told them that if you don't collect bills you'll never have a hospital.

In fact, Ida once even went into a saloon to collect a bill. She said she knew people had money to pay their bills if they went in there to do nothing but drink. "I went right in and the place became very quiet, everyone in town knew me. But I got my money!" Ida stated.

During her days in Big Fork, Ida began her writing career. She started writing because she liked to write. She had never studied journalism or writing. She wrote a weekly column for the local newspaper called "Hospital Window Reflections." She wrote about the hospital "to let the people in the town know how the hospital was doing." Ida was the only registered nurse in the hospital during her years there. She trained high school girls to

become nurses' aids. When she left she planned to return to Upsala; however, in those days few people retired so she went to work at Ashland, Wisconsin, for two years to build up her social security. There she worked at Trinity Hospital as a registered nurse.

Finally, in 1960, Ida retired and returned to Upsala to write her family history and travel. She has visited her ancestral Sweden three times, the Holy Land, southern Europe, Alaska, Cuba, Mexico, and Russia. She also writes a weekly column for the *Stearns-Morrison Enterprise*. Although she never studied writing, she "makes good use of her encyclopedias." She is very proud of her church work, especially the work she does for the archives. She says she feels she has been a true pioneer in many ways. At age three months she came to the wild area of Upsala as a pioneer, she pioneered at the Lutheran Bible Institute in their first class, she was a pioneer as one of the first nurses at Immanual Deaconess in Omaha, she was again a pioneer in Big Fork, and says, "I like that. I might write about being a pioneer one day. My dad wanted us to go to school and I appreciate that."

Today Ida lives very comfortably in a little apartment in Upsala surrounded by her memories, memorabilia, and antique furniture that she brought from the farm. Her nephew takes care of her business now. "I'm glad he took over," she stated.

A favorite poem of Ida's, by Elizabeth Akers Allen, reminds her of her childhood on the farm where Swedish traditions coupled with a zest for living were the cornerstones of her satisfying life.

Backward, turn backward
  O time in your flight
Make me a child again
  just for tonight.

1 Ida C. Ryberg, "The Ryberg Saga: A Story of Swedish Immigrant Parents," Unpublished Family History, 1968.

2 Personal interview with Ida C. Ryberg, 26 May 1981. All quotes, unless otherwise indicated, are from that interview.

3 Ida C. Ryberg, "Ryberg Saga," *Stearns-Morrison Enterprise*, 5 October 1976.

4 *Stearns-Morrison Enterprise*.

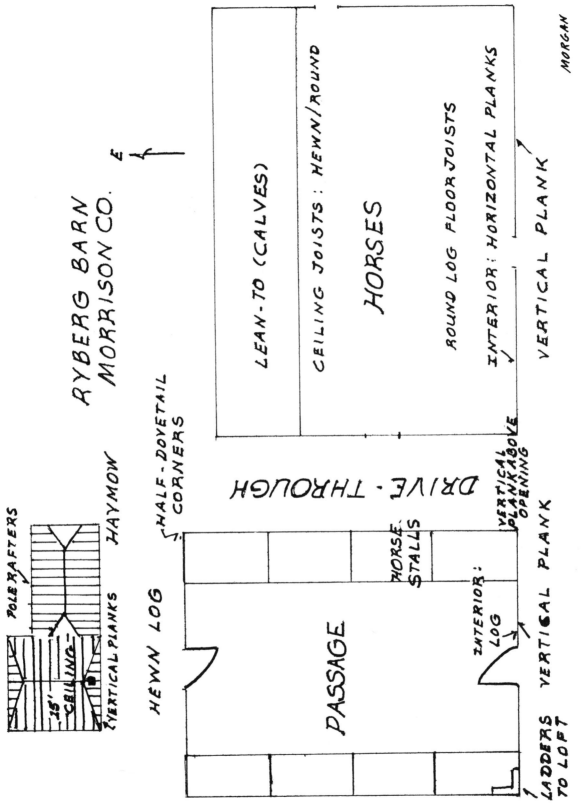

RYBERG BARN
MORRISON CO.

E

POLE RAFTERS

HAYMOW

15' CEILING—

VERTICAL PLANKS

HEWN LOG

HALF-DOVETAIL CORNERS

PASSAGE

HORSE STALLS

INTERIOR: LOG

LADDERS TO LOFT

VERTICAL PLANK

DRIVE-THROUGH

VERTICAL PLANK ABOVE OPENING

LEAN-TO (CALVES)

CEILING JOISTS: HEWN/ROUND

HORSES

ROUND LOG FLOOR JOISTS

INTERIOR: HORIZONTAL PLANKS

VERTICAL PLANK

MORGAN

HEWN LOG WALL

117

Joe Gasperlin

Joe Gasperlin is a resident of the Mother of Mercy Nursing Home in Albany, Minnesota. He is a quiet man of eighty-six who likes to tell visitors about the old days in St. Anthony, Minnesota, where he was born and where he lived most of his life on a small farm on the outskirts of the tiny village.[1]

Joe Gasperlin, resident of Mother of Mercy Nursing Home, Albany, Minnesota.

Joe said his parents, John and Theresa (Maschisnick) Gasperlin homesteaded the farm in the late 1860s. They emigrated from the Republic of Slovenia, Yugoslavia, then under Austrian rule, because they were very poor and many of their fellow countrymen were emigrating to America. Joe said:

> There were too many people in the old country and not enough food. My mother often said that here a lady had more lard on her clothes than she had in a pan over there!

Like many other Slovenians and Germans of this period, the Gasperlins heard about America and the rich farmland in Minnesota from the missionary priest, Father Francis X. Pierz, by way of letters and newspaper articles imploring his fellow countrymen to emigrate and enjoy the rewards of life in his wonderful adopted land.

The Gasperlins left Slovenia with a small group of countrymen who eventually settled together in central Minnesota where other Slovenians were already established. Later they formed the tiny village of St. Anthony, in Krain Township, Stearns County.

A large log house, by the standards of the day, was home to the growing Gasperlin family. It was built by John of hand-hewn oak logs, native to the area. It had three large rooms upstairs and two large rooms downstairs, plus an addition used as a summer kitchen. Thirteen children were born to John and Theresa. Along with the joys of a large family, however, they suffered the loss of three children to cholera in childhood, leaving empty places at the dinner table and in the hearts of the other members of the family. "It was sad," lamented Joe.

Two log barns were built on the site, one for horses and one for cattle, and a hog barn, a chicken barn, a corncrib, plus a smokehouse. The family smoked and cured all of their own meat—six

The original Gasperlin log house was moved to this site and used as a granary, blacksmith shop, and storage place.

hogs and a beef at one time. They rendered their own lard and made their own sausage. The chicken barn was always a building with lots of activity. The eggs were gathered, washed, and stored in a root cellar under the house. The hogs were fattened in the hog barn, often fed garden and fruit surpluses. Horses were kept for work in the fields, and about forty to fifty head of cattle supplied the beef and milk as well as income for the family. The family raised corn, oats, and alfalfa.

Theresa always planted a large garden and canned and preserved a great amount of vegetables, also stored in the root cellar. To supplement the vegetables, John planted a large orchard over the years: Two kinds of apple trees, cherry trees, chokecherry bushes, plum trees, rhubarb plants, and various flowers and shrubs were planted in a neat pattern around the house and yard. These were complemented by a number of shade trees: There were locust and willow trees, a large catalpa tree that John bought as a sapling, and numerous evergreens, making the farmsite a beautiful and productive place. Today the site is kept well-manicured by the new owners and a number of blue spruce were planted in recent years by Robert Radamacher. He obtained them as seedlings as part of an FHA project in high school. In a sense, he has continued the idea that John Gasperlin pioneered on the farm.

Much of the farm fruit was sold—strawberry crab apples sold for $1.00 per bushel, and some years the apples were so abundant that sacksful were given away or fed to the pigs. Today the apple trees still bear, as do the other fruit trees; and passersby often pick the fruit when visiting the site at the outskirts of town. No one lives there today and the buildings are empty.

As a young man Joe attended a two-room grammar school in St. Anthony. Although the family spoke German and Slovenian at home, in school they were required to speak English. Joe said religion was more important when he was a young man than it is today. He and his brothers and sisters received catechism instructions in St. Anthony for six months before they could receive their First Holy Communion at age twelve. "Everything was more strict in those days. Different than it is nowadays," Joe said.

With a large growing family, the log house became too small so the Gasperlins purchased the old parish house in St. Anthony when the parishoners decided to build a new one for their pastor in 1915. This is a large, white, frame house in Greek Revival style, measuring about 30′ by 60′. This was an exciting time for the Gasperlins. As Joe said:

A guy from St. Cloud came out and moved it with planks and rollers. It took one-and-a-half days to move it from one end of town to the other. Everybody watched the whole thing.

The house has large windows, including a few of stained glass, and it stands on a slight rise in the midst of other farm buildings and the lovely productive orchard. It has an ornate open staircase running the entire length of the house from the kitchen to the living room which Joe said he liked very much and as children they played on it. There are eight large rooms with high ceilings. In 1939 the Gasperlins had electricity installed in it, but it has never had indoor plumbing. A cistern under the house provided their water for washing and laundry and a privy was located behind the house.

In time, the Gasperlins sold most of the log buildings but the log house was moved to a new site close by and was used as a granary and blacksmith shop and for storage. It still stands today with its weathered logs and noticeable axe marks. The bottom five courses use large, carefully hewn, half-dovetail joints, 15″ to 18″ high. There is a plank staircase on the interior leading to a full loft where the children slept.

When the family was younger, Joe said, everyone helped with the farmwork. Then, as they grew up, most of them married and left the farm. Joe and his brother Pete didn't marry and Joe took over the family farm. He took over completely after his father died in 1925 and farmed with his mother until her death at age 84. After which, his uncle came to live with him until he also died at age 94. Joe farmed as long as he was able to, building a new rainbow roof barn and contemporary silo in the 1960s. Unfortunately, no one in the family wanted to continue the farm after Joe was forced to retire. He said, with a note of sadness in his voice:

I was done then. Why should I fix everything up? I had plenty of room for the cattle and everything. Now it's too late. If I wasn't so crippled up and in this nursing home, I'd go out there and investigate the place again. It used to be so nice.

In 1975 Joe sold the farm to Paul and Evelyn Rademacher. They now farm the land, but the buildings are vacant and will deteriorate rapidly if they are not cared for properly. The log house is a gloomy vestige of the life and activity that once prevailed in it—a ghostly remnant of the pioneer past of St. Anthony.

1   Personal interview with Joe Gasperlin at Mother of Mercy Nursing Home, Albany, Minnesota, 25 November 1980.

The Warren-MacDougall Homestead: *Two Rivers* and *Riverside*

On the flat open prairie of central Minnesota, stands the farm of Peter MacDougall, the last brother of a family of Scotch-Canadian emigrants who settled in the region between 1849 and 1873, and whose descendants farmed the site until 1968.[1]

Peter and Martha MacDougall at *Riverside*.

In 1847, the site was the home of William Whipple Warren, a noted scholar of Indian life, whose cabin stood on the later MacDougall farmstead. While only a ground depression exists where Warren's log cabin stood, the MacDougall homestead is remarkably intact, and includes a two-story house with attached kitchen, summer kitchen and woodshed; a machine shed, barn, workshop, two corncribs, a chicken coop, two storage sheds, and a windmill. A smokehouse is the only building that has disappeared. At the time of Warren's residence, 1847-1853, the site was known as *Two Rivers*; the MacDougalls named it *Riverside*.[2]

The Warren-MacDougall homestead overlooks the west bank of the Mississippi River. The farm buildings are in a cleared site which is surrounded even today by hardwood stands of oak, elm, ash, and virgin white pine. A tamarack swamp is located north of the farm and several open areas, which the MacDougalls called "the old fields," are situated about the site in three directions. High prairie bluffs to the southwest look down upon the river and a floodplain island (MacDougall Island) and white pine stands nearby serve as nesting for blue herons. The landscape surrounding the farm buildings is highly varied and topographically exciting because of the river's presence, the abundance of trees and wildlife, areas of natural meadowland, and the remnants of cultivated fields from the days of large-scale farming. To the east and south lie great stretches of flat land, dotted by windbreaks, that typify the prairie landscape of Morrison County. In the splendor of its wild isolation, this region even today possesses a strong sense of the frontier past.[3]

The area that later became the MacDougall homesite was visited as early as 1805 by Zebulon Pike. The *Two Rivers* designation refers to the Lake River (now Little Rock) and the Clear River (Platte)—names given to the Mississippi tributaries by Pike. In 1847, William Whipple Warren settled on the site.[4] Warren was the descendant of a prominent New England family which included Richard Warren, who landed at Plymouth in 1620, and Revolutionary War General Joseph Warren. In 1818, William W. Warren's father, Lyman, emigrated to the Lake Superior region where he engaged in the fur trade. At LaPoint in the Apostle Islands, Lyman married Mary Cadotte, daughter of a French fur trader and an Ojibway woman. William was born 27 May 1825 and in his youth became fascinated with the lodge stories and legends of his Ojibway people.[5]

In 1836, William's grandfather took him East where he received his formal education until age 16. According to J. F. Williams, Warren was "greatly devoted to reading and read everything he could get, with avidity."[6] In 1842, after his return West, he married Matilda Aitkin, daughter of William A. Aitkin, a well-known Indian trader.[7]

In 1845, Warren brought his family to Minnesota where he eventually became a farmer, interpreter, and in 1850 a member of the Minnesota House of Representatives. Under the urging of Col. D. A. Robertson, editor of *The Minnesota Democrat*, Warren began writing a series of stories on Ojibway life for the newspaper. The first feature appeared 25 October 1851 as "A Brief History of the Ojibways in Minnesota, as Obtained From Their Old Men."[8] The success of Warren's writings led to work on a book which he carried out while struggling with a severe lung ailment. The exhaustion caused by an unsuccessful trip to New York to seek publishers in the winter of 1852-53, coupled with his continuing illness, led to his premature death in St. Paul, 1 June 1853, at age 28.[9] Warren's *History of the Ojibways Based Upon Traditions and Oral Statements* was not published until 1885.

Two Rivers was Warren's home between 1847 and his death. During that time he built a cabin and a trading post. From this post Warren became part of the fur trading operation along the Pembina Oxcart Trail, the major commercial route between St. Paul and the Red River Valley. Six miles north, his father-in-law, William Aitkin, established another post at Swan River, Morrison County.[10] Scholar, interpreter, writer, trader, politician— William W. Warren was an important figure on the Minnesota frontier.

In the spring of 1849 Duncan MacDougall, the first of four Canadian brothers to emigrate to Morrison County, arrived and in 1852 began farming one mile north of the *Two Rivers* site. This brother later became a county commissioner, supervisor, and county treasurer.[11]

The first MacDougall to settle at *Two Rivers* was James who arrived sometime in the early 1850s. James operated a post office for settlers located across the Mississippi to the west. This post office, now a ground depression, stood near the present blacksmith shop. In 1857, the third brother, Donald, settled on the adjacent homestead north of *Two Rivers*. He became a town clerk, county sheriff and surveyor.[12]

The present configuration of the *Two Rivers* site is the result of the labor of the last brother, Peter, who arrived in October 1873 by covered wagon pulled by a horse and an ox.[13] While living in James' cabin Peter oversaw construction of the barn in 1874 and the house soon after. Peter's family became responsible for the success of the *Two Rivers* site.[14] Peter was born in Bredalbane, Ontario, in 1819, was educated in Canada, and worked for ten years in lumber camps. He then moved to County Huron and from there to Morrison County. Peter married Martha Gibson of New Brunswick and eleven children were born to them. Peter died in 1904; Martha in 1921.[15]

The Peter MacDougall family named the homestead *Riverside*. From the beginning the farm prospered and became an excellent example of pioneer self-sufficiency. Early crops included wheat and potatoes which the pioneers raised on the rich prairie sod east of the buildings. They had a large garden and planted a plum orchard. Fences made from trees cut from the woods enclosed the house, garden, and field sites to keep animals out, as the entire wooded area was pasture. Chickens, turkeys, and guinea hens roamed around the buildings; and until the 1960s, partridges, Hungarian pheasants, and prairie chickens made up the wildlife in the area. The MacDougalls did not wantonly expend their woods; they used only dead or dying trees as fuel. Also, they trimmed the lower pine branches and grazed about twenty head of cattle and six to eight horses in the pasture area to keep it free of underbrush. In the early days the oaks were the tallest trees as today the pines are.[16]

The MacDougalls supplied the house with water by an ingenious system of pipes connected to the pump which was activated by the windmill. Clothes were washed in the summer kitchen. Potatoes were kept in a root cellar under the house which was served by a chute that sifted out the dirt as the potatoes were rolled into bins. Peter raised bees for honey, cattle for milk and meat.

Horses were the MacDougall's real love. Peter's son, Thomas, had a team of roan Belgians which weighed 4200 pounds harnessed. Clover was raised to feed these animals, and only the horses were allowed to drink from the tank near the house; cattle had to go to the river.

When Peter died in 1904, Thomas took over the farm. As time passed, the rich prairie soil became depleted of its natural nutrients and yields decreased. Between 1900 and 1910 rye became the main crop since it required fewer nutrients. Between 1910 and 1930 severe sandstorms created the need for diversified farming. Since the Mac-Dougalls were excellent farmers and farmed a large operation for their time, they planted windbreaks and rotated their crops annually. After 1915, the MacDougalls were planting corn, soybeans, oats, wheat, and buckwheat, in a fixed order of succession, and they used organic fertilizer (green manure). Their main source of hay was wild hay—good fodder for horses.

After Thomas' death in 1940, the land slowly began to return to its natural state. The last pasturing occurred in about 1945. Selective logging of hardwoods, cutting of basswood for fuel, and, in the 1960s, pine, spruce, and cedar plantings have been made.[17]

Architectural Analysis of MacDougall Buildings

The workshop lies approximately 35 yards southwest of the house. This frame structure was built probably about 1910 and is still in very good to excellent condition. According to Katherine DuFrene, the men would always retire here to smoke after dinner. Like the machine shed and corncrib, the workshop utilizes drop-siding and is painted red. The building's dimensions are 16' 4" north/south by 26' 4" east/west and the structure sits on a field boulder and cement foundation. Of particular interest esthetically are the capped

chimney of yellow brick and the hand-crafted hardware on the entrance door. The interior contains workbenches and a few tools which show the building's original use and suggest a possible direction for future restoration. Katherine DuFrene said that the missing smokehouse stood about 15' northeast of the shop. It was covered with vertical plank siding.

One of the finest vernacular buildings in central Minnesota is the machine shed which lies 10' southeast of the blacksmith shop. [Fig. 2] This building is 40' north/south by 27' 10" east/west. The machine shed is esthetically pleasing because of its clean lines, solid rectangular mass, and unpretentious honesty in its use of materials. The textural quality of the roof (now gently sagging in the center) is an interesting contrast to the smooth surface and straight lines of the walls. The machine shed fronts the farmyard driveway and is located within relatively convenient range of the house and barn. The east facade contains a sliding door, a

2. The machine shed is a most beautiful vernacular building.

3. Handwrought iron hardware.

122

single door, and double doors: the latter two sets have truncated corners. Handcrafted hinges, similar to those used on the blacksmith shop, grace the doors. [Fig. 3]

A drive-through corncrib/equipment shed stands 21' to the south directly in line with the machine shed. [Fig. 4] Keystone-shaped, the

4. Keystone-shaped corncrib.

corncrib is constructed of 1″ by 4″ slats on the crib section (north) and drop-siding for the equipment area (south). A sliding door faces the farmyard to the east. This structure, like the other outbuildings, is well crafted and in its simple form esthetically most pleasing.

Directly west of the corncrib is the original corncrib. [Fig. 5] This once handsome structure, also keystone-shaped, is now in a state of collapse. Its construction is of unpainted boards and slats fastened with square-headed wrought nails throughout. Stone piers and heavy sills formed a foundation. Even in its present dilapidated condition, the corncrib is very picturesque with its weathered, vine-covered boards. If no measures are taken to restore this structure, it will soon become another vanished relic on the central Minnesota landscape.

5. Weathering patterns and square nails mark the side of the original corncrib.

In terms of size, craftsmanship, and esthetic value, the English-style barn constructed by the MacDougalls in 1874 is probably the most significant rural structure in central Minnesota. [Fig. 6] Of a style common to rural Canada and northeastern United States, a barn of this type and size is rarely found in the midwest. The MacDougall barn is a gabled structure, rectangular in shape, containing four bays separated with handcrafted, mortise-and-tenon, post-and-beam construction. A granary was added on the north side in the 1880s and a dairy shed was attached on the southwest probably as late as the 1920s. An enclosed cattle shed on the north has been torn down. The entire structure is in good to excellent condition.[18]

6. English-style barn constructed by the MacDougalls in 1874.

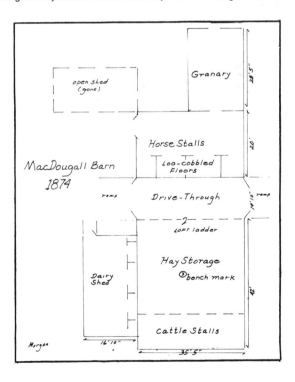

MacDougall Barn 1874

open shed (gone)

Granary

Horse Stalls

Coo-cobbled Floors

ramp

Drive-Through

ramp

loft ladder

Hay Storage

bench mark

Dairy Shed

Cattle Stalls

Morgan

16'10″

35'5″

The MacDougall barn contains enormous space (76' 10" north/south by 35' 5" east/west) for a structure built in this region in the 19th century. Brick embossed gray metal siding, an esthetic distraction, was added in 1903. This material covers a wall of vertical white pine planking nailed to an exposed interior surface of studs and heavy hewn girts. The entire structure sits on a field boulder foundation set in heavy mortar. Except for the transom lights and single upper-level windows on the north and south, the only source of illumination is from the doors. A metal cupola of late origin surmounts the roof at the barn's center.

Anyone viewing the barn's exterior is not prepared for the contrast presented by the interior. An analysis of each bay reveals its unique beauty and level of craftsmanship.

The most accessible entrance to the barn is on the west through double doors that lead to the four horse stalls (north bay)[Fig. 7] These stalls are

8. A unique, log-cobbling floor used in the horse stalls.

7. The horse-stall bay looking east.

9. The drive-through bay looking west.

framed with huge hand-hewn oak posts and beams, carefully mortised and tenoned and pegged throughout. A unique feature is the log-cobbled stall floors which are constructed of sapling pieces, 4" to 6" in diameter by 10" in length. [Fig. 8] These logs are set into the floor in an upright position to form a hard and dry surface for the horses' hooves. This kind of surface is extremely rare in the United States, and may have Russian, Scotch, or Canadian antecedents.[19] The circular pattern formed by the log-ends and the straight lines of the stalls make this bay esthetically pleasing.

At the end of the stalls, a narrow passage turns right into the central barn area. From this passage, the drive-through [Fig.9] (north middle bay) and hay storage area (south middle bay) can be observed. The initial reaction is one of great surprise, for one does not expect to find the soaring height of the cathedral-like interior. [Fig. 10] From this perspective one sees that the builders conceived of this space as having esthetic as well as practical proportions.

The drive-through bay is also entered through large (12'-wide) double doors on the east and west. These doors are constructed of 9"-wide vertical

124

planks and reach to the eave line, allowing entrance for two loaded wagons side-by-side. Twelve-pane transom lights above each set of doors illuminate this bay. The drive-through floor is of plank construction. Feed boxes opening into the horse stalls line the north wall of this bay.

The hay storage area [Fig. 11] is separated from the drive-through by a three-foot plank wall. From this point the entire framing can be observed: Rafters, purlins, struts, plates, knees, girts, and studs. All major timbers are hand-hewn oak or mill-sawn white pine boards. The floor itself is dirt and is slightly recessed from the adjoining bays.

10. A view of the hay storage area.

11. The interior roof is supported by gigantic hand-hewn struts and braces.

The cattle stalls (south bay) are closed off from the threshing floor by a wall of 12"-wide mill-sawn oak planks. This area is isolated from the other bays and can be entered only from the west. The dairy shed (actually a lean-to) adjoins the south bays and is entered on the north and south. A cement ramp on the north was imprinted with horseshoes when it was wet making an interesting design. A cement floor and steel pipe stanchions indicate the shed's later vintage. More in keeping with the integrity of the barn's design is the granary on the north. This addition (1880s) is now filled with stored lumber, including partition boards that were used to change the size of the granary during heavy or light harvests.

The MacDougall house is a vernacularized version of Georgian architecture. Even though it is quite simple in design, it is uncommonly elegant for its time and place. Built in the late 1870s, it is a two-story frame structure, 24' 5" by 28' 5", joined on the west by a kitchen, summer kitchen (1880s), and a woodshed, built *c.* 1900. These smaller one-story additions form an "L" to the main house. In style, these three units are in keeping with the traditional New England "continuous architecture" plan, [20] although the most direct sources were the MacDougall and Gibson Canadian homesteads, pictures of which exist in the MacDougall Scrapbook.

The entrance (south) facade is rigidly symmetrical. Proportion of window to wall space is well articulated and esthetically pleasing in conception. A central, paneled door, flanked by two windows, mark the ground floor. Three windows illuminate the second floor. (All openings are large-paned, 2 over 2 windows that appear to be original). The window-placement on all sides is well-designed, providing ample light to the second floor bedrooms through full use of southern exposure. Exterior trim is minimal and in keeping with a vernacularized interpretation of classic forms. These include thin corner boards, slightly capped on the north, and simple cornice window heads all around. Thin, white clapboard siding (1/4" × 5¾" × 4') has been utilized. Elegant, though somewhat austere, the MacDougall house symbolizes the comfortable surroundings of a prosperous rural family.[21]

The kitchen/summer kitchen is 22' by 23', has standard lapped siding, and a capped chimney. A central door is flanked by two windows. Preservation of the original hardwood flooring and wainscoting, plus a large Monarch range, suggest the feeling of the original interior. The adjoining woodshed is slightly smaller, has similar materials, a single door and window on the north and south sides, plus beveled corner boards. This area has been totally sealed off except for the door leading to the summer kitchen. The continuous plan as utilized on the MacDougall homesite is both a practical solution to the problems of climate and a handsome addition to the rural central Minnesota landscape.

The Warren-MacDougall site is an important part of the vanishing rural landscape of late 19th century America. Preservation, and possible restoration, rests on recognizing its significance as the home of a prominent historian and an immigrant farm family whose buildings, farm layout, and agricultural practices reveal valuable insights into architectural and social history.

1 Material for this chapter is drawn from several sources, including ten site visits in 1980-1982. Intensive on-site investigation was carried out by the authors with the help of Muriel Poehler, Royalton, Jan Warner, Weyerhaeuser Museum, Little Falls, and Dale Olmstead, St. Cloud. Diane Wade and Bob Fox of the Nature Conservancy also gave valuable assistance.
Personal interviews on 6 May and 2 June 1982 with Katherine DuFrene, granddaughter of Peter MacDougall, and her husband Clement were invaluable. Besides reading this chapter, Clement DuFrene provided on-site building descriptions and drew a floor plan of the MacDougall house. The DuFrenes own albums, scrapbooks, tools, and furniture from the MacDougall estate. An emigrant chest, brought from Ontario to Morrison County, is in their possession.

2 Hagdis Tschunko, "Brief History of MacDougall Homestead," unpublished manuscript, Charles A. Weyerhaeuser Memorial Museum, undated, p. 3.

3 The herons are now protected by the Nature Conservancy which controls the MacDougall Homestead. Under their jurisdiction are 215 acres that include the island and a hardwood forest, a prairie, the homestead, and the heron colony. Mrs. William Mandery, born on the west side of the river in 1895, remembers herons on the site as a child. The MacDougalls designated areas of the farm by name: The Big Woods, The Pines, The Big Hill, The Grove, The Lane, The Hollow. (Tschunko, p. 3-8).

4 Tschunko, p. 1.

5 J. Fletcher Williams, "Memoirs of William W. Warren," in William Whipple Warren, History of the Ojibway Nation (Minneapolis: Ross & Haines, 1957), p. 9.

6 Williams, p. 13.

7 Williams, p. 14.

8 Williams, p. 16.

9 Williams, p. 18.

10 "William Warren Two Rivers Cabin Site and MacDougall Homestead," National Register of Historic Places Inventory—Nomination Form, Minnesota Historical Society, 1977. Two cellar depressions west of the MacDougall barn constitute the remains of Warren's shelters. The cabin site is the northernmost one; the other may be either his barn or trading post.

11 J. Fletcher Williams, History of the Upper Mississippi Valley (Minneapolis: Minnesota Historical Company, 1881), p. 597. Duncan settled in Section 20, Bellevue Township. Two Rivers is in sections 28 and 29.

12 Tschunko, p. 2.

13 Harold L. Fisher, The Land Called Morrison (St. Cloud: Volkmuth Printing Co., 1972), p. 87. The site was originally deeded to Silas Barrett, a New Hampshire private in the War of 1812. Peter MacDougall purchased the land from John B. and Ruth A. Dearing, 17 Sept. 1873. (Warranty Deed, DuFrene Papers).

14 Tschunko, p. 5.

15 Clara K. Fuller, History of Morrison & Todd Counties Indianapolis: B. F. Bowen & Co., 1915), p. 621. Also see, "Peter MacDougall Obituary," Royalton (Minn.) Banner, undated. Martha's mother was born in Roxboroshire, Scotland, and emigrated at age 15 to Stanley Township, New Brunswick, which was described as a "vast wilderness" in her obituary. (DuFrene scrapbook).

16 Tschunko, pp. 3-4.

17 Tschunko, pp. 9-11.

18 In the fall of 1981, workers began to cover the leaking roof with cedar shingling.

19 Nomination Form, p. 4. A similar construction called stovewall occurs as wall nogging. It occurs in Canadian lumberjack shelters. Richard W. E. Perrin, The Architecture of Wisconsin (Madison: The State Historical Society of Wisconsin, 1967), pp. 27-32.

20 Continuous architecture may have originated in New Hampshire where high snow prevented farmers from reaching their outbuildings. This style is rare in central Minnesota. For a discussion of continuous architecture see Eric Sloane, An Age of Barns (New York: Ballantine, 1975), pp. 48-49.

21 Window and door placement of the MacDougall facade closely resembles that of the John Wilson Printer Museum, Deerfield, Mass., 1816. This simple Georgian building is illustrated in Curt Bruce and Jill Grossman, Revelations of New England Architecture (New York: Grossman Publishers, 1975), pp. 74-75.

The Cater Farmstead

The Joshua Otis Cater homestead, Haven Township, Sherburne County, includes a white clapboarded house, an English-style barn, garage, granary, and a corncrib. Adjacent to the quiet farmsite, highway 10 carries traffic past this important 19th century architectural landmark.

The Cater house is still a showplace, although it went through an extensive remodeling in 1940. Originally, the house was Gothic Revival in style with an intermingling of features from the Georgian and Federal styles. The hipped roof and widow's walk are the only surviving elements from the original design.[1] Built *c.* 1870, the house had a large, one-story porch with a balustrade, paired windows with pointed arches, and twin chimneys. Window-placement was radically changed in the remodeling, producing a facade with a slightly discordant asymmetrical appearance. The interior, radically remodeled in 1968 after lightning struck the house, provides space for four bedrooms upstairs and a kitchen, living room, dining room, parlor, and bedroom downstairs. The grounds are well-kept and include a large lawn, neatly planted young trees, shrubbery, flowers, and a large vegetable garden.

The Cater house and farmsite are reminders of a family and a way of life that is significant to the area. The Cater family were New England immigrants who became the first wheat farmers in Sherburne County. At one time the family owned between 8,000 and 10,000 acres of land in central Minnesota.

The family is of English and French descent. Three brothers came to America in 1635 and settled in North Barrington, New Hampshire. One brother, Stephen, fought in the War of 1812. The family name was initially DeCater; however, only one brother kept this surname, another changed it to Cates, and the Minnesotans dropped the "De." The Cates branch of the family has since died out; consequently, family reunions today include only Caters and DeCaters.

Ephraim Cater was the patriarch of the Minnesota Caters. Because his farm in New Hampshire was rocky and unproductive, his family income was supplemented by factory work. Joshua

Otis Cater, Ephraim's son, met his wife Louisa Woodis "a little Quaker girl of Scotch-Irish heritage," in one of these factories. Their daughter-in-law, Kate Snow Cater, simplified references to the Cater ancestry by "referring to them all as 'Yankees,'" according to Ben Scherfenberg, a great-grandson of J. O. and Louisa Cater.

J. O. Cater was born in New Hampshire in 1822. He purchased a small farm adjoining his father's in 1844 and married Louisa in 1846. In 1856, he and his three brothers, Joe, Martin, and Andrew, traveled to Minnesota as land speculators. They found Minnesota favorable to their needs and desires. Joe filed a claim in Sherburne County before they all returned to New Hampshire where Joe married before he and Martin returned to Minnesota to settle on a farm near Princeton. In 1860, J. O. traded his farm in New Hampshire for 480 acres of prairie land in Haven Township. He, Louisa, and their five sons, Levi, Jim, Eph, Trask, and Arthur traveled to Minnesota where they stayed with Martin and Joe for a short time. (Herbert was later born in Minnesota). Levi's story about their journey was documented by his daughter, Ruth Cater Scherfenberg:

> We came as far as LaCrosse on the train and up to St. Paul by boat. Father bought a three-year-old heifer and calf there. But he had no money for horses or oxen so he hired a man with a team and wagon to take our trunks up to Princeton. Mother drove the team and father, the man, and I walked behind the wagon. The smaller boys walked part of the time. The cow couldn't travel very fast, but it wasn't much of a road and we were barefoot. It was about eleven o'clock in the forenoon when we got to Uncle Mart's at Princeton. He and a neighbor were breaking together and they had six oxen on the plow. They left me to drive while my uncle went up to the house with the rest of the family. Maybe I wasn't scared to take that goad-stock! I had never driven such a team and they said one big fellow wouldn't keep the furrow. But when we went in to dinner the neighbor praised me, and I drove the team six weeks.[2]

The Caters had left New Hampshire because the land was rock-strewn, but since the land near Princeton was tree-covered and full of stumps, they only substituted one problem for another. Therefore, after less than two years, the sons persuaded their father to move on to their prairie land in Haven. Although the prairie farm seemed potentially bountiful, the work was still difficult. The family immediately broke and planted 100 acres into wheat that had to be cut with a cradle, bound by hand, and threshed with a flail because they could not afford mechanical equipment. In hot weather, they often slept during the daytime and worked into the night. They also had 160 acres of meadow hay that had to be mowed and bunched by hand. Money was scarce, flour cost $17.00 a barrel, and wheat brought only forty cents. At one time they bartered ten bushels of wheat for two fine two-year-old steers. A team of oxen cost $150.00 and five hundred tamarack poles brought $50.00. One year the Caters broke eighteen acres of land for a neighbor and were paid two fine buffalo robes for their efforts. Twelve percent interest was paid on borrowed money.

Indians were often a problem. Once, when an attack was expected, all of the livestock was turned loose and the people gathered together in one large house. When nothing happened after three days, the livestock was again collected and brought home. "Another time when grandma was alone with the children, Indians butchered a steer in the yard in full view of the house and carried it off with them," Martha Cater Scherfenberg wrote. Usually, however, the Indians wanted only food, and once fed, would leave. Martha also wrote that "perhaps the white people were just as surely a curse to them as they were to the whites because the white people gave them whiskey and then tried to cheat them and play dirty tricks on them."

While the Cater brothers were establishing themselves in the new state of Minnesota, their parents remained in New Hampshire. In 1860, Charlotte wrote J. O. to lament the conditions in New Hampshire that had led her sons to emigrate and to express her own grief over the loss of her family:

> It has been some time since we heard from you. . . . The mills are stopped and hundreds are out of work, and war is upon us. Money scarce. . . . We are all well at present, but your father and I are growing old and cannot do but a little. We want to hear from you all. . . . We are very lonesome. No one to come to see us. I very often look out to see some of you coming, before I think. Then, I will sit down weak and faint. . . . We have not sold none of your things since I wrote you. We cannot sell them. Times are so hard. Everyone has as much as they can do to live. We want to see you all very much.

> Father and I talk of coming out there after we have done haying if nothing happens and Martha is well enough to leave, but don't put too much dependence so to be disappointed. I want you to write how you get along and how the children is, how Trask is, and how Ehpraim is. . . . I must close. I have a little money for you which I thought to send to you but I shall not send it until I see whether we come or not. I will bring you all we can. Write as soon as you get this from your

> Mother Charlotte Cater[3]

Unfortunately, Ephraim and Charlotte never found the money to come to Minnesota. However, good fortune, combined with hard work, brought a measure of success to J. O. and his brothers in their new environment. J. O. had to borrow $20.00 in gold to pay for his first breaking plow, and later they worked together to acquire mechanical equipment to make their work go faster and easier. Their first reaper cut the grain, but did not bind it; the second allowed two men to stand on it and bind; the third to cut a wider and faster swath. In 1899, Herbert built an impressive barn. Levi improved his premises with new buildings, Arthur managed a vegetable canning factory, and James was awarded the prize for the largest load of wheat brought to the Clear Lake mill. The Cater family was publically recognized as very progressive. Arthur Dare, editor of the *Sherburne County Star News*, noted:

> Joshua O. Cater is a pioneer who has done well and is so comfortably situated that he can enjoy the decline of his life without worry. He came to Haven in the 1850s and devoted his life to improving his farm which happens to be the first in the township.[4]

By 1904, when Joshua died, the Cater farms totaled thousands of acres in Sherburne County.

The Cater family was also active in township and county government. Joshua was one of the organizers of Haven Township and its first town chairman. In 1892, Barret Cater was township supervisor in Bladwin Township and Levi was supervisor of Haven Township. In 1884, J. O. Cater and twenty other citizens petitioned the county board for a new highway that would connect more than one town in the county.[5] Finally, Joe Cater was one of the first postmasters in Princeton where his home served as post office for a number of years.

While the Caters were progressive farmers and loyal citizens, one member, Joshua, had a stubborn streak, according to Ben Scherfenberg.

Joshua believed so strongly in the right of ownership of land that he fought the Northern Pacific Railroad when tracks were laid "cornerwise" through his property. During one summer he kept crews away, using a shotgun as persuasion. Eventually, the tracks were laid, but the Cater family could ride the train free anytime and anywhere—and the company held only a lease on the land.

Another incident involved J. O.'s refusal to permit the Northwestern Telephone Company from placing its poles on a roadway passing through his land. J. O. and his family had already petitioned for a road to run along the Mississippi River instead of through Cater land. However, the telephone company attempted to follow the old trail by cutting trees and setting poles for lines. In the end, the road and telephone lines were placed along the river instead of through Cater property, though not until J. O. took the case to the Minnesota Supreme Court.

The Cater homestead has been in the family for four generations. The farmsite consists of the house, barn and cement-stave silo, granary, a two-bin corncrib, and a windmill with a working water pump.

The barn built by Benjamin Snow *c.* 1870 is an English barn, a three-bay structure which includes a central driveway flanked on either side by animal stalls on the ground floor and haymows above.[6] Now used for storage, the ground floor was designed for horses, and had double-floor planking (now removed), a feed bin, and nine stalls. Below ground level, set into a hill on the east, is a basement once used for calves and cattle on the north and poultry on the south.

The barn's exterior is of board-and-batten construction, painted red, and like all English style barns, is quite elegant. Measuring 40' by 60', it sits on a foundation of oak sills with a granite-chunk foundation of stone from the State Reformatory quarry. Twelve-inch wide double doors with an eleven-pane transom dominate the south entrance. The gable end is opened by a four-pane window set into the wall as a triangle. A small entrance door opens into the stalls at the far right.

The west wall is flanked by a shed-door that leads to the basement, a square board-and-batten

A view of the Cater barn as seen from the widow's walk.

silo chute, and a cement-stave silo. The silo resembles similar wooden stave silo structures in form and is topped by a bowl-shaped roof. To the east is a poured concrete wall broken by windows and doors that open into the basement level with a board-and-batten wall above.

To truly appreciate the beauty of the Cater barn, one must see its interior. All interior work is hand-hewn post-and-beam construction (heavily axe-marked) with pegged mortise-and-tenon joints throughout. The walls are supported by four large bents with 9½" by 10" posts, 6" by 6" beams, and 4" by 4" braces. The roof is supported by struts and pole rafters and a ridgepole is used. The timbers

The south facade has large double doors topped with a transom light. A triangular window allows light to enter the haymow.

form a handsome support system—an outstanding example of folk art craftmanship.

Near the north end of the barn stands a drive-in corncrib, 19′ by 32′. This is a picturesque structure with its heavily-weathered brown and gray siding covered with vines. The crib sections are covered with 1′ × 5″ board siding and 7″-wide horizontal planking is utilized in the gable ends. The gable is opened through a vertical plank door. Square nails are used throughout.

A tall, frame granary, 16′ north/south by 24′ east/west of red-painted 4½″-wide clapboard, stands immediately north of the house. Like the crib, this structure is also picturesque. In design and use of materials it appears to be of an early date, *c.* 1870. The building sits on a granite-chunk foundation set in heavy mortar and has a large root cellar. The supporting members for the granary above are all handwork with 10″ by 10″ posts, 8″ by 8″ summer tie beams, and joists left in the round and chiselled to fit the beams. An entrance porch with concrete steps opens to the cellar on the south. This area was at one time used as a chicken barn. Access to the granary is through large double doors on the east.

Joshua Otis Cater and his descendants have played a vital and, at times, a colorful role in the early history of central Minnesota. The Cater buildings constitute an extremely interesting site. It is rare in central Minnesota to find a farmsite made up of buildings from a single era. With the exception of a modern garage on the east, the Cater farm represents a fine example of a late nineteenth century pioneer Minnesota homestead, and is hence a valuable heritage landmark.

The English-style barn is somewhat unusual in the seven-county central Minnesota region.

The crossbeam of the Cater barn reveals the craftsmanship of mortise/tenon work. Handmade pegs hold beams in place.

The rather stately Cater house was the home of Joshua and Louisa Cater, early settlers in Sherburne County. The Cater homestead is one of three adjacent farms forming "Caterville"—part of vast land holdings once held by pioneer Cater families.

1   All information documented in the Cater family history was obtained from Ben and Vera Scherfenberg in personal interviews on 27 May 1980 and 9 December 1980. Personal letters from ancestors and personal anecdotes written down through the years by Martha and Ruth Scherfenberg were used and quoted from.

2   Ruth Cater Scherfenberg files.

3   Charlotte Cater Scherfenberg files.

4   Cynthia Seelhamer and Mary Jo Masher, *The Growth of Sherburne County: 1875-1975* (Becker, Minn.: Sherburne County Historical Society, 1980), p. 115.

5   Seelhamer and Masher, p. 16.

6   The English or New England barn is described by Eric Sloane, *An Age of Barns* (New York: Ballantine Books, 1975), pp. 38-41. The design of the Cater barn may have been taken from a book of plans, a common source for early builders. The Cater barn also resembles a style described as "English Barn, Bank Barn Subtype." William L. Montell and Michael Lynn Morse, *Kentucky Folk Architecture* (Lexington: The University Press of Kentucky, 1976), p. 99.

Peter and Maggie Lind

Peter and Mary (Maggie) Lind emigrated to America from Halsingland, Sweden, in the summer of 1870. Married in 1865, they lost a daughter at age one and later adopted three children. For a short time Peter and Maggie lived in Anoka, Minnesota. Although in Sweden Peter had been engaged in lumbering, in America he turned to farming. After a few months in Anoka, the Linds bought an 80-acre farm in Sherburne County. By 1881, after several years of hardship, the farm was considered prosperous.[1] Peter died in 1903 at age 66. Maggie remained on the farm until four years before her death in 1918 at age 76.[2]

Carl and Anna Tingquist are in their 90s. As neighbors of the Linds, they hold memories of the family that extend back to the turn of the century. In 1914, Carl moved the widowed Maggie Lind back to Anoka after she sold the farm. Carl said that the trip took one day by horse and wagon and that they stopped in Elk River to eat their meal and to water the horses. Carl recalled that Maggie was a "small, wiry, smart woman who used her wits," and that she was "rather happy-go-lucky." According to Anna Tingquist, the Linds claimed descent from Swedish royalty. Anna said that the Linds operated their farm by employing the labor of emigrants who came from Sweden to work for them until they had earned enough money to establish their own homesteads. The Tingquists said that there were always a large number of people living on the farm and that they worked hard under Lind's management.[3]

Even in its present ruined condition, the Lind farmsite reveals patterns of the thoughts and feelings of the settlers. Architecturally, its value stems from its uniqueness as a site which contains a cluster of buildings, rather than a single dwelling, from the era of log construction. To fully appreciate what it was like to live in the Minnesota wilderness during the late nineteenth century, a careful study of each structure was made, including structural measurements. The site was walked over several times to allow the recorders to appreciate how the Linds may have felt living there. Building dimensions, number of structures, and an evaluation of the level of craftsmanship indicate a highly developed and complex lifestyle and a successful achievement of substantial economic goals.[4]

Although only a shell of the farm exists today, this shell reveals that the Linds strove to carve out a home of rough grandeur from the wilderness. The site chosen by the Linds was well treed with bur oaks that predate settlement. Six of these giant, gnarled oaks still stand. The site also reveals that the homestead was carefully planned in terms of available timber for shelter, land for crops, and proximity to wild game and water. Located on high ground facing a branch of the Snake River to the east, the Lind home had a fine view of the countryside. Along the eastern boundary runs the Santiago Road. Adjacent to the road, Peter Lind constructed a cruck fence, using an oak tree as a corner post, and Maggie planted strawberry rhubarb, lilac bushes, iris, raspberry bushes, chokecherry, and Canada plum trees.[5]

According to the Tingquists, the Lind home was a local showplace. The site where a 16′ by 22′ log-and-frame house stood is now a hole filled with tree stumps. Originally, however, the house was a two-room log structure which was later expanded to an "L" by the addition of a frame parlor to the east with two bedrooms above. The entire structure was eventually covered with tongue-and-groove siding

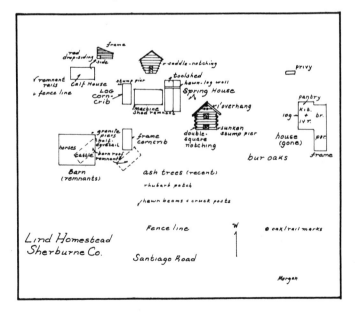

Lind farm plot reconstruction from site measurements.

and painted white. Unfortunately, this house burned to the ground in 1950.

The Lind farmsite is roughly rectangular. The north to south line extends approximately 200' along the Santiago Road. From east to west the site is 100' deep. The log-and-frame house stood on the highest point of the northeast corner facing east. Two extant log structures in semi-ruined condition still stand to the south of the house. Of these, the larger structure may have been a springhouse with a lean-to toolshed. The smaller structure was a corncrib. A frame calf house stands 33' south of the corncrib. Near the southeast corner are the ruins of a 35' by 40' cattle-and-horse barn from which only a heap of half-dovetailed logs remains. A frame privy and a frame corncrib, along with the calf house, are the only standing frame structures. All of the standing buildings are in an advanced state of disrepair and within a few years will be reclaimed by nature.

The most important log building for study is the springhouse. Standing 130' south of the house site, it measures 14' east/west by 27' north/south.

The Lind springhouse is part of a cluster of log buildings belonging to Swedish emigrants who settled in Sherburne County in the 1870s. At one time it may have been living quarters for the Linds while they were building a larger home, hired hands' sleeping space, and a springhouse. To the rear is a workshop or storage place.

Positive identification of its former use has been difficult to determine. According to Carl Tingquist and Rose Hanson, the building was used as a granary, but the absence of a grain-door and the use of fitted logs without chinking seems to rule out this use. It may have been a multi-use building, including shelter for hired hands.

The east (entrance) facade of the springhouse contains a low opening 4' high. This doorway and a small window above it are the only sources of light. Two small, round holes, flanking the projecting ridgepole have been sealed shut. The low door, a sand floor, and large pegs for hanging vegetables or meat indicate an area designed originally for cool storage. Heavy round joists, now fallen to the floor, appear to have been supporting beams for a loft. (Notches cut into the north and south walls probably received these timbers). The loft may have been used for sleeping or hay storage, its use changing through the years.

Esthetically, the springhouse surpasses many log structures in central Minnesota. The east facade is carefully handcrafted in hewn tamarack and joined by double-square notching. This method of joinery had not been observed elsewhere in this region. Its interior is most pleasing. Measuring 12' 9" by 17', the interior west wall of smoothly-adzed log rises 16'. This impressive room has a distinctly warm and homey feeling.

A small room on the west end of the spring-house also defies positive identification, but its appearance suggests use as a toolshed, workshop, or storage place. It contains a window and a low gate-door on the north. Heavy round joists at head-level may have supported shelves. Several bits of broken metal and a china plate were found near the surface of the dirt floor. Although the walls of this room are plank, the continuous ridgepole from the

This log corncrib is joined to the springhouse by a machine shed. This structure sits on stump piers and is of round-log construction.

132

log spring house would indicate that it was built at the same time.

South of the springhouse are the remains of a 22′ long machine shed which spans the space between the springhouse and corncrib. Constructed of plank, the shed was 15′ deep and approximately 5′ in height. This shelter also may have served as a protective shelter for summer cooking and eating—an ideal place for feeding field crews.

At the south end of the shed stands the smaller log corncrib. Keystone shaped, the crib measures 10′ 4″ at the widest point of the east (front) facade, 16′ 8″ north/south, and has a height of 8′. Round-log, saddle-notched construction has been used throughout. The crib has a ridgepole, a one-foot overhang, and facing boards on the gables—in design, a smaller version of the springhouse.

Interestingly, the corncrib's interior, like that of the springhouse, looks as if it had once been lived in. Except for the total lack of chinking, it could have been used for housing. (Two organ keys found beneath the dirt floor add to this feeling). Stumps have been used as corner piers on both log structures—a rare construction technique for this region.

Thirty-three feet south of the corncrib is a frame structure, 12′ by 18′ 8″, that appears to have been used as a calf-house. Constructed of drop-siding painted red, the structure certainly postdates the log buildings.

To the east of the calf-house are the remains of a cattle-and-horse barn. Measuring 40′ east/west and 35′ north/south, this barn must have been a massive structure. Although little remains of the original structure, remnants again suggest a high level of craftsmanship. The only structure wherein stone was employed, this barn rested on granite piers. Still intact upon this foundation rests an 11″-high sill (west wall) and three remaining 4½″-high half-dovetailed logs. A portion of the extant north wall reveals smoothly-adzed logs of the high quality found in the springhouse. A portion of the roof, now twisted into a cone as if hit by a storm, shows a ridgepole and 9″-wide cedar shingles. Even in its deteriorated condition, one can sense the beauty of this forgotten building.

An 8′ 3″ by 16′ frame corncrib north of the

barn completes the Lind complex. According to Carl Tingquist, it was moved in after the farm's abandonment and was used as an icehouse by neighbors.

The Lind farm belongs to the past. The wilderness surrounding the site is fast reclaiming the remnants of this once prosperous farm, and the tillable land has been purchased by neighbors. Although the site is only a relic, it must have been at one time a productive and beautiful place.

Detail, Lind springhouse. Existing examples of the double-notch are extremely rare. The Lind springhouse is the only structure found in a seven-county area that utilizes this Scandinavian notch type.

1   N. H. Winchell, Edward D. Neill, William J. Fletcher, and Charles S. Bryant, *History of the Upper Mississippi River Valley* (St. Paul: Minnesota Historical Society, 1881), p. 314.

2   Personal interview with Mrs. Rose Hanson, 21 August 1980, Mrs. Hanson, Big Lake, is compiling a history of the Snake River area that includes the Lind site. (The site is the south ½ of the northeast ¼, section 10, township 34, range 28). The warranty deed cites sale from the U.S.A. to Peter Lind, 1 October 1880. By law, only 80-acre sites could be homesteaded within 50 miles of the Twin Cities.

3   Personal interview with Anna and Carl Tingquist, Becker, 4 June 1981.

4   Intensive site analyses were made by Morgan and Dale Olmstead, 4 June 1981. The area is filled with nettles, three-leaf ash trees, poison oak and ivy. Hawks circle above the site. Lying two miles west of the Sherburne National Wildlife Refuge, the Lind site evokes even today a strong impression of pioneer conditions.

5   Survey and identification of plant life was made by botanist Mary Johnson, 23 May 1981. Lyn Johnson found the artifacts cited above.

Skandar-Legatt Vertical Log House

Vertical log houses are very rare in the United States. One of eight recorded in Minnesota stood in St. Stephen, Brockway Township, Stearns County, until April 1981 when it was dismantled for the purpose of using the squared timbers in a new, earth-sheltered house.

Fortunately, over a two-year period, the authors had photographed, measured, and documented the background of this unusual architectural landmark prior to its destruction.

The vertical log house was built by a Slovenian emigrant, John Skandar, for his family about 1865. It is not known why it was built with the logs placed vertically—a method common to French colonial settlers in North America. A common theory says that it was done to discourage marauding Indians from scaling the logs. Since no

Blaise Legatt (left) and Mae Legatt (right) talked with Marilyn Brinkman about the house. Hand-hewn ceiling joists can be seen above.

other vertical log structures are found in the area, this theory is doubtful. Also, the vertical log structure should not be confused with palisade construction, an early method of upright, *round-log* building used for purposes of fortification.

Blaise Legatt, who was "born between those logs" on 3 January 1901, proudly told us the history of the vertical log house and his own family history in it.[1] He said that each year he had tried to make a pilgrimage to his boyhood home. Three days before it was razed, Blaise, accompanied by his wife, Mae (Long) Legatt, showed us the vertical log house in person.

Blaise's parents emigrated from a town in Slovenia called Jyor (pronounced *gor*), meaning "lower mountain" in Yugoslavian, where they had also lived in a log house. This house was still in use when Blaise and Mae visited it recently. Marked with the date it was built—1737—the logs and stones, like the materials used in the Skandar house, were indigenous to the area. The logs were set horizontally, however.

Blaise told us that he did not know there was anything unusual about the Skandar house when he lived there. As far back as he could remember, it had been clapboarded. He remembers the house as

The north facade of the Legatt house. Above the openings the upright logs can be seen. For as long as Blaise Legatt can remember, the hand-hewn upright logs were clapboarded.

being very cold in winter. Although the family was poor, they were, Blaise told us, "quite happy because we didn't know any better way of life."

The vertical log house and a nearby fieldstone and log barn were built on a hill overlooking a tamarack hollow where Blaise and his brothers played baseball and in winter slid down the slope on homemade sleds. Wolves and wildcats, as well as other wild animals and fowl, could be found in the area. (Even today deer are seen in the neighborhood). Pheasants were so plentiful and tame that Blaise once caught one with his bare hands.

Since only a few trees grew on the hill, cold winter winds chilled the house. The original house was a simple square structure with a sleeping loft. Blaise's father, Matthew, added a frame "lean" on the north side for the children's bedroom and a pantry. Behind the steps leading to the loft was another pantry and storage area. Blaise once found a snake there. Another time, he was bitten by a rat—a scar he carries today—when he tried to chase it out of the house. Beneath the kitchen floor was a root cellar with wooden steps leading down to it. Blaise remembered that whenever the parish priest visited their sick mother, he walked very carefully over the sagging kitchen floor because he was sure the floor would collapse one day.

The house itself, however, was well-built of sturdy, large, white and red oak timbers chinked with red clay, stones, and blocks of wood. The walls were carefully mortised and tenoned into the sills and girts and pegged in place. Several yards away, lie the ruins of a log and stone barn, built by Skandar in the 1860s, a once handsome and well-crafted structure, one bay of which was constructed of massive half-dovetailed tamarack logs, the other

Blaise Legatt stands in the window of his boyhood home.

of gigantic glacial boulders. Blaise recalled the family always kept a number of good work horses on one side and six to eight dairy cows on the other. The barn had low, narrow doors and a few small windows. As a young man, Blaise had the unpleasant task of pitching manure through the windows into wagons outside.

As children, the Legatts raised rabbits. Blaise believes they burrowed under the foundation, weakening the heavy, gabled roof which peaked where the stone and log walls met.

Four boys and one girl were born to the Legatts in the vertical log house, one dying in infancy. They had a hard life. The father was 55 when he married a young woman of 25. Both died when the family was quite young, the mother of cancer after a lengthy illness at age 38. The father died five years later of a stroke. The children were placed in homes with relatives. During this time the farm was rented out until the oldest boy, John, was old enough to take it over and farm the land himself.

Blaise remembers many incidents of their childhood, both sad and happy. John once set fire to a straw pile and neighbors helped to save the house and barn. Another time, Blaise opened a cornhusk mattress and set fire to it. "My father whipped me with a leather belt for that!" Blaise said. "Mother finally told him to quit. She thought I had had enough." Children did not wear shoes in summer, and Blaise often walked barefooted to the mailbox in winter.

Blaise said that when John married, friends gave an "old-fashioned chivaree," but it was overdone "as often happens when young people get together." Blaise said that on this occasion someone put a half-gallon of kerosene in the cookstove oven. "Fortunately, no one was hurt," he added.

After John Legatt left the farm, it was rented out for many years to a number of people. Since 1950, it has been abandoned and ownership has changed many times. No one has lived in the house or used the barn since that time. The land and buildings lay in a state of deterioration and neglect until 1981 when new owners took advantage of the picturesque location and the beautifully weathered logs of the vertical log house to create a new homestead.

1   Personal interview with Blaise and Mae Legatt, 30 March 1981.

BIBLIOGRAPHY

Anderson, Clay, Ronald M. Fisher, Stratford C. Jones, Bill Peterson, and Cynthia Ramsey. *Life in Rural America*. Washington, D.C.: National Geographic Society, 1974.

Anderson, Elaine. "History of Sherburne County." Unpublished MS, Sherburne County Historical Society. n.p. n.d.

Apps, Jerry, and Allan Strang. *Barns of Wisconsin*. Madison: Tamarack Press, 1977.

Arthur, Eric, and Dudley Witney. *The Barn*. Ontario: M. F. Feheley Arts Company, 1972.

Atkinson, Brooks, ed. *Selected Writings of Ralph Waldo Emerson*. New York: The Modern Library, 1950.

Bealer, Alex W., and John O. Ellis. *The Log Cabin*. Barre, Mass: Barre Publishing Company, 1978.

Berry, Wendell. *Clearing*. New York: Harcourt Brace Jovanovich, 1970.

––––––––––. *Farming: A Hand Book*. New York: Harcourt Brace Jovanovich, 1970.

––––––––––. *Openings*. New York: Harcourt Brace Jovanovich, 1980.

Blegen, Theodore C. *Minnesota: A History of the State*. St. Paul: 1949.

––––––––––. *The Land Lies Open*. St. Paul: University of Minnesota Press, ·1949.

Brinkman, Marilyn, and Marcelline Schleper. *Centennial: St. Catherine's Parish, Farming, Minnesota*. Albany, Minn.: Weber Printing, 1979.

Burris, Evadine A. "Frontier Homes and Home Management." Master's thesis, University of Minnesota, 1933.

Campbell, Marie. "Frontier Women: Pioneers or Outcasts?" Paper presented at Popular Culture Association, Eleventh Annual Meeting, Cincinnati, Ohio, 27 March 1981.

Cather, Willa. *My Antonia*. Boston: Houghton Mifflin, 1918.

––––––––––. *O! Pioneers*. Boston: Houghton Mifflin, 1913.

Condit, Carl W. *American Buildings: Materials and Techniques From the First Colonial Settlement to the Present*. Chicago: University of Chicago Press, 1968.

Conrat, Maisie and Richard. *The American Farm: A Photographic History*. San Francisco: California Historical Society, 1977.

Davey, Norman. *A History of Building Materials*. New York: Drake Publishers, Ltd., 1971.

Dick, Everett. *The Sod-House Frontier 1854-1890*. New York: D. Appleton-Century Company, Inc., 1937.

Drache, Hiram M. *The Challenge of the Prairie*. Fargo: North Dakota Institute for Regional Studies, 1970.

Fisher, Harold L. *The Land Called Morrison*. St. Cloud, Minn.: Volkmuth Printing Company, 1972.

Foley, Mary Mix. *The American House*. New York: Harper and Row, 1980.

Fox, Jon Michael. "The Fox House: Alternative for an Historical Structure in the Sherburne National Wildlife Refuge: Sherburne County, Minnesota," Private report. 6 June 1978.

Furlan, William P. *In Charity Unfeigned*. Paterson, N.J.: St. Anthony Guild Press, 1952.

"George Kulzer, 1831-1912, A Continuing Story of a Stearns County Pioneer." *The Albany* (Minn.) *Enterprise*, June-July, 1976.

Giedion, Sigfried. *Space, Time and Architecture*. Cambridge: Harvard University Press, 1954.

Gilman, Rhoda R., and June Drenning Holmquist, eds. *Selections from Minnesota History*. St. Paul: Minnesota Historical Society, 1965.

Glassie, Henry. *Pattern in the Material Folk Culture of the Eastern United States*. Philadelphia: University of Pennsylvania Press, 1969.

––––––––––. "The Wedderspoon Farm." *New York Folklore Quarterly*, 22:3 (September, 1966), 165-187.

Halsted, Byron D. *Barns, Sheds, and Outbuildings*. New York: Grange Ludd, 1881.

Hart, John Fraser. *The Look of the Land*. Englewood Cliffs, N.J.: Prentice Hall, Inc., 1975.

Haupt, Walter. "Frank A. Lemke." Genealogy Files. Stearns County Historical Society, 7 February 1938.

––––––––––. "Fred Christen." Genealogy Files. Stearns County Historical Society, 5 May 1937.

History of Wright County Minnesota. 2 Vols. Chicago: H. C. Casper Jr. and Company, 1915.

Hodgkinson, Ralph. "Tools of the Woodworker: Axes, Adzes, and Hatchets." Nashville: American Association for State and Local History Technical Leaflet, 28 May 1965.

Hubbard, Earle R. *My Seventeen Years with the Pioneers, Thistles, and Hay-Needles*. Raymond, S.D.: Privately printed, 1950.

Jackson, John B. *American Space: The Centennial Years, 1865-1876*. New York: W. W. Norton, 1972.

Jarchow, Merrill E. *The Earth Brought Forth, History of Minnesota Agriculture to 1885*. St. Paul: Minnesota Historical Society, 1949.

Johnson, Loren C. "Louis J. Moser Homestead." National Register of Historic Places Inventory—Nomination Form. 21 December 1978.

Jordan, Terry G. "Alpine, Alemannic, and American Log Architecture." *Annals of the Association of American Geographers*. 90, #2 (June, 1980), 154-180.

––––––––––. *Texas Log Buildings: A Folk Architecture*. Austin: University of Texas Press, 1970.

Ketchum, Richard, ed., *The Pioneer Spirit*. New York: American Heritage Publishing Company, Inc., 1959.

Klampkin, Charles. *Barns: Their History, Preservation, and Restoration*. New York: Hawthorn Books Inc., 1973.

Kniffen, Fred, and Henry Glassie. "Buildings in Wood in

the Eastern United States, A Time-Place Perspective." *Geographical Review* 56 (1966): 40-66.

Krutch, Joseph Wood, ed., *Thoreau: Walden and Other Writings.* New York: Bantam Books Inc., 1962.

Lahr, Mary. "There's No Rush During Slovak's Little Christmas." *St. Cloud Daily Times*, 7 January 1981, Sec. B, P. 1, cols. 1-3.

Lawrence, Barbara. "Two Women: Good News and Bad News." Paper presented at Popular Culture Association, Eleventh Annual Meeting, Cincinnati, Ohio, 27 March 1981.

Leitch, William C. *Hand-Hewn.* San Francisco: Chronical Books, 1976.

Lovelace, Maud and Delos. *One Stayed at Welcome.* New York: John Day Company Inc., 1934.

MacFarlane, Rosemary, ed. *Currents.* 4 Vols. St. Paul: Minnesota Valley Restoration Project, Inc., 1979.

Madden, Betty I. *Arts, Crafts, and Architecture in Early Illinois.* Urbana: University of Illinois Press, 1973.

Mann, Dale, Richard Skinulis, and Nancy Shanoff. *The Complete Log House Book.* Toronto: McGraw-Hill Ryerson Ltd., 1979.

Marin, William A. "Sod House and Prairie Schooners." *Minnesota History*, 12 (June, 1931), 135-136.

Marshall, Howard Wight. *Folk Architecture in Little Dixie: A Regional Culture in Missouri.* Columbia: University of Missouri Press, 1981.

Massachusetts Department of Community Affairs. *Built to Last: A Handbook on Recycling Old Buildings.* Washington, D.C.: Preservation Press, 1977.

McKee, Harley J. *Introduction to Early American Masonry.* Washington, D.C.: National Trust for Historic Preservation, 1978.

Meier, Peg. *Bring Warm Clothes.* Minneapolis: Minneapolis Star and Tribune Co., 1981.

Minnesota Historical Society and Minnesota State Planning Agency. *Historic Preservation for Minnesota Communities.* St. Paul: Minn. 1980.

Minnesota Trends: A Report to the People. St. Paul: University of Minnesota Social Science Research Center of the Graduate School, 1954.

Mitchell, William Bell. *The History of Stearns County Minnesota.* 2 vols. Chicago: Cooper and Company, 1915.

Moberg, Wilhelm. *The Emigrants.* New York: Fawcett Popular Library, 1971.

_____. *The Settlers.* New York: Fawcett Popular Library, 1978.

_____. *Unto a Good Land.* New York: Fawcett Popular Library, 1954.

Montell, William Lynwood, and Michael Lynn Morse. *Kentucky Folk Architecture.* Lexington: University Press of Kentucky, 1976.

Morgan, William T. "Strongboxes on Main Street: Prairie-Style Banks." *Landscape* 24:3 (1980), 35-40.

Morris, Lucy Wilder, ed. *Old Rail Fence Corners.* 1914; rpt. St. Paul: Minnesota Historical Society Press, 1976.

Morris, Wright. *God's Country and My People.* New York: Harper and Row, 1968.

Morrison, Hugh. *Early American Architecture.* New York: Oxford University Press, 1952.

Nelson, Lowry. *American Farm Life.* Cambridge: Harvard University Press, 1954.

_____, Charles E. Ramsey, and Coolie Verner. *Community Structure and Change.* New York: The MacMillan Company, 1960.

_____. *The Minnesota Community: Country and Town in Transition.* Minneapolis: University of Minnesota Press, 1960.

Olmstead, Dale. "Benton County Log Structure." Unpublished paper, St. Cloud State University, December 1980.

Parson, Ruben L. *Ever the Land.* Staples, Minn.: Adventure Publishing, 1978.

Perrin, Richard W. E. *The Architecture of Wisconsin.* Madison: Wisconsin State Historical Society, 1967.

Plowden, David. *The Hand of Man on America.* Washington, D.C.: Smithsonian Institution Press, 1971.

Poppeliers, John, S. Allen Chambers, and Nancy B. Schwartz. *What Style Is It?.* Washington, D.C.: The Preservation Press, 1977.

Ristuben, Peter John. "Minnesota and the Competition for Immigrants." Master's thesis, University of Oklahoma, 1964.

Rolvaag, O. E. *Giants in the Earth.* New York: Harper and Brother Publishers, 1929.

Rozycki, Anthony T. "The Evolution of the Hamlets of Stearns County Minnesota." Master's thesis. Univeristy of Minnesota, 1977.

Rural Women in Minnesota: A Needs Assessment. Center for Human and Community Development Booklet. Collegeville, Minn.: St. John's University, n.d.

Ryberg, Ida C. "Ryberg Saga." *Stearns-Morrison Enterprise*, 5 October 1976.

_____. *The Ryberg Saga: A Story of Swedish Immigrant Parents.* Privately printed, 1968.

Saint Anthony Parish Centennial Book. (Stearns County, Minn.), 1974.

Sandburg, Carl. *The People, Yes.* New York: Harcourt Brace, 1936.

Schroeder, Fred E. H. "Educational Legacy: Rural One-Room Schoolhouses." *Historic Preservation*, July-September, 1977, pp. 4-7.

Scully, Vincent. *American Architecture and Urbanism.* New York: Praeger Publishers, 1969.

Seelhamer, Cynthia, and Mary Jo Masher. *The Growth of Sherburne County 1879-1975.* Becker, Minn.: Sherburne County Historical Society, 1980.

Sloane, Eric. *An Age of Barns.* New York: Funk and Wagnalls, 1955.

——————. *American Barns and Covered Bridges.* New York: Funk and Wagnalls, 1955.

——————. *A Reverence for Wood.* New York: Funk and Wagnalls, 1965.

Snyder, Margaret. *The Chosen Valley.* New York: Norton and Company, Inc., 1948.

Soloth, Barbara Ann. "Women on the Farming Frontier of Minnesota, 1849-1890." Master's thesis, Mankato State College, 1965.

Stratton, Joanna L. *Pioneer Women: Voices From the Kansas Frontier.* New York: Simon and Schuster, 1981.

Tasker, A. E. *Early History of Lincoln County.* Lake Benton (Minn.): Lake Benton News Print, 1936.

The Church Steeple: St. Stephen Parish and Community Newsletter. 1979-1981.

Thielen, Lois. "Christmas Celebrated by Russian Orthodox." *Stearns-Morrison Enterprise,* 15 January 1981, p. 5.

Tschunko, Hagdis. "Brief History of MacDougall Homestead." Unpublished manuscript, Historical collection, Charles A. Weyerhaeuser Memorial Museum, n.d.

Upham, Warren. *Minnesota Geographic Names: Their Origin and Historical Significance.* 1920; rpt. St. Paul: Minnesota Historical Society, 1966.

Van Ravenswaay, Charles. *The Arts and Architecture of German Settlements in Missouri.* Columbia: University of Missouri Press, 1977.

Wagner, William J. *Sixty Sketches of Iowa's Past and Present.* Des Moines: Brown and Wagner, 1967.

Warren, William Whipple. *History of the Ojibway Nation.* Minneapolis: Ross and Haines, 1957.

Wheeler, Thomas C., ed. *The Immigrant Experience.* New York: Penguin Books, 1975.

Wilhite, Orville L. *1979 Census of Agriculture, Stearns County, Minnesota.* United States Department of Commerce Bureau of the Census, 78-A71.

"William Warren Two Rivers Cabin Site and MacDougall Homestead," National Register of Historic Places Inventory—Nomination Form, 1977.

Winchell, N. H., Edward D. Neill, J. Fletcher Williams, and Charles S. Bryant. *History of the Upper Mississippi River Valley.* St. Paul: Minnesota Historical Society, 1881.

Wright, Frank Lloyd. *The Natural House.* New York: Horizon Press, Inc., 1954.

Yzermans, Vincent A. *The Mel and The Rose.* Melrose, MN: Melrose Historical Society, 1972.

PERSONAL INTERVIEWS

Christen, Theresa. 13 February 1982.

Clancy, Jeanette. 11 June 1980.

Du Frene, Katherine and Clement. 4 June 1982.

Erickson, Wanda. 9 June 1980.

Franzen, Nancy. 9 June 1980.

Garner, Perry. July 1982.

Gasperlin, Joe. 25 November 1980.

Gilk, Merylyn. 10 March 1981.

Gogala, Andrew, Joseph, Tony and Agnes. 1980-1982.

Grausam, Math. 6 August 1980.

Guzy, Gregg. 1979-1982.

Hansen, Rose. 21 August 1980.

Horton, Jack and Penny. July 1982.

Jameson, Marion. 17 July 1980.

Klein, George. 30 March 1981.

Kohorst, Herman and Liz. 1979-1981.

Legatt, Blaise and Mae. 30 March 1981.

Mischke, Sylvester. 20 November 1980.

Peternell, John. 1980-1981.

Petrich, John and Anna. 1980-1982.

Pilarski, Frank and Mary. 4 September 1980.

Poehler, Muriel. 9 June 1980.

Rausch, Agnes. 11 November 1980.

Rolfes, Bertha. 1979-1981.

Ryberg, Ida C. 26 May 1981.

Salzl, Henry and Cecelia. 1979-1982.

Scherfenberg, Ben and Vera. 1980.

Schmitt, John and Marie. 28 August 1980.

Schwieters, Cyril and Olivia. 6 March 1981.

Supan, Frances and Steve. 9 October 1980.

Swan, Fred. 3 March 1981.

Symanietz, Clara and Vincent. 1980-1982.

Tingquist, Anna and Carl. 4 June 1981.

Trettle, George and Ben. 23 October 1980.

Thielen, Lois. 4 September 1980.

Voronyak, Irene and Ed. 19 May 1981.

Warner, Jan. 7 August 1980.

Westrum, Caroline. 1979-1982.

Zniewski, Bertha. 11 August 1980.

MAP LEGEND

1. Founding of individual counties

1. Benton County, 27 October 1849. Named for Thomas Hart Benton, United States Senator, Missouri; 1821-1851.
2. Stearns County, 20 February 1855. Named for Charles Thomas Stearns, Member of the Council of the Territorial Legislature, 1854-1855.
3. Todd County, 20 February 1855. Named for John Blair Smith Todd, Commander of Fort Ripley. (Cousin of Mary Todd Lincoln).
4. Wright County, 20 February 1855. Named in honor of New York statesman, Silas Wright.
5. Morrison County, 25 February 1856. Named in honor of William and Allan Morrison, Minnesota fur traders.
6. Sherburne County, 25 February 1856. Named in honor of Moses Sherburne, Associate Justice of the Supreme Court of Minnesota Territory, 1853-1857.
7. Mille Lacs County. 23 May 1857. Named for the lake of the same name—thousand lakes.

2. Families/Counties/Townships (all in Minnesota)

1. Steve and Frances Supan, Stearns, Brockway
2. Blaise Legatt, Stearns, Brockway
3. John and Anna Petrich, Stearns, Brockway
4. Vincent and Clara Symanietz, Stearns, Brockway
5. Anton Gogala Farm, Stearns, Krain
6. Math Grausam, Stearns, Krain
7. Joseph Gasperlin, Stearns, Krain
8. Cyril and Olivia Schwieters, Stearns, Grove
9. Peter and Martha MacDougall, Morrison, Two Rivers
10. Ida Ryberg, Morrison, Elmdale
11. Habas-Voronyak, Morrison, Elmdale
12. Fred Swan, Benton, Glendorado
13. Joshua Otis Cater, Sherburne, Haven
14. Peter and Maggie Lind, Sherburne, Santiago

3. Structures

#	Owner/Name	Structure	Location
15.	Ferdinand Mielke	Dugout	Maine Prairie TS (Stearns)
16.	Louis Lemke	Log/stone barn	Farming TS (Stearns)
17.	Fred Christen	Barn	Farming TS
18.	District 175 (St. John's)	Stone School	Collegeville TS (Stearns)
19.	Mathew Justin	Forebay barn	Brockway TS (Stearns)
20.	Victor Lauer	Straw shelter	Farming TS (Stearns)
21.	Frank Pilarski	Log barns	Holding TS (Stearns)
22.	Perry Garner	Octagonal barn	Elk River (Sherburne)
23.	Joseph Brever	Root cellar	Todd County
24.	Unknown owner	Springhouse	Mille Lacs County
25.	Thelen Brothers	Chicken house	Farming TS (Stearns)
26.	Otto Christen	Tamarack pole corncrib	Farming TS (Stearns)
27.	Herbert M. Fox	Plank house	Santiago TS (Sherburne)
28.	Joseph Brever	Brick house	Todd County
29.	Eleanor E. Simpson	Victorian frame house	Mille Lacs County
30.	James C. Cater	Victorian frame house	Haven TS (Sherburne)
31.	Mathew Hall Lumber	Office	St. Cloud (Stearns)
32.	T. J. Anderson	Store	Belgrade (Stearns)
33.	Herman Athmann	Blacksmith shop	Farming TS (Stearns)
34.	Aloys Willenbring	Shoe/harness repair shop	Farming TS (Stearns)
35.	Farmers Cooperative	Creamery	Brooten (Stearns)
36.	Sauk Centre House	Hotel	Sauk Centre (Stearns)
37.	Soo Line Railroad	Depot	Paynesville (Stearns)
38.	Church of St. James	Church	Wakefield TS (Stearns)
39.	Elmer Grant	Kiln	Ronneby (Benton)
40.	South Santiago Lutheran	Church	Santiago TS (Sherburne)
41.	St. Stephen's	Church	St. Stephen (Stearns)
42.	Protestant church	Frame church	Ronneby (Benton)
43.	State Bank of Rockville	Bank	Rockville (Stearns)
44.	St. Mark's Episcopal	Church	Corinna TS (Wright)
45.	St. Anthony's	Church	St. Anthony (Stearns)
46.	North Prairie	School	North Prairie (Morrison)
47.	St. Martin's	Church	St. Martin (Stearns)
48.	Fairhaven	Mill	Fairhaven (Stearns)